*From Heads of Household to
Heads of State*

This work is a partial representation of *From Heads of Household to Heads of State* by J.L. McIntosh, a multimedia work of scholarship published in the Gutenberg-e online history series. As such, this print edition does not include the images, maps or the index contained in the online edition. The Gutenberg-e series is part of our commitment to create new kinds of scholarly and educational publications through new media technologies. Our mission is to make these works as innovative, efficient, and cost-effective as possible. We encourage reviewers and readers to also consult the complete work online at the free access site: http://www.gutenberg-e.org/ or through ACLS Humanities E-Book (HEB) at: http://www.humanitiesebook.org/series_GUTE.html

The online version of this work contains all the printed text here, in addition to digital images, artwork, audio, video, and hyperlinks that allow the reader to experience the full meaning of this scholarly work. The organizing structure, content, and design of the online work was created by the author in collaboration with a team of editors, web developers, and designers in order to give the richest meaning to the historical narrative and argument. The intellectual content of this work is designed to be read and evaluated in its electronic form. This text is not a substitute for or facsimile of the online version of this work.

From Heads of Household to Heads of State

The Preaccession Households of Mary and Elizabeth Tudor, 1516–1558

J.L. McIntosh

www.gutenberg-e.org

COLUMBIA UNIVERSITY PRESS

NEW YORK

Columbia University Press
Publishers Since 1893
New York   Chichester, West Sussex
Copyright © 2009 Columbia University Press

Library of Congress Cataloging-in-Publication Data

McIntosh, Jeri L. (Jeri Lynne)
From heads of household to heads of state : the preaccession households
of Mary and Elizabeth Tudor, 1516–1558 / J.L. McIntosh.
p. cm.
Includes bibliographical references.
ISBN 978-0-231-13550-4 (cloth : acid-free paper) — ISBN 978-0-231-50955-8 (e-book)
1. Mary I, Queen of England, 1516–1558.   2. Elizabeth I, Queen of England,
1533–1603   3. Royal households—Great Britain—History—16th century.
4. Great Britain—History—Mary I, 1553–1558.   5. Great Britain—
History—Elizabeth, 1558–1603.   I. Title.

DA347.M356 2009
942.05'4092—dc22
2008049364

www.gutenberg-e.org

Columbia University Press books are printed on permanent
and durable acid-free paper. This book is printed on paper
with recycled content. Printed in the United States of America.

c 10 9 8 7 6 5 4 3 2 1

References to Internet Web sites (URLs) were accurate at the time
of writing. Neither the author nor Columbia University
Press is responsible for URLs that may have expired
or changed since the manuscript was prepared.

CONTENTS

Preface   vii

Dedication and Acknowledgments   ix

List of Abbreviations   xi

Introduction: The Corporate Household   1

1. *The Material Household and the
   Politics of Ostentation   15*

2. *The Princely Household: Patronage and
   Corporate Loyalties   66*

3. *Property and Politics: Land Acquisition
   and Political Status   119*

4. *Accomplishing the Female Succession: The Succession
   Crisis of July 1553 and Its Aftermath   148*

*Conclusion: The Female Succession, Elite Households,
and Further Research   194*

*Appendix A: Henry VIII's Will and the Bequests to
Mary and Elizabeth, 1547*   201

*Appendix B: The Fraudulent Claims in Mary's and
Elizabeth's Patent Letters, 1547*   219

Appendix C: Mary's Aborted Flight, 1550   231

Appendix D: Creating and Investing a Prince of Wales   237

Select Bibliography   241

PREFACE

Wherever possible, I have presented quotations in the original spelling and punctuation. I have followed scholarly convention and used a modern dating system starting the year on January 1, rather than using the regnal year, which contemporaries employed in official documents.

DEDICATION AND ACKNOWLEDGMENTS

DEDICATION

In loving memory of my mother, Michele A. Sherlock

ACKNOWLEDGMENTS

I would like to thank, first of all, the American Historical Association and Columbia University Press for awarding my dissertation, "Sovereign Princesses: Mary and Elizabeth Tudor as Heads of Princely Households and the Accomplishment of the Female Succession in Tudor England, 1516–1558," the Gutenberg-e prize as one of the six best dissertations on Women and Gender for 2000–2003.

I completed the dissertation at Johns Hopkins University under the guidance of Richard Kagan. I am grateful to him for agreeing to supervise a student working in an area outside of his own field. I benefited greatly from the opportunity to submit my work to a nonspecialist whose breadth of knowledge about European history in the sixteenth century enabled him to offer pertinent comments and forced me to recognize the possible implications of this study beyond the confines of England. Indeed, I was most fortunate to complete my graduate studies at Johns Hopkins in the mid-1990s and to work with historians such as J. G. A. Pocock, Gabrielle Spiegel, Orest Ranum, and John Marshall. I am particularly grateful for the interest and encouragement of J. G. A. Pocock. All of these scholars were then in residence at JHU and ensured that those of us fortunate to study with them understood the useful and necessary interplay between methodology and archival work within a premodern European historical context.

It has been my privilege to know and receive advice from many scholars whose insights have helped me to crystallize my thinking. Unfortunately, space does not permit me to name all of them, but I feel I must at least make some attempt to give credit to a few here on the understanding that many who have helped me remain unlisted. I would like to thank, in particular, the members of the Early Modern Spain seminar at Johns Hopkins University from 1993 to 1996 and also the members of three seminars at the Folger Shakespeare Library from 1993 to 1995. I am grateful to all of my colleagues at the University of Tennessee, but I mention here those who were kind enough to listen to my ideas about this and to offer suggestions—Chad Black, Lorri Glover, Bob Morrissey, and Lynn Sacco. Whatever shortcomings remain in this work are entirely mine and, no doubt, are the result of not following or understanding their advice. I also must mention Eric Carlson, Helen Hackett, Barbara Harris, Felicity Heal, Ralph Houlbrooke, Christine Johnson, Carol Percy, Paul Seaver, Penry Williams, and Natalie Zacek.

Most of these individuals have become my friends, but they have not put up with me nearly as long as Mary Anne, Carol, Pam, and Kay Stafford have, and I am in awe of their forbearance as well as grateful for their insights and encouragement. My family has always supported and encouraged my scholastic efforts. I also express my gratitude to Michele Sherlock, Alvin and Adeline Parker, Steven Parker, and Geraldine Eichelman. I am indebted to the Stammtischers and to the Hackett family for many dinners, drinks, and endless diversions. Most of all, I blame my husband, Paul Cobb, for all of this.

LIST OF ABBREVIATIONS

APC   *Acts of the Privy Council of England.* New Series, ed. J. R. Dasent
          [London, 1890]
BL   British Library
BP   C. R. Manning, "State Papers relating to the custody of the Prin-
          cess Elizabeth at Woodstock, in 1554 . . . ," *Norfolk Archaeol-
          ogy* . . . , 4 (1855), pp. 133–226
CPR   *Calendar of the Patent Rolls. Preserved in the Public Record Of-
          fice. Edward VI and Mary,* multivolume [London, 1924]
CSP   *Calendar of Letters, Despatches and State Papers Relating to the
          Negotiations between England and Spain. Preserved in the Ar-
          chives at Vienna, Simancas, and Elsewhere,* vols. II–IX [London,
          1866–1912]
          Calendar of State Papers Edward VI, ed. C. S. Knighton [Lon-
          don, 1992]
          Calendar of State Papers, Mary, ed. C. S. Knighton [London,
          1998]
CW   *Elizabeth I: Collected Works,* ed. L. S. Marcus, J. Mueller, and
          M. B. Rose [Chicago University Press, 2000]
LP   Brewer and Gairdner, eds. *Letters and Papers, Foreign and Do-
          mestic of the Reign of Henry VIII* . . . [London, 1864–1905]

Loades	David M. Loades, *Mary Tudor: A Life* [Oxford, 1989]
Madden	Frederick Madden, *The Privy Purse Expenses of the Princess Mary* [London, 1831]
Prescott	F. M. H. Prescott, *Mary Tudor* [London, 1952]
PRO	Public Records Office
Starkey	D. Starkey, *Elizabeth: Apprenticeship* [London, 2001]
TNA	The National Archives, Kew (formerly PRO)

INTRODUCTION

The Corporate Household

Every Mans proper *Mansion* House and *Home*, being the
Theater of his *Hospitality*, the *Seate* of *Selfe-fruition*, the *Com-
fortablest part* of his owne *Life*, the *Noblest* of his Sonnes *Inheritance*, a kinde of priuate *Princedome* . . .
    — Sir Henry Wotton, *Elements of Architecture* [1624], p.82

Despite the popular fame of Mary I and Elizabeth I, their political lives before
acceding to the throne has received surprisingly little attention from scholars.[1]
It is the intention of this study to shed some light on an aspect of the Tudor
queens, which has not yet been the focus of a study based on original published
research: their preaccession political careers. Their preaccession political careers grew out of their roles as heads of their own independent households.
Their political activity, and the household context that made it possible, in turn,
has potential to add new complexities to how one views the daily practice of
politics at the elite level in Tudor England. I will argue here that Mary and
Elizabeth eventually were able to wield sovereign power not only because they
were the legal heirs to the throne (through the 1544 Act of Succession) but also
because they were heads of their own independent households.

    The research is not based on some undiscovered cache of documents that
historians have overlooked. It is both the blessing and curse of the field that

many of the records of the English past have been not only been preserved but also calendared and even transcribed in reliable printed editions. The benefits of this are obvious, but the downside is that a scholar can rarely justify their work on the basis of making a new discovery of previously unconsulted sources. This study will therefore use sources that are both widely available and consulted with reasonable frequency by scholars.

The contribution made by this study is to read these sources—state papers, household instructions and accounts—with a different sensibility from that usually found in works originally conceived on a more grand scale. The more limited scope of this study allowed me to privilege seemingly "dry" or "objective" documents like property transactions, patent letters, wills, and household accounts. Because these documents were central to the topics at issue in this project, they have been scrutinized here as if they were novels containing authorial intent, plots, and foreshadowings—in short, all the elements present in more obviously narrative documents such as letters and prescriptive literature. These latter sources have been used here, too. It is the connections between these apparently disparate and unrelated sources that has linked this initially small study of Mary's and Elizabeth's preaccession households to the wider political and conceptual context of mid-Tudor England.

The cross-comparison of sources as outlined earlier, the recognition of embedded agendas within them, and the paleographic analysis conducted here has resulted in this study having relevance to discussions on the separation of the private and public spheres as they related to the household; the political opportunities available to elite women heading or managing their households; how patron-client relationships were articulated within the informal domestic household; and the impact of these relationships on the more formalized patriarchal political network that governed Tudor England.

Establishing the connections between property documents and more traditional sources has the further benefit of reintegrating Mary and Elizabeth Tudor as women of their time.[2] True, as inheriting females, the Tudor princesses are "disproportionately visible in contemporary documents," but this is something they have in common with other contemporary landed women of the period.[3] By contrast, their status as single unmarried women living in their own households ensured that their experience was similar to that of many contemporary women, especially nonelite women.[4] They need no longer be discussed primarily as "exceptions" whose experience was separate and remote from that of other women both elite and nonelite of sixteenth-century England. Certainly, as royalty, the Tudor princesses shared more cultural assumptions with other elites than they did with those lower down the social scale. But, as I will argue, Mary and Elizabeth headed their own households in much the same way widows from various economic backgrounds during this period did. Just as the wife of a nobleman, especially if she was a propertied heiress in her own right, was in reality the source of local patronage, so, too, did the Tudor princesses acquire political clients by exploiting the patronage opportunities attendant on their roles as substantial property owners.

The household here serves as a prism through which Mary and Elizabeth are viewed not simply as belonging to the elite class but also as women who, in common with other elite women, were able to exploit one of the crevices in a formally patriarchal system: the authoritarian role of the high-born housewife in an elite household. The hierarchal status of the Tudor princesses merely allowed them to exploit certain fissures—in particular, the resources of the household—to their fullest potential.

One of the things that the Tudor princesses shared with many of their contemporaries, both female and male, was that they presided over their own households. What set the princesses apart was that they were able to exercise authority formally as did male householders and informally in ways similar to female household managers. The terms "formal" and "informal" are useful but fail to convey the complexities involved. The authority of an elite noblewoman over her servants, tenants, and neighbors was openly and explicitly acknowledged. To apply the term "informal" to the authority of an elite housewife should not be read as an argument advocating that the noblewoman's authority was merely tolerated as a practical necessity. Even in the harshest prescriptive literature regarding the subordination of a wife to her husband, there was no suggestion that a male servant had any cause for evincing superiority to his female mistress. By the same token, a man's "formal" and legal headship of his household did not necessarily translate into him having more authority over his servants than his wife did. A complex interplay of personalities, economics, kinship ties usually determined whether it was the husband or the wife who commanded greater respect and obedience from servants, tenants, and neighbors.

The complexities involved in applying the terms "formal" and "informal" should not detract from the overall insight provided by examining the preaccession households of the Tudor princesses. In studying the household as an abstract political concept (as it often appeared in Tudor prescriptive literature[5]) and the related connection between political agency and property ownership, it has become clear that Mary and Elizabeth were able to exercise political patronage *before* their accessions by virtue of their positions as heads of households.

Indeed, this study will present evidence demonstrating that Mary and Elizabeth Tudor lived more like other women of their time than any English princess before or since. The only female predecessor in the royal family that headed her own household was their paternal great-grandmother, Lady Margaret Beaufort.[6] Mary's and Elizabeth's ambiguous status as potential future sovereigns constrained both their father and brother to treat them more as if they were noble (male) cousins rather than as their dependent female royal relations. Mary and Elizabeth did not share the usual fate of English princesses of living as dependents of the monarch until marriage. Rather, Mary and Elizabeth lived as other elite women lived in Tudor England, presiding over a household, in possession of valuable property both real and moveable, and dispensing the patronage attendant on those properties in their possession.

That wealthy/propertied women were able to circumvent some of the more formalized strictures of patriarchy—exclusion from educational, political (except the crown), and judicial offices and institutions—is not an insight original to this study.[7] Barbara Harris's overview of elite women's ability to exercise agency in their political and professional lives due to their wealth and social status focused on the political and public role of elite households.[8] This study follows this model by exploring the political and public roles Mary and Elizabeth enjoyed *before* their accessions by virtue of their preaccession status as householders and property-owners.

This study argues that Mary and Elizabeth exploited the resources of their independent households—display, corporate identity, and property—to establish themselves as viable authority figures before their accessions. When Princesses Mary and Elizabeth received visitors, such as foreign ambassadors or their noble friends, they did so in their own manor residences, the furnishings of which were designed to impress onlookers with their wealth and political status. As heads of household, Princess Mary and Princess Elizabeth could draw on the loyalty of their staff, who were sworn to their service.[9] These servants provided each princess with a corps of dedicated agents who helped to create readily identifiable public personas for their mistress. As property owners, princesses Mary and Elizabeth could dispense offices on their estates, collect revenues so they could patronize scholars, and secure political clients through grants of reversionary interests in their lands. In times of crisis, princesses Mary and Elizabeth could call on their tenants, neighbors, and clients—their affinity—to supply them with military arms, men, and munitions. This enabled Princess Mary to literally enforce her accession in 1553 when it was challenged on behalf of Lady Jane Grey.[10] Mindful of this, Princess Elizabeth called out her affinity in 1558 in case her accession was challenged as was Mary's.

In a society in which women were excluded from all major institutions of power—government, education, the church—the consecutive accessions of two women to the sovereign power must be explained. I argue that the female succession was not inevitable once Henry VIII failed to sire more than one son. Normally, women who were the last representatives of a patriline, as were Mary and Elizabeth, would be quickly married off in the hopes that such female heirs would transmit their blood claims to their male offspring. Although common law (which governed the royal succession) allowed women to inherit real property and, for royalty, sovereign power, in practice heiresses were usually married off with their inheritance rights enjoyed by their husbands and male offspring.[11] This was the strategy most often employed by the English polity to avoid the spectacle of a female sovereign in a patriarchal state. It was more common for royal women, if they were, like Mary and Elizabeth, the last survivors of the direct patriline, to *transmit* their claims to the throne rather than to *inherit*.

One of the more famous royal heiresses in English history, Matilda, only surviving adult child of her father Henry I, failed, in the twelfth century, to repel a challenge from her male cousin for the throne that was hers by right of inheritance. In the end, her son, Henry Plantagenet, was able to accede to the English throne as Henry II by claiming he inherited through his mother. Matilda was able to transmit her claims but not inherit outright. Within the Tudor family itself, women transmitted their blood claims to the throne rather than claimed in their own right. Margaret Beaufort transmitted her claims to her son Henry VII, the first Tudor king. His queen, Elizabeth of York, was the Yorkist heir to the throne, being the eldest surviving child of her father Edward IV. She did not claim the throne herself but, rather, strengthened the far more dubious blood claim of her husband, Henry VII, and transmitted her blood claims to her offspring including her son Henry VIII.

The strategy to neutralizing the threat to the patriarchal status quo posed by a female heir to the throne was to accept the inevitability of dynastic change and marry the female heir suitably so she could transmit her blood claims to her male offspring. Initially, this was the expectation behind the marriage negotiations for Princess Mary's hand throughout the 1520s. Later, when Edward IV attempted to disinherit Mary, his first thought was to designate his Protestant cousins, Frances or (her daughter) Jane Grey as *transmitters* of blood claims by nominating the male offspring of these women as his heir. It was only when his illness began to proceed rapidly that he recognized he would not survive to see the birth of this male heir and so designated Jane Grey herself.[12]

Not overburdened with many skills in forward planning, Henry VIII failed to arrange marriages for his daughters and so they remained single heiresses-at-law during his reign and that of his son, Edward VI. Nevertheless, Mary and Elizabeth still faced many challenges before they could accede to the throne. I contend that their elite households allowed Mary and Elizabeth to succeed to the throne in spite of rival male claimants, their own statutory illegitimacy, their gender-based subordination, and the hostility of incumbent monarchs like Henry VIII and Edward VI. One of the most important, although until recently largely overlooked, factors crucial in allowing them to succeed to the English throne was that they took advantage of the opportunities available to them as heads of household and landed magnates. This allowed Mary and Elizabeth to supplement their blood claims with the resources of their elite households.

When I first began to research, in 1998, the political significance of the pre-accession households of Mary and Elizabeth, few scholars had published any serious work involving original research on the topic. David Loades's 1989 biography of Mary Tudor stood alone as the major study of Mary that paid any attention to Mary's preaccession household. Since the completion of my own study (as a Ph.D. dissertation) in 2002, there is now a small but growing interest in the households of the Tudor princesses.[13] This study will contribute to the growing consensus that Mary and Elizabeth acquired, as heads of household, important political status *before* their accessions.

TERMS AND CONDITIONS

The term "household" as used here will serve a dual function both abstract and real. In sixteenth-century England, the term designated an economic and political abstraction.[14] Conceptually, a "household" referred to the actual collection of people living together as well as the material contents, like furniture, therein. According to Natasha Korda, the material culture of the household assumed greater importance in the sixteenth century because of "England's rapidly expanding market of consumer goods" and this was reflected in increasingly popular linguistic and legal designation of "householdstuffe."[15]

Although due attention will be paid to the material culture of Mary's and Elizabeth's households (see Chapter 1), this study concentrates mainly on the personal and economic *relationships* that constituted a household: the head of household (householder) and their dependents (kin, servants, tenants). This collection of people was recognized at law and for tax purposes as a "household" no matter the place of residence.[16] A "household" could move from place to place, residential manor to manor, and still remain an household. Sixteenth-century England recognized a further abstraction of the concept in that a person in Tudor England could be a member of another's household but not live with that person. This earlier concept of "household" incorporated those who were nonresident but still associated with the head of household either through ties of economic dependency or clientage based on service, proximity, lineage, and so on.[17]

Therefore, in this study, "household" refers to a collection of people who were identified in contemporary documents—such as accounts and legal documents—as members of a particular household whether or not such persons shared a residence with the head of household. This is fairly straightforward. Further clarification of relationships of nonresident clients of the householder was not always so uncomplicated. In the case of Elizabeth's household, for instance, Foxe related a story involving a grocer who was not resident in Elizabeth's household but identified himself as a member of her household and in service to Elizabeth as his "mistress."[18] This was a household relationship based on economics and patronage and is not confirmed in any other source. Yet another client of Elizabeth's, one who received from her a reversionary interests in some of her lands, was Edward Fiennes, Lord Clinton who clearly was not a member of Elizabeth's household but, rather, presided over his own independent establishment.

Because this study is more concerned with how members of these royal households *related* to each other rather than with the specific details of who was a member of one of these households at any given time, this study will adopt a conservative approach in assigning people as members of either Mary's or Elizabeth's preaccession household. Only when the evidence explicitly indicates their membership, especially their resident membership, will people be listed under the rubric of one or the other's household. So Robert Rochester will be listed here as a member of Mary's household because he is listed as her treasurer or "comptroller" in state documents and he appears regularly in her privy chamber accounts, whereas Robert Wingfield, whose *Vita Mariae* indicates more than a passing familiarity with Mary's household staff, will not be claimed even as a nonresident member of her household because there are no contemporary documents that identify him as such.

Another important term, one that bears directly on how "household" is discussed here, is "corporate." It is a term used here to characterize the relationships within a household, particularly of the relationship between the head/manager of household and the other members of the household. The aim here is adhere as closely as possible to sixteenth-century usage. Thus, it is employed here to signify a "corporate body" similar to Tudor discussions of the "body politic." The term is used here to designate a "corporate body," a "persona" created by individual members of the household and represented as a corporate individual by the head of household.

This conceptualization of the household as a corporation is the leitmotif of this project. This is a study of Mary's and Elizabeth's household as an organizing concept: a deployment of people and resources to further not just the interests of the householder but also the interests of the household itself as a larger collective body. This sense of corporate identity expressed itself visually in the liveries and badges worn by the household staff, marking them as the loyal servants of the householder. Even common household tools, like masking irons, carried the insignia of the head of household.[19]

The preaccession households of Mary and Elizabeth Tudor were "corporate" bodies in the sense that the whole of the household was greater than the sum of the individual members. The head of household received formal and ceremonial oaths of loyalty from members of their household and these individual members often identified with the aspirations and views of the head of household. This is not to argue that only the head of household shaped and determined the agenda and identity of the corporate household body. In the case of Elizabeth's household, her staff formed a conception of the household that did not always agree with Elizabeth's representations of herself or her household.

These households will be discussed here "corporate bodies" because the individual members identified with a common goal even if individual members did not always work in harmony toward that goal. This study will present instances of internal conflict within the household but the most serious conflicts often resulted from an external political crisis that threatened to undermine the existence of the household itself and certainly destabilized the political status of the nominal head of household. Mary's and Elizabeth's elite households were "corporate bodies" in the sense that their contemporaries employed the term "body politic," a collection of individual members subordinated to the authority of the head but necessary to continued existence of the body as a whole.[20]

There are two other terms that are relevant here: "affinity" and "family." Affinity, as understood in sixteenth-century England, meant the tenants and neighbors or clients of a landowner.[21] Part of this affinity would be informal "retainers." These were neighbors and friends of a landlord who behaved as if they were formally sworn to the military service of the landlord. Landlords, on the scale of the Tudor princesses after 1547, were, as the largest property owners in a particular area, also usually the regional patron who had many clerical and local offices in their gift. Additionally, regional magnates—as Mary and Elizabeth were from 1547 until 1558—could secure local clients by awarding reversionary grants in their lands. In return for this patronage, magnates expected their clients, tenants, and neighbors—their "affinities"—to support them with men, arms, and money when the magnate needed military resources. Thus, when Princess Mary called out her affinity to take the throne by force during the succession crisis in 1553, those who responded behaved as if they were her sworn retainers.[22] Nevertheless, they acted in the capacity as members of her "affinity" in providing military service when requested by the princess as their neighbor and patron.

The other term that needs to be clarified here is "family" whose modern usage is at considerable variance with that of sixteenth-century England and the early modern period in general.[23] In the Tudor period, "family" did not mean blood relations as it (mostly) does today but, rather, those who lived together in one household.[24] The head of household would refer equally to live-in relatives and servants living under his roof as his "family." Blood relations not living in the household were termed "kin" or, more usually, in a generic usage, as "cousin." Indeed, the terms "family" and "household" carried almost the exact opposite cognitive meaning in the sixteenth century from that of today. The domestic servant was "family," whereas the relative was "kin." Today householders would not refer to their servants (living with them or nonresident) as "family" but a sixteenth-century householder would have done so. These terms will be deployed here according to their sixteenth-century usage, although "family" will be used as little as possible in an attempt to avoid confusion.

OVERVIEW

This study presents evidence demonstrating that Mary and Elizabeth exploited the resources of their elite households, most especially those concerning display, corporate identity, and property, in order to take full advantage of the political status inherent in their preaccession positions as heads of household. Therefore, Chapter 1 concentrates on "display" with an examination of the material culture of the preaccession households of Mary and Elizabeth Tudor. This chapter discusses the interconnection between material display and political status.

Henry VIII regulated the quality and quantity of the material resources of Mary's and Elizabeth's childhood households (also that of his son Prince Edward) to indicate publicly which of his three children was his preferred heir. Domestic nobility and foreign emissaries judged the political status of a princely householder by the quality of hospitality offered, which itself was determined by the quality of the material goods within the household. After the death of Henry VIII, the princesses were able to assume full control in furnishing their households. Both Mary and Elizabeth demonstrated that they had learned the value of the relationship between political status and its outward display by deliberately selecting textiles from Henry VIII's Inventory, which underscored the history and benefits of female rule.

Chapter 2 traces the development of the distinct court cultures of the princesses' households. This chapter focuses on the interaction between the princesses and their household officers. The evidence will indicate that Princess Mary's household was an expression of her will; her staff rendered unquestioning loyalty and she ruled absolutely. In contrast, Princess Elizabeth's household staff treated their young mistress with a mixture of parental indulgence and dominance. She, in turn, relied on her household staff for emotional and political support. Both households exhibited strong corporate identities which provided the princesses with dedicated followings. At times of political crisis, princesses Mary and Elizabeth relied on the efforts of their household staffs to shield them from blame and to publicize their political and religious agendas.

Chapter 3 will then examine the princesses' careers as property owners. Land acquisition was the preferred method for consolidating political and social power amongst the elite in sixteenth-century England. Land was the currency of patron-client exchanges. By considering princesses Mary and Elizabeth as landowners, this study restores to them their full participation in this traditional form of political maneuvering.

To a certain extent, this move to situate Mary and Elizabeth within the same sociopolitical context as other contemporary elite women runs counter to current trends within feminist scholarship. It is now considered more useful and historically valid to emphasize the economic and social differences between women in the past.[25] This is a trend that I wholeheartedly support. It is not the intent of this study to generalize about the experiences of all women in Tudor England by claiming that Mary and Elizabeth were representative of contemporary female experience. Indeed, as single, never-married women, even among the landed aristocracy (which included female heiresses), Mary and Elizabeth were anomalous in their status as regional magnates and householders in their own right.[26] The intent here is to question the necessity for perpetuating the stereotype that Mary and Elizabeth functioned as honorary men in their society. Considering them primarily as "exceptions" proving the rule of Tudor patriarchy has resulted in the Tudor princesses being studied, not as historical figures responding to and contributing to the events and culture of their particular society, but rather as aberrations whose lives and choices provide insight only into their individual selves and not into their society. This study will advance the argument that the Tudor princesses functioned in similar ways as both elite men and elite (although married) women in heading and managing their own households. In this way, Mary and Elizabeth enjoyed the same social, economic, and political status as that of other elite male householders and elite female household managers before their accessions. Like other contemporary householders, the princesses exercised political authority. What makes this particularly interesting is that the princesses thus functioned as authority figures many years before they became sovereigns.

Chapter 4 details how princesses Mary and Elizabeth, through their position as heads of household, exercised political agency in much the same way as contemporary widows, heiresses, and other elite women who either headed their own household or managed that of their husbands. The position of head of an elite household, which often entailed owning land, endowed the head with authority as overlord over her/his servants, tenants, neighbors, and clients. The chapter closes by examining the way in which the princesses harnessed all three of the households' primary assets—display, corporate identity, and property—to ensure their accessions.

The Conclusion will present conclusions drawn from the evidence. Questions concerning the representativeness of these households, the role they may or may not have played in the female succession, and how this study contributes to a further understanding of the period in general will be considered here. The overriding issue for this chapter is whether or not the evidence presented adequately demonstrates the validity of the title of the study. Did Mary and Elizabeth enjoy an easier and smoother transition to becoming heads of state because they had first been heads of elite households?

One final point to bring this Introduction to a close: some of the initial findings offered in this Introduction will strike many readers as startling. Women's history now has a long and distinguished record that continues to offer novel insights.[27] This is not always welcomed in fields with established "grand narratives" such as Tudor history. This grand narrative has predetermined how Mary and Elizabeth are regarded as political actors before their accessions and even, to a certain extent, after their accessions.

Few scholars question the depiction, as established by Lawrence Stone and Mortimer Levine, of Mary and Elizabeth as "genealogical accidents."[28] In this interpretive context, Mary and Elizabeth were women who were forced to assume the traditionally male role of authority figures much to the anxiety of themselves and their male contemporaries. For the period under consideration here, 1516–1558, evidence for this gender-based anxiety is sparse.[29] Except for a few stray remarks by Henry VIII, there little evidence for widespread dread over the possibility of a female succession. Rather, the evidence suggests that those who thought about the succession, before 1553, preferred Mary as their next ruler in preference to the leading male candidates such as James V of Scotland, Henry Hastings, Earl of Huntingdon, or the Darnley brothers (sons of Margaret Douglas Lennox).[30]

What this study asks of the reader is to evaluate the quality of the evidence presented here which indicates that it was precisely because Mary and Elizabeth functioned very much as other elite contemporary women—heading/managing households, dispensing patronage, presiding over household staffs—that their future subjects already regarded them as authority figures *before* their accessions. In a society as hierarchal as Tudor England, the social status of a person—female or male—counted as much as gender (perhaps more in some cases) toward their ability to implement their political agendas. I will present a conclusion here that took me by surprise as I completed my research: it was the household, traditionally depicted as the place of women's containment and marginalization from political power, which played a determinative role in the elevation of two women in succession to the throne in a patriarchal society. It is the goal of this study to ensure that by the time the reader finishes the book that what was a surprise to me in the course of my research will strike the reader of this book as painfully obvious.

NOTES

1. The most published recent work that devotes substantial attention to Mary's and Elizabeth's preaccession careers is a popular biography: D. Starkey, *Elizabeth: Apprenticeship* [London, 2001]

2. Mary and Elizabeth, as princesses, exploited their households and roles as property owners in much the same way as the women studied by Barbara Harris in *English Aristocratic Women, 1450–1550: Marriage and Family, Property and Careers* [Oxford UP, 2002]

3. Harris, *English Aristocratic Women*, p. 22

4. A. L. Erickson, *Women and Property in Early Modern England* [London, 1993], p. 192

5. For example, R. Cleaver, *A Godly Form of Household Government* . . . [London, 1603], p. 13

6. M. K. Jones and M. G. Underwood, *The King's Mother: Lady Margaret Beaufort Countess of Richmond and Derby* [Cambridge UP, 1992], pp. 93–170 and F. Kisby, "A Mirror of Monarchy: Music and Musicians at the Household Chapel of Lady Margaret Beaufort, Mother of Henry VII," *Early Music History*, 16 (1997), p. 212

7. See, in particular, Jones and Underwood, *Lady Margaret Beaufort* . . . , p. 5

8. For public and political importance of elite households from late medieval to early modern period, see D. Herlihy, *Medieval Households* [Harvard UP, 1985]; D. Starkey, "The Age of Household: Politics, Society, and the Arts, 1350–1550," in S. Medcalf, ed., *The Context of English Literature in the Late Middle Ages* [London, 1981]; and K. Mertes, *The English Noble Household* [Oxford, 1988]

9. I use the term "princess" here in the modern sense to refer to royal female heirs to the throne. In sixteenth-century parlance, powerful unmarried royal women were often referred to as "my lady" like Margaret of Austria was when she was the widowed Regent of the Netherlands for her nephew Charles V; e.g., *L&P Hen.VIII*, 3/2, 58. Before her disinheritance in 1536, Mary bore the title "my lady princess" analogous to the modern "princess royal"; e.g., *L&P Hen.VIII*, 3/2, 118

10. Since my initial treatment of the determinative role played by Mary's household in the 1553 succession crisis, in "Sovereign Princesses: Mary and Elizabeth Tudor as Heads of Princely Households and the Accomplishment of the Female Succession in Tudor England, 1516–1558" [Ph.D. thesis, Johns Hopkins University, 2002], others have begun to document the importance of Mary's household; see especially A. Whitelock and D. MacCulloch, "Princess Mary's Household . . ." [2007]

11. E. Spring, *Law, Land and Family: Aristocratic Inheritance in England, 1300–1800* [North Carolina UP, 1993], p. 15

12. M. Levine, *Tudor Dynastic Problems, 1460–1571* [London, 1973], p. 81; Levine assigns to John Dudley, Duke of Northumberland, sole agency in diverting the succession away from Mary to Lady Jane Grey

13. D. Starkey's popular biography of Elizabeth centers on her preaccession career and household, *Elizabeth: Apprenticeship* [London, 2201]; Whitelock and MacCulloch, "Princess Mary's Household and the Succession Crisis, July 1553," *Historical Journal* 50/2 (2007), pp. 265–287

14. For example, R. Cleaver, *A Godly Form of Household Government . . .* [London, 1603], p. 13

15. N. Korda, *Shakespeare's Domestic Economies: Gender and Property in Early Modern England* [Pennsylvania Press, 2002], pp. 1–2

16. D. Herlihy, *Medieval Households* [Harvard UP, 1985], p. v

17. See, e.g., Sir Thomas Smith, *De Republica Anglorum*, pp. 23, 29, as cited in V. Comensoli, *Household Business: Domestic Plays of Early Modern England* [Toronto UP, 1996], p. 17

18. Foxe, *Acts and Monuments . . .* [1570], Bk.12, p. 2296; available at http://www.hrionline.ac.uk/johnfoxe/main/12_1570_2296.jsp

19. See list of Princess Mary's household items in *LP* IV, pt.1, 1577, which notes that the princesses' insignia was branded on her household masking irons

20. The classic discussion of the political dimensions of premodern corporate identities is E. H. Kantorowicz, *The King's Two Bodies: A Study in Medieval Political Theology* [Princeton UP, 1957].

21. D. Loades, *Mary Tudor*, p. ix

22. Further support for this view can be found in A. Whitelock and D. MacCulloch, "Princess Mary's Household and the Succession Crisis, July 1553," *The Historical Journal*, 50/2 (2007), pp. 265–287

23. C. Shammas, "Anglo-American Household Government in Comparative Perspective," *William and Mary Quarterly*, 3/52 (Jan.1995): 104–144; esp. p. 105

24. R. Houlbrooke, *The English Family 1450–1700* [London, 1984], p. 19

25. M. E. Wiesner, *Women and Gender in Early Modern Europe* [Cambridge UP, 2000], pp. 3, 7

26. Harris, *English Aristocratic Women*, p. 88. Harris's study does not encompass heiresses—the sole primogeniture family heir to land and title—who never married, presumably because such heiresses often came under intense pressure to marry and were betrothed at young ages by their families to secure political, economic and social alliances

27. Wiesner, *Women and Gender in Early Modern Europe*, p. 3

28. L. Stone, "The Rise of the Nuclear Family in Early Modern England: The Patriarchal Stage," p. 50 from *The Family in History*, ed. C. E. Rosenberg [Pennsylvania, 1975]; M. Levine, "The Place of Women in Tudor Government," p. 109 from *Tudor Rule and Revolution: Essays for G.R. Elton from his American Friends*, ed. J. D. Guth and J. W. McKenna [Cambridge 1982]

29. A. Shephard, *Gender and Authority in Sixteenth-Century England* [Keele UP, 1994] unearthed six treatises in the sixteenth century debating the advantages and disadvantages of female rule; only four of the six were printed

30. *LP*, XI, 1246. Printed in Fletcher, *Tudor Rebellions*, p. 128; see also M. Bateson, "The Examination of Robert Aske," *English Historical Review*, V, [1890], pp. 652–654

1. THE MATERIAL HOUSEHOLD
AND THE POLITICS OF OSTENTATION

First, as you know, my house within the city
Is richly furnishèd with plate and gold,
Basins and ewers to lave her dainty hands;
My hangings all of Tyrian tapestry.
In ivory coffers I have stuffed my crowns,
In cypress chests my arras, counterpoints,
Costly apparel, tents, and canopies,
Fine linen, Turkey cushions bossed with pearl,
Valance of Venice gold in needlework,
Pewter, and brass, and all things that belongs
To house, or housekeeping.
—William Shakespeare, *The Taming of the Shrew*, 2.1

THE PHYSICAL AND CONCEPTUAL LAYOUT
OF AN ELITE HOUSEHOLD IN TUDOR ENGLAND

From 1547 to 1553, Princess Mary and Princess Elizabeth resided in manors that were arranged to display their social position and financial resources. Stray references to Mary and Elizabeth having privy and presence chambers—at least as departments if not actual rooms—are found in their accounts and checker-olls. I have not been able to locate any floorplans or detailed descriptions of their manors, but the physical arrangement of rooms from presence chamber to bed chamber was quite common for the period. Knowledge about the lesser royal manors that were placed at the disposal of Princess Mary and Princess Elizabeth after 1547 allows for some informed speculation on what a visitor to one of their residences would have found.[1]

A visitor to one of Mary's or Elizabeth's manor residences would likely find themselves ushered on arrival into a public reception room known as the Presence Chamber (or "Great Chamber"). There the guest would await a formal reception by the princess. The Presence Chamber was clearly delineated as a space separate from the Great Hall or the house, either by intervening structural elements, such as walls or columns, or else by furnishings (tapestries, for example). Privileged guests would be taken to the Privy Chamber. The Privy Chamber served primarily as a private dining area though it might typically contain an elaborately decorated bed on which the princess could recline during the daytime. If the manor was of recent construction and the visitor of suitable rank or perhaps a close relative or friend of the princess, then the visitor would be received in the bedchamber, which would, of course, also have a sumptuously dressed bed. An overnight guest would expect to sleep in their own bedchamber (rather than in a dormitory as in early medieval times). This "guest room" would contain a bed furnished as appropriate to the guest's own social and political standing.

This layout of rooms and furnishings along with their function was typical of sixteenth-century manor houses transitioning, in the arrangement of interior space, from medieval military headquarters to primarily domestic establishments. This transition was not novel to the sixteenth century but had been in process for some time.[2] Long-term residency in fortified manors fueled the late medieval trend of communal rooms giving way to compartmentalization. The head of household and his immediate family now occupied rooms reserved for them alone, separated from the large reception rooms such as the great hall. As households came to serve more overtly as administrative and political centers, in addition to continuing their traditional function as regional military headquarters, it became necessary (especially by the sixteenth century) to regulate the crush of place-seekers, suitors, and clients. Hence, large rooms that once contained dormitory-style accommodation were now divided into cellular lodgings for the head, his immediate family, and guests, in which access was subject to restrictions.

The physical separation of the elite kin group from the living spaces reserved for guests and servants was not primarily to preserve the modesty of the head of household but, rather, to clearly demarcate the social hierarchy within the establishment.[3] At the apex of the domestic social pyramid was the householder whose relative isolation within the establishment made visible his/her unique status within it—paradoxically by making the householder less visible to the majority of her/his staff.

There was a paradox at the heart of the elite domestic interior. The "private" chambers of the householder and their immediate relatives was, in fact, an indication of their "public" status. Only the elite, the economically advantaged, could reside within houses large enough to accommodate the division of interior space. The "public" nature of the householder's "private" rooms manifested itself in other ways. Perhaps the most notable is that the householder would use these rooms to receive guests in a way that few modern householders would. There are reports of Elizabeth, as sovereign, receiving her ministers in her bedchamber. Both she and Mary, as princesses, took especial care in the furnishings of bedrooms and their beds. This, and other accounts of how restricted rooms were used, all suggest that elite householders received important guests in their bedrooms in order to indicate the esteem the householder "publicly" evinced toward the guest.

Indeed, these restricted rooms were furnished in the full expectation that important guests would regularly visit them. These cellular chambers and limited-function rooms furthered the early-modern drive toward the display of luxury items that made visible the householder's social and political standing.[4] Collectively, the presence chamber, privy chamber, private chapel, and bedchamber contained many of the elaborate tapestries, cloths of estate, ornate beds, and sumptuous cushions that displayed the wealth of the householder to the guests that they wished to impress.

Royalty and the nobility no longer proclaimed their political and social importance exclusively on the battlefield or through the maintenance of an impressively armed escort. They also made political statements through architecture and furniture. Or, as Natasha Korda phrased it, the "relations between subjects within the home became increasingly centered around and mediated by objects."[5] This trend would culminate later in the sixteenth century with elaborate architectural showpieces such as that of socially prominent figures including Elizabeth Talbot, Countess of Shrewsbury, builder of Chatworth and Hardwick Hall.[6] Royalty and nobles regularly commissioned portraits of themselves, which included their most prized residences and/or furniture as indicators of their wealth and status. Architecture and furniture functioned not simply as a reflection of a person's social and political position but also as a form of self-aggrandizement. Building a large house and furnishing it lavishly, including such things in one's portrait, was a means by which householders publicized both their current standing and the status to which they yet aspired.

Indeed, it was not only royalty and the aristocracy that practiced this form of the "politics of ostentation."[7] William Harrison noted in his *Description of England*, printed in 1577, that anyone with any means at all laid claim to status via the materiality of their households:

> Likewise in the houses of knights, gentlemen, merchantmen and some other wealthy citizens, it is not geason [uncommon] to behold generally their great provision of tapestry, Turkey work, pewter, brass, fine linen, and thereto costly cupboards of plate . . . the costly furniture . . . descended yet lower, even unto the inferior artificers and many farmers, [who] . . . for the most part [have] learned to garnish their cupboards with plate, their joint beds with tapestry and silk hangings, and their tables with carpets and fine napery whereby the wealth of our country . . . doth infinitely appear.[8]

It was not only noble guests who would be impressed with the visible households of the princesses but also the servants, the suppliers, the temporary laborers, the messengers from other households who lived, worked, and visited their manors. Material display in a household setting was universally appreciated as a method for proclaiming status.[9] Also, in an age before mass media, household display and hospitality were the mechanisms by which the fame, wealth, and status of the householder became public knowledge. As contemporaries recognized, the household was the "theater of hospitality."[10] Domestic display highlighted the political and economic importance of the householder.

THE EARLY HOUSEHOLDS OF MARY TUDOR, 1516–1519

Initially, however, Mary's and Elizabeth's residences reflected Henry VIII's understanding of their status. As royal offspring, their childhood households were dependent adjuncts of the king's own domestic establishment. Since the medieval period, it was customary for all royal children to live together either at court or in nursery households in country manors.[11] Only the heir, the eldest son, resided in his own separate establishment. The household of a Prince of Wales (the title reserved for monarch's eldest son) was a distinct corporation, separate from the king's household and funded by revenues from the Prince's own estates.[12] If the royal couple produced several offspring, as did Henry VII and Elizabeth of York, then their younger children often shared one household. At times, the Prince of Wales shared accommodation with his younger siblings in country manors. Even during such periods the prince would continue to employ his own separate and substantial staff. To my knowledge, spinster princesses always lived in shared accommodation either with their siblings in country manors or at court with their parents.

If the royal couple's first child was a girl, as Mary was, the princess would technically have her own household but only in the very limited sense that she was the first occupant of a nursery household. Other than such cases, I have found no record of an unmarried English princess maintaining her own household for a great length of time before Mary. Before marriage, English princesses did not head their own independent establishments funded from their own property revenues. Even adult unmarried princesses lived at court rather than in their own separate households, as did Mary's aunt, known (later) as Mary the French Queen, up to the time of her first marriage. The elder Mary Tudor, sister to Henry VIII, in 1514 had married King Louis XI of France. After his death, she married Charles Brandon and they returned to England in 1515.[13] Before her marriage, Mary, the French Queen, lived either with her siblings (during her father's lifetime) or at the court of her brother, Henry VIII.[14]

The Mary Tudor who is one of the two subjects of this study was the daughter of Henry VIII and Catherine of Aragon, born on February 18, 1516. As the king's eldest child, Mary initially had her own separate establishment. Mary's establishment, however, reflected her status as the king's only legitimate child rather than a reflection that she might be the next monarch of England. Indeed, the king clearly hoped that Mary would soon share her household with other royal children, preferably male children. Shortly after Mary's birth, in a conversation with the Venetian ambassador, Henry famously reasoned: "If it was a daughter this time, by the grace of God the sons will follow."[15] There are indications that Henry was not alone in taking this view. When Lord Mountjoy wrote to congratulate the king on Mary's birth, he described it as a good beginning.[16] The king evidently considered Mary to be no more than a placeholder in the succession until a son was born. Although Mary was, by default, the king's heir until and unless the royal couple produced a son, Henry refused, in the two full years after Mary's birth, to make an official announcement to that effect.

The scale and expenditure of Mary's initial household reflected Henry's hope that he would soon have son to displace Mary as his successor. Princess Mary's household was, initially, little more than an *ad hoc* collection of staff transferred from the king's and queen's own households. The earliest records pointing to the formation of Mary's first household are preserved in "the king's payment book," which listed the actual costs of Henry VIII's Privy Purse expenses as well as estimates for recurring costs.[17]

The payment book lists only seven officers serving in Princess Mary's household including four female "rockers vnto ye prices," who, as their title suggests, rocked the infant princess to sleep. In November, the accounts list a "gentylwoman to the prîces" who received her wages for three quarters of the year. The account books indicate that the infant princess had a chaplain who doubled as her clerk, the aforementioned gentlewoman attendant, as well as a nurse, laundress and the four rockers. There was also mention of a nurse, who was probably Katherine Pole and who received two annuities as the princess' nurse in July 1517.[18] The king's expense account records the quarterly payments to these servants in March, June, September, and December 1517 and March 1518.[19]

Henry VIII's accounts are not sufficiently comprehensive to allow an estimate of the total number of Mary's first household staff, or even of the number serving in a particular capacity. Clearly, her initial staff must have been far larger than the few individuals mentioned explicitly in the king's surviving accounts. Even the minimum staff of seven, as outlined earlier, would have required others to prepare their food and care for their horses.

These kitchen, stable, and other staff may have been assigned initially from Henry's own household, and so their wages do not appear separately in his accounts; nor would they be considered, at this stage, to be permanently attached to Princess Mary's household. Richard Sydnor, for instance, may have been a typical example. In 1518, Sydnor received wages as a member of Henry's household, although he was clearly employed on the princess' business (obtaining horses for her litter).[20] It is also possible that some of the princess' staff came from Catherine of Aragon's household. Mary later demonstrated a great knowledge of Catherine's staff, which may have begun when the queen's staff served temporarily in the young princess' establishment. There is no indication that any of these servants, even those specified as Mary's exclusive staff, wore any livery but that of the king's or queen's households. There may have been no outward sign that they were the princess' servants.

Moreover, Mary's household was such ad hoc affair that at least one of her senior officers held two positions in her household. Henry Rowle served both as Mary's clerk of the closet and also as her chaplain.[21] That Mary's clerk doubled as the chaplain for her household further evidences the modest scale of her initial household. That at least two of the princess' senior officers were either still technically part of the king's household (Sydnor) or served in more than one capacity (Rowle) suggests that Mary's first household was little more than an appendage of the king's own establishment. As late as 1518, when Mary was two years old, her household expenses were still listed as part of the daily expenses of the king's household rather than as a separate establishment as it would be later.[22]

The strongest indication of her status as merely a placeholder until a male heir was born was that Mary was granted none of the trappings of firstborn royal male children. In contrast to firstborn infant royal sons, Mary enjoyed no landed revenues from which to fund her household. No evidence has survived indicating that, until she reached the age of two, Mary's household expanded much beyond more than half-dozen or so staff.

Traditionally, firstborn sons were treated differently in the English royal family. Edward IV's eldest son nominally presided over a viceregal household in the Welsh Marches when he was only six months old. Edward IV further granted his infant son the Welsh Principality from which the young prince's lavish household was funded.[23] Although Mary was officially the heir to the throne in the same way that Edward IV's son was, the scale of her first household suggests strongly that Henry VIII, as he indicated to the Venetian ambassador, considered her as merely a harbinger of better things to come, and certainly not as the next ruler of England.

A comparison between Mary's household during her infancy and those of her future siblings Elizabeth and Edward demonstrates Henry's unwillingness to fund Mary's household on a princely scale. After the births of his younger children, Henry VIII could not take the political risk of failing to support publicly their succession rights, as he had with Mary. Elizabeth was born of a marital union that was recognized only by the English church, and not by Roman Catholics in England or abroad. Henry was obliged to declare Elizabeth the heir to the throne immediately after her birth as a public reaffirmation of his commitment to the Boleyn marriage and his rejection both of Catherine Aragon as his wife and of Mary as his heir. Furthermore, Henry pressured Parliament into passing the first Act of Succession 1534, which declared Elizabeth the successor to the crown.

Although very little documentation survives for Elizabeth's first household, it is clear that her initial household was much more lavish that of Mary's first household. The one stray reference to her household expenditure dates from March 1535 when Elizabeth's steward, Sir John Shelton, promised the king that he would attempt to rein in costs for the coming half-year.[24] He promised not to exceed substantially a total of £1,000 for the following six-month period. This suggests that the household of the two-year-old Elizabeth had already cost the king at least £2,000 per annum. This was roughly twice the cost of Mary's household from 1516 until 1533. Until she was nine, Mary's household rarely required the king to lay out more than the £1,400 that he spent in 1518. As late as 1523, when Mary was seven, her household cost the king just under £1,100.[25] For comparison purposes, the king's household averaged around £13,000 until the late 1530s.[26]

After the birth of king's son, Prince Edward, in 1537, Henry VIII wasted no time in declaring him heir the throne and conferring on him the title of Prince of Wales. The king proceeded to confer several titles on the infant prince, making him Prince of Wales, Duke of Cornwall, and Earl of Chester; the revenues from all these estates were available to fund the prince's household. Mary's initial household would not have possessed similar funding sources because she held no landed titles as Prince Edward did from infancy. Initially, however, the king did not wait for a rogation day to collect the necessary revenues for the young prince's household. By May 1538, when the prince was only seven months old, the king had already spent £6,500 from his own coffers on his son's household.[27] This was an enormous sum. In the late 1530s, per annum expenses for the king's own household averaged around £25,000, so the Prince's household expenditure was roughly equal to 10 percent of the king's own annual household expenditure.[28]

The later financial worries of the Henrician regime make it unlikely that the king was able to continue maintaining such a lavish establishment even if Edward's household could draw on the revenues of Wales, Cornwall, and Chester. Some retrenchment is suggested by Edward's household later sharing accommodation with Elizabeth and Mary. This retrenchment, however, appears to have been temporary. Prince Edward's household independence was reemphasized in 1543 when he ceased to share accommodations with his sisters. At this time, preparations were underway to invest Prince Edward with a viceregal household in Ludlow, the traditional residence of the Prince of Wales. The plans for Edward's viceregal household/court in Ludlow exist in draft form.[29]

Another indication that Elizabeth's and Edward's first households were much more complicated establishments than Mary's first household was that the king took more time to institute them. Henry's household accounts support David Loades's suggestion that Mary's household took shape very shortly after her birth.[30] In contrast, the time lapse between, on the one hand, the births of Elizabeth and Edward and, on the other, the commencement of their households indicate that Henry VIII spent months recruiting staff, assigning offices, and establishing regulations for the households of his younger children. The king did not officially constitute Elizabeth's household until December 1533, over three months after her birth.[31] Edward's household officers did not receive their appointments until March 1538—five months after his birth.[32] As noted earlier, Henry VIII's accounts indicated that he patched together Mary's household quickly and minimally within weeks of her birth.

Yet another testament to the importance of Edward's first household, in contrast to Mary's, and among the reasons that it took so long to establish Edward's household, are the elaborate procedures that Henry VIII commissioned to ensure the boy's safety. Among them was a set of instructions to the prince's household officers, who by rank and number were indicative of a substantial household. In order to ensure the proper "keepinge oversight care and care [sic] of his ma[jes]ties and the holl realmes most precyouse jewell the Princes grace," Edward's initial household had the full complement of departments such as kitchen, buttery, larder, scaldinghouse, and so on. Overseeing these departments was a complete staff of senior officers including a chamberlain, vice chamberlain, steward, and a controller, all supported by "yomen and gromes of the hall" as well as "sundry boyes, pages and seruants."[33] No such instructions survive for Mary's first household or even any indications that, initially, she had similar departments or officers.

The comparison with Elizabeth's and Edward's households shows clearly that the small size and limited financial resources of Mary's first household reflected Henry VIII's 1516 statement to the Venetian ambassador that she was only a temporary placeholder in the succession, soon to be supplanted by a Prince of Wales. Both Mary and her younger siblings technically enjoyed, at separate times, the same official status as the king's only heir, but only Elizabeth and Edward were immediately given households commensurate with the status of future monarchs.

Mary was Henry's only child until the illegitimate birth of Henry Fitzroy in 1519, and remained his only legitimate child until 1533 when Elizabeth was born. Although Edward was born after his two sisters, he was, legally, the king's only legitimate child until 1544 as both Mary and Elizabeth were declared illegitimate in the second Act of Succession (1536). It was not until the third Act of Succession in 1544 that Edward became only the first in a line of three heirs when Mary and Elizabeth were restored to the succession order (while still remaining illegitimate).

The gap between Mary's official status in 1516–1518 as the king's heir and his personal opinion that she was merely, as David Loades put it, the "token of hope" heralding the birth of the real heir (a son) was clearly demonstrated by the hasty formation, minimal staffing, and limited scale of her first household.[34]

MARY'S CHILDHOOD HOUSEHOLD, 1519–1525

The scale of Mary's household expanded from 1519 onward as her political status rose. Since Mary's birth in 1516, Henry VIII and Catherine of Aragon had not produced a child, let alone a son. It was looking increasingly likely that Mary would remain the king's only heir. Catherine of Aragon did not conceive again until 1518. This was Catherine's sixth pregnancy (at least) since her marriage to Henry in 1509 and so far, she had given birth successfully only to Mary and, earlier in 1511, to a son who lived but a few weeks. All the others had ended in stillbirths and miscarriages.[35] This sad history of unsuccessful pregnancies combined with Catherine's health (she had likely begun menopause in 1519)

made Mary's succession ever more a realistic outcome as she grew from an infant into a healthy toddler.

Despite Henry VIII's clear reluctance to acknowledge Mary as his probable
successor, Mary's status was rising in the international marriage market based
on her increasingly likely future as the next monarch of England. These negotiations would have immediate consequences for the princess' household. In
1518, Henry entered into negotiations with the French for an alliance to be cemented by a marriage between the princess and the French dauphin. The
French negotiators insisted the Henry finally acknowledge that Mary was his
only heir. Accordingly, the terms of the marriage contract contained a stipulation that Mary was Henry's next successor in default of any future sons that he
might have.[36] A month after the betrothal ceremonies took place in October
1518, which bound Mary to the dauphin, Catherine gave birth to a stillborn
daughter. This was a "vexatious" outcome, according to Sebastian Guistinian.
The Venetian ambassador was convinced that Henry would not have agreed to
the clause naming Mary as his immediate successor in the French marriage
contract if he were not that Catherine would shortly give birth to a healthy son
who might make such an acknowledgment irrelevant.[37] After the November
1518 miscarriage of a daughter, Catherine would not conceive again. Hence, the
acknowledgment in the French marriage treaty of Mary's succession rights became the default political reality from late 1518 until Mary's disinheritance in
the wake of the Henry's divorce from Catherine.

Mary's household began to reflect this new reality. From 1519, Mary's household steadily increased its staff, and by implication, its scale. In this year, the
king authorized the purchase of liveries for sixteen newly hired servants.[38] The
household acquired an additional six new gentlemen, nine valets, and four
grooms. Now three years old, Mary no longer needed rockers; her former rockers became gentlewomen of her privy chamber.[39]

As the king's (reluctantly) acknowledged heir, tradition required that Mary
preside over a household that showcased her potential as the next sovereign.
Her household performed this function during Mary's reception of unnamed
French envoys in early July 1520.[40] At the time, the king and queen were in
Calais for the famous meeting, known as the Field of the Cloth of Gold, with
the French king, François I. As the betrothed of the dauphin and potentially
the next queen-consort of France, Mary's presence at this event was assumed
by the French. Mary, however, did not attend. It is unclear what prompted
Henry and Catherine to leave their daughter at home. The important thing for
this study are the repercussions of this decision. Evidently suspicious that Mary
was too ill to come to France, François I sent envoys to England to report back
on her physical and mental development.[41] The king's chief minister, Thomas,
Cardinal Wolsey, warned the privy councilors, in charge of the government in

Henry VIII's and Wolsey's absence, of the arrival of the envoys. Wolsey instructed the councilors to ensure that the four-year-old Mary was shown to best advantage.

On short notice, the council decided that it was time for Mary and her household to overawe the envoys with royal hospitality.[42] Mary was too young to preside over a banquet but, apparently, she could host a reception. The councilors installed Mary and her household at the king's palace of Richmond, which was usually reserved for the royal court only when the sovereign was in residence. Mary's household expanded to include the noble ladies who had not accompanied Queen Catherine to France. Their function was to impress on the French envoys that Mary was not the usual type of princess whose future merely contained a consort's crown. The council ensured that Mary appeared before the French envoys as a princely figure, the next sovereign of England, more than worthy to be also the next queen-consort of France. The account of the meeting comes from a letter from the Privy Council to Henry VIII. It is worth quoting at some length as it underscores the household's central role in offering hospitality on a politically important occasion.

> . . . [the] gentilmen of ffraunce of whose commyng and ent[ainment] we had aduertisement by my lorde Cardinall . . . being well accompanied by [the] Lorde darcy and others repared to yor derest doughter the [princess] at Richmounte/ where they founde her grace right honorable [and well] accompanied wt your counseill and other lordes booth sp[irit]uãll and temporall/ and her house and chambers right well appointed and furnished wt a goodly company of gentilmen and tall yomeñ/ And as vnto ladies ther were in the chamber of presence attending on her grace besides the lady gõu[er]nes and other her gentilwomen the duches of Norff[olk] wt her iij doughters/ the lady [Margaret] wiff to the lorde herbert countesse of Worcestre/ the ladies gray and nevill/the lord Johns wiff wt sondery other ladies and gentilwomen/ and in the great chamber wer many goodly gentilwomen well apparailled/ And at the commyng of the said gentilmen of ffraunce to the princes presence her grace in suche wise showed her self vnto theym furst in welcommyng and enterteynyng of theym wt moost goodly countenence/ proper commyunycacõn and pleasant passe tyme in playing at the virginalles that they greately marveled and reioyesed the same her yong and tendre age considered/ And soe after they departed ageine to London . . . [43]

A copy of the letter sent to Wolsey added that Mary's household offered the envoys "strawberes wafers wyne and ypocras in plenty" for their "goodly chere."[44] In these letters, the privy councilors list Mary's household staff as second in importance only to the privy councilors themselves and the nobles present. The household staff were the laudable "furnishings" of the chamber and as such, crucial in creating what the Privy Council hoped was a good impression in the minds of the envoys.[45]

In July 1520, the Anglo-French alliance was, in many respects, predicated on Mary's continued survival and eventual inheritance of the English throne. It was, therefore, vital that the Privy Council ensure that Mary appeared before the French envoys as a princely hostess (and a healthy one) against a material background that indicated the king's acknowledgment of her future as the next ruler of England. The central element of the setting in which Mary received the ambassadors was her household: her noble governess (Margaret Plantagenet, countess of Salisbury), tall servants and smartly dressed gentlewomen. The rest— bishops, nobles, councilors—were there to lend extra support and weight as were the aristocratic women mentioned in the Privy Council's letter. The importance of this household reception (and Henry VIII's particular interest) is demonstrated by the Privy Council's letters in which the council claimed that Mary's household reception was the only real noteworthy political event that had occurred recently in the king's absence.[46]

It is unlikely that Mary's more modest establishment before 1519 could have "appointed" her chambers with such a socially (and physically) impressive staff or offered hospitality to a standard required "in plenty" for such an occasion. Additionally, it would appear that Salisbury had ensured that the toddler performed her duties as a political hostess by training Mary in "proper commmyunycacõn."

It would appear that Mary's household offered hospitality to more than just the French envoys during the king's absence. In their letter to the king, the Privy Council reported that the princess made a good impression upon "all such as repaire vnto her presence" and indicated that they themselves were frequent visitors.[47] In the absence of the king and his consort, Mary's household served as *the* royal court in England.

Significantly, from 1519, Mary's household now disbursed sums directly to household officers. Mary's staff now received their wages as members of her household rather than as the king's agents temporarily assigned to her service as had been the case from 1516 until 1518. Her establishment was no longer merely an adjunct of the king's own household; it was now too large and complex to be conflated with the king's own household accounts.[48] Her accounts also witness her household's continued expansion throughout the 1520s. The princess' 1522 and 1523 household accounts reveal that her establishment now contained the full complement of departments and staff found in contemporary aristocratic households. As with other royal and elite households, she had her own household Privy Council that managed her household affairs.[49] During these years, Mary's household continued to take on staff by adding ushers, valets and grooms of the chamber. In 1521, the king furnished the princess' chamber with seventeen liveried servants.[50] According to accounts her treasurer submitted to the crown, by

September 1522, Mary's privy chamber staff alone now included thirty-six members: six gentlemen ushers, ten valets, fifteen grooms, a stable boy, three children of the kitchen, and a woodbearer.[51] None of these accounts provides a complete list of her household staff but these stray references make it likely that her establishment employed around seventy-five staff members, a number common to many aristocratic households, although short of the two-hundred found in ducal households.[52]

Her household accounts from the early 1520s suggest that the king had provided her with furnishings that finally reflected her status as his next successor. The 1523 accounts list her table linens as made from the finest Holland cloth and Brussels linen. The seven-year-old Mary received important visitors while sitting under a cloth of estate made of cloth of gold tissue. This cloth of estate was an important indicator of her status and not just because of its ornate material. Customarily, only the king or those who received his special permission were allowed to sit beneath a cloth of estate. In fact, the king had furnished the princess with four. The other three were nearly as lavish as the first, being made of "brocade," blue cloth of gold, and crimson velvet. Her household was now decorated with several sets of tapestries and her beds were dressed with satin and velvet linens. She sat on chairs cushioned in crimson and purple velvet, as well as red cloth of gold, and satin. The tapestries depicted the story of Hercules, the siege of Damascus, Christ's Passion, scriptural allegory, and Alexander the Great. Her bed linens were of crimson satin embroidered with deer, lions, and falcons. Others consisted of gold and green velvet. Admittedly, many of these textiles were listed by her treasurer as "old." This does not necessarily indicate that they were in poor condition. Usually, an item that was clearly in need of replacing would be designated not simply as "old" but "old and worn." None of Mary's goods were so described; rather, "old" here referred to her goods being secondhand rather than newly purchased.[53]

Not all this domestic splendor resulted solely from the king's generosity. The nobility, following the king's lead, presented Mary with objects intended for household display. Her accounts list a set of hangings with the duke of Buckingham's coat of arms in the border, suggesting that he gave them to her along with matching bed curtains. In 1522, Cardinal Wolsey gave her a gold cross, the Countess of Devon sent two silver flagons; and the princess' aunt, Mary the French Queen, gave her solid gold pomander. In 1523, the king gave her a silver cup, Wolsey sent her a gold salter, and the countess of Devonshire gave her a gold cross.[54] In 1524, the same countess gave her a silver gilt image of the Virgin, Wolsey gave her a saucer of gold, and the Duke of Norfolk sent her a silver cup.[55]

These were clearly not children's toys but household ornaments of the richest kind. The gift-givers did not intend for these objects to divert the princess but to exalt her through domestic display. This display formed the backdrop to the household's important function as a center of hospitality.

In addition to the reception of the French envoys in 1520, her household offered hospitality on a grand scale around Christmas. In 1522, John Thurgood, selected as the Lord of Misrule, submitted costs to Mary's treasurer for expenses incurred in orchestrating the entertainments. These included the live butchering of a calf (!), a play on a naval theme, a skit with a friar, dancers with staves, a "disguising" that involved twelve men playing animate haystacks, and an unknown entertainment featuring gunners and gunpowder. On a more sedate note, John Stenton led the clerks of the Windsor College in the singing of ballads before Mary and her household on Christmas Day.[56] For the next year, 1523, the scale of Christmas entertainments is suggested by the bloated entry for foodstuffs and table linen for the month of December in the accounts, for example, the household consumed six pounds of pepper in December as compared to the more usual £1 per month. Additionally, the unusual amounts of liquorice and comfits as well as gold and silver leaf argues for sumptuous and ornate culinary creations. It is little wonder that an extra cook was employed for the twelve days of Christmas in 1523 to help out with "the gilting of divers subtleties."[57] For this Christmas, Mary's household commissioned the forest wardens in Essex to provide her table with, at least, twelve deer. The hearty diners in Mary's household would have been able to eat in a civilized manner using brand new linen napkins and towels and some of them would have enjoyed the twelve new napkins made out of the more expensive and delicate "diaper" cloth—all prepared the month before. Moreover, they would have dined on the brand new pewter plates and saucers. The feast was prepared using new kitchen equipment purchased for the occasion including copper pots and new wooden trays and bowls. Serenading the household and guests were three musicians sent by Mary the French Queen.

The dishes at her table were flavored with expensive spices such as saffron, cloves and mace.[58] Records of the establishment's meat and seafood consumption suggests the scale of her newly expanded household. From October 1522 to September 1523, her household digested 22 bulls, 158 sheep, 45 calves, 8 large pigs and 48 small ones, 163 stock-fish, 4 barrels of white herrings, and an uncalculated number of chickens, which alone cost the household the not inconsiderable sum of £35.[59] To put the £35 poultry sum in perspective, the costs for the entire household including wages, tips, and other consumables were just under £1,400. To serve all of this food, the household commissioned a London silversmith to make two dozen platters, four dozen dishes, and two dozen saucers out of pewter.[60]

It is not easy to compare the scale of this display and the level of hospitality in Mary's household with those of her contemporaries; records for other elite households have not survived in sufficient quantity. Certainly, her household hospitality was less lavish than that offered at the king's court. Comparing Mary's household expenditure to the duke of Buckingham's during these years provides a clue as to how her household compared with others. In 1519, the duke's household expenses totaled nearly £2,500. As noted, Mary's expenses during the early 1520s averaged around £1,100.[61] This suggests that Mary's household could not compete with the establishments of the high aristocracy. By contrast, for a landless minor, Mary's household was impressive.

For the heir to the throne, it was still modest. Historians have not examined Henry's and Mary's household accounts during these years for clues to the king's attitude toward a female succession. It is, however, clear from these records that initially, Henry did not regard Mary as his heir. Furthermore, although the scale and furnishings of her household expanded and improved in keeping with her increasing chances of succession in the early 1520s, the king was still unwilling to spend the lavish sums on her household that he would spend later on the households of his younger children to ensure their public acceptance as his heirs. Yet there was a brief moment in early 1525 when the king finally seemed resigned to Mary's succession, which he characteristically indicated by significantly altering the scale and material furnishings of his daughter's household.

PRINCESS OF WALES BY HOUSEHOLD: MARY'S HOUSEHOLD IN THE WELSH MARCHES, 1525–1528

In 1525, at the age of nine, Mary finally received a household that approached the scale normally found in the household of a king's successor. In the summer of 1525, Henry VIII bestowed on Mary a viceregal household and dispatched her to the Welsh Marches to govern the counties and the Welsh Principality in his name. Even at this stage, Henry refused to bestow on Mary the status—via her household—as his only heir. Just before Mary left for Wales, the king elevated her illegitimate half-brother, Henry Fitzroy, to the peerage. In June 1525, Henry created Fitzroy as duke of Richmond and Somerset and dispatched him up north with a household on a scale commensurate with Mary's. Henry was, essentially, backing two horses. The long-term effects Richmond's household might have had on his credibility as a successor were frustrated by his early death in 1536.[62]

Queen Catherine had not conceived since 1518. It was clear that Mary would be the only child of the marriage. In accordance with shifting alliances in 1521,

Mary was betrothed to her cousin, Charles V, Holy Roman Emperor. Imperial negotiators, like the French before them, had insisted that the marriage contract contain Henry's acknowledgment of Mary as his heir.[63] In early 1525, when the king began making preparations to send Mary to the Welsh Marches, the princess' future looked very promising. Not only was she likely to be the next ruler of England but also the consort of Western Europe's most powerful monarch.

Mary's position was strengthened with Henry when Charles won a major victory over the French king at Pavia in Italy in February 1525. The French king was taken prisoner by Charles' army. On hearing this news, Henry hoped to enlist his future son-in-law to help him invade France. Henry argued that Charles should support him militarily in this because Charles would eventually inherit Henry's French conquests through his marriage to Mary.[64]

It was amid these plans to invade France with Imperial support that Henry planned to send Mary to Wales. Given that it later took Henry five months to establish Edward's household in 1538, it is reasonable to assume it took a similar amount of time to gather together Mary's new viceregal household. Mary's household was fully constituted by July 1525 suggesting that the king began planning the household in late February/early March, that is, shortly after Charles V's victory at Pavia. He intended to present her to the English and Welsh people as their future monarch and to indicate to Charles the importance of his future consort and, by implication, the importance of the Anglo-Imperial alliance.

In the event, by the time Mary left for Wales in August, she was no longer betrothed the Emperor and Henry's plans were in ruins. Her new household, however, had already taken shape and, due to a recent power vacuum, a royal presence was needed in the Welsh Marches. According to the payroll, Mary's new household officially commenced around the beginning of July 1525.[65] Charles V had suddenly broken off his betrothal to her only a month before. The crown was short of representatives in 1525, which, in part, justified the king's decision to implement his plan to send Mary to Wales despite Charles's repudiation. In March 1525, the king recalled Charles Brandon, Duke of Suffolk, from his role as justiciar of North Wales and, in south Wales, the long-time crown agent, Sir Rhys ap Thomas, had died in the spring.[66] This household was to have a profound effect on Mary's political status and composition of future households.[67]

Mary left for Wales in August 1525 and returned sometime in mid-1528. Of all her childhood households, this one has left the most substantive documentation. These documents comprise accounts submitted by her household to the crown, lists of servants and furnishings, correspondence between her new household council and the king's chief minister, Cardinal Wolsey, and sets of instructions for the household and its Privy Council. The most detailed of these documents is the "Instruction Book," preserved in a manuscript from the Cotton collection, and now in the British Library.[68]

Henry's primary intention in sending Mary to the Welsh Marches was for her household to serve as a royal hospitality center. In the instructions that the king commissioned for the regulation of the new household, he specified that the goal of the establishment was to ensure that the local population was "by meanes of good hospitalitie refreshed."[69] It was customary for the English monarch to govern Wales through a combination of a council and royal agents as justiciars, especially when there was no Prince of Wales.[70] Henry dispatched Mary to Wales so her household, in common with other elite and royal households, could perform the one governing function—offering hospitality—that worked best with a viceregal figure even if that figure was little more than a figurehead.[71] The king's "Instructions" reveal a general expectation that Mary's household would quickly become the center of elite social life in the region:

> . . . the gentlemen vshers yomen of the chambers, groomes and others belonging to the chambers to giue their due attendance every one as to his rome [job] and place doeth appertayne so that the chambers be always seruised as the tyme and case shall requyer /That is to say Sondayes Saturdayes and other principall seasons when there shallbe accesse or recourse of noblemen or other straungers repayring vnto that court or that it be as festiviall dayes or tymes or other thinges requisite to haue a great and honorable p[e]rsonne then all the officers and ministers of the chambers to giue their continuall attendance for that tyme . . . [72]

A council of the king's commissioners accompanied Mary's household and also served as her personal household council. One of the council's main tasks was to ensure that her household was performing its hospitable functions. John Vosey, bishop of Exeter and Lord President of the council, wrote anxiously to Wolsey about the preparations Mary's household should make for the public celebration of Christmas at Tewkesbury Castle in the marches in 1525:

> Please it youre grace for the great reparre of straungers supposed vnto the princesse honorable householde this solemne fest of Cristmas. We humbly beseche the same to let vs knowe youre gracious pleasure concernñyg aswell a ship of silver for the almes dysshe requysite for her high estate/ and spice plate/ as also for trumpettes and a rebek to be sent/ and whither we shall appoynte any lord of mysrule for the said honorable household/ previde for enterludes disgysynges or pleyes in the said fest/ or for banket on twelf nyght . . . [73]

Vosey's letter indicates that Mary's Welsh household, like other satellite royal households and the royal court itself, used Christmas as an occasion for conspicuous display and hospitality.[74] The "Instructions" and Vosey's letter suggest the scale of Mary's household. This household was so lavish that Henry, for the first and only time, granted Mary lands to help defray the costs of the establishment.

The cost of her new household was around £4,500 per annum for her two and half year residency. This was over three times her household expenditure in the preceding years.[75] Although women could hold legal title to land in England, it was still rare for them to receive grants in their own right, especially if they were unmarried or minors and Mary was both. According to the final folio of the "Instructions," Henry bestowed on Mary the counties of Bromfield, Yale, and Chirkland for "the supportacōn and maintenance of the chardgs for thestate and household of the said Princess," that is, to draw the necessary revenues to support and maintain the lavish scale of her household.[76]

In relation to the household, these grants are an important testimony to its scale. Mary's household was now on a princely scale. It had the full standing and function of a regional court. As such, Henry anticipated that it would attract local magnates and gentry to witness Mary's "high estate," her sumptuous lifestyle. Mary now finally presided over a household worthy of an heir to the throne.

When the locals repaired to Mary's household, they would have found that the king had outfitted it to high standards. Her servants—all 213 of them—wore liveries of damask.[77] Among the furniture that traveled with her to the Welsh Marches were goods to furnish three altars. These included two cushions of cloth of gold and another two of crimson velvet. Her keeper of the Wardrobe took a delivery of cloth of gold on August 11. Her privy chamber ladies were instructed to wear gowns of black velvet. She had a throne in the presence chamber.[78]

From measuring instruments to senior staff, all household personnel and goods identified themselves as extensions of her rank and privilege. Her senior servants wore damask liveries of her colors: blue and green. Her senior officers who also doubled as her privy councilors would have worn their own clothing but their servants, who were on Mary's payroll, would have worn her colors. This was an important indication of Mary's status. Her servants wore her colors, rather than the king's. Even the keeper of the princess' horse was expected to wear the damask livery (although presumably only on ceremonial or public occasions). Nothing was too small to escape identification with the princess, including the masking iron used for measuring that also bore her badge.[79]

Although the household's grandeur was primarily intended to reflect glory on the king, he had, perhaps with some personal misgivings, substantially enhanced Mary's credibility as his successor. Henry's elevation of Fitzroy to the dukedom of Richmond immediately after Charles V repudiated his betrothal to Mary in June 1525 may reflect these misgivings. Henry sending Richmond to the north with his own viceregal household adds further credibility to the idea that the king was ambivalent about having Mary as his only heir now that she was no longer the linchpin in an Anglo-Imperial alliance, which had at one point looked likely to help Henry relive the conquest of France accomplished by Henry's already legendary ancestor and namesake, Henry V.

Whatever Henry's own intentions were, by allowing Mary to preside over a viceregal household, just as male Princes of Wales had before her, fostered the impression that she was unquestionably the heir to the throne, the next ruler of England, and a *de jure* as well as a *de facto* Princess of Wales. Contemporaries now generally, if erroneously, referred to her as "Princess of Wales." Juan Luis Vives dedicated his educational treatise, Satellium, to her as "Princeps Walliae."[80] The Imperial ambassador designated her as the Princess of Wales in his dispatches.[81] This was not simply an error made by foreign observers. Official documents bore some of the responsibility by shortening the official title of her household council from "the king's commissioners with my lady Princess" to "the princess' council."[82]

David Loades has uncovered evidence that her Welsh household servants remained on the crown payroll as late as 1532, apparently in case Mary should return to hold court again in Ludlow Castle (the principal residence of the Prince of Wales, which Mary briefly occupied in 1526).[83] Her former household council continued to govern the region under the name of "the princes council" until 1536—eight years after Mary left the Marches and two years after she was declared illegitimate by the first Act of Succession.

Part of the explanation for this confusion over Mary's official status may be because her household, most particularly her Privy Council, performed very much as the households and councils of her male predecessors—actual Princes of Wales. By the mid-sixteenth century, it was customary to provide outlying borderlands like the Welsh and Scottish Marches with a royal viceregal figure to represent royal authority in areas where the actual sovereign would likely never visit. It was also customary by this point to draw these viceregal figures from the royal family. English sovereigns often dispatched their firstborn sons to the Welsh Marches in order to provide a satellite royal court, a visible manifestation of the English crown's control of the Welsh principality.

In 1525, Henry and Wolsey reached the conclusion that both the Scottish and Welsh Marches required more direct supervision by royal officials. But the king had no legitimate son. He had no Prince of Wales to send to the Welsh Marches as his father, Henry VII, had sent Prince Arthur. Nor did he have a second son to dispatch to the Scottish Marches. Yet, both places had recently become nearly ungovernable: the Scottish border was the scene of mutual raiding on both sides and the attempt by Charles Brandon, Duke of Suffolk, to stabilize the Welsh Marches had ended in failure.[84] Generally, when there was no suitable royal male offspring, then the monarch selected a nobleman with a substantial landed presence in or near Wales. The obvious choice in the 1520s was the Duke of Buckingham, whose patrimony included many substantial estates along the Welsh border. But English kings from Richard III to Henry VIII had a complicated relationship with the Buckingham family, the Staffords, which recently had resulted in the judicial execution of the last two dukes, including Edward Stafford, third Duke of Buckingham, in 1521.[85] Something needed to be done about Wales, but the pool of viceregal figures available to the crown was depressingly small. Henry must, perforce, use the children he had: a bastard son and a legitimate daughter. Accordingly, he sent his son, Henry Fitzroy, to the Scottish marches along with a princely household and dispatched his daughter to the Welsh marches with nearly the same fanfare and household as if she had been a male Prince of Wales.

The lavishness of Mary's household in the Welsh Marches created confusion as to whether or not she had been granted the title of "Princess of Wales" by her father. This confusion was, perhaps, exacerbated by idiosyncratic nature of how the title was bestowed and invested. The royal tradition for designating the monarch's firstborn son as "Prince of Wales" has remained remarkably stable for centuries. The associated procedures and legal status of the title are the same today as they were in late medieval England. The title "Prince of Wales" is (and has always been) in the sovereign's gift. The title is reserved only for the monarch's firstborn son. The sovereign, however, can withhold the title. The monarch can elect not to bestow the title on their firstborn son. However, the sovereign does not have complete discretion over the granting of the title. Most important, the monarch cannot bestow the title "Prince of Wales" on anyone but the firstborn son and that son must be the issue of a legally valid marriage. So Henry VIII could not bestow the title on his illegitimate son, Henry Fitzroy. The other relevant caveat for this study is that at that time the sovereign could not (and never could) bestow the title on a female.[86]

Although these strictures are widely known among jurists, what is less appreciated is the informality that has always been attendant on the initial bestowal or designation of the monarch's first born son as "Prince of Wales." A Prince of Wales is "created" or granted the title by the monarch informally. The sovereign can "create" (designate) their firstborn son as "Prince of Wales" shortly after birth as Edward IV did for his son, the future Edward V and later Henry VIII would do for his son, the future Edward VI. This designation can be nothing more than a witnessed verbal declaration, which finds confirmation in subsequent written documents. Edward VI's right to the title of Prince of Wales was confirmed by the crown as when Henry VIII issued instructions for Edward's first household of in which the infant was referred to as "prince of Wales and duke of Cornwall."[87]

"Investing" a prince with the title "Prince of Wales" is another much more public matter. When sovereigns designated their infant firstborn sons as Prince of Wales, the investiture often did not take place until years later when the prince was judged of sufficient age to withstand the ceremony. The "investiture" of a prince with the title involves not only elaborate ceremony but also a confirming act of Parliament. The confusion over "creating" and "investing" a royal offspring with the title was aggravated in the sixteenth century by the imprecise terminology employed on this issue even by those most vitally concerned. For instance, the first entry in the chronicle kept by Edward VI refers to his "creation" as Prince of Wales and how this ceremony was to take place but was cancelled when his father, Henry VIII, died and Edward acceded to the throne.[88] Edward, however, was referring to his "investiture." He had held the title "Prince of Wales" since infancy and even signed himself "princeps" in his personal correspondence but had not yet been invested with title ceremonially. It was the ceremony that had been cancelled, not Edward's assumption of the title of Prince of Wales.[89]

This disjunction between the designation and the ceremonial investment of a Prince of Wales is something not widely appreciated in the sixteenth century. Edward VI, before his accession, was styled "Prince of Wales" in royal documents even though he never underwent a formal investiture ceremony.[90] In this, he followed in his father's footsteps. After the death of Arthur, Prince of Wales, his father Henry VII declared verbally that his younger son, Prince Henry, was now Prince of Wales. But Prince Henry (the future Henry VIII) did not undergo a formal investiture ceremony nor was he granted the revenues of the principality as enjoyed by his brother before him. Despite this lack of ceremonial and public confirmation of the title, contemporaries understood in both cases that these princes held the title "Prince of Wales."

It is not surprising, therefore, that some of Mary's contemporaries drew the erroneous impression from her household on the Welsh Marches (which so resembled in scale and function those of preceding Princes of Wales) that she, too, had been granted the title. Given all this ambiguity, it appears that the scale of Mary's household in the Welsh marches, evoking as it did the establishments of previous male Princes of Wales, was taken as a sign by many that Mary held the title officially.

To ensure that modern readers do not share in this confusion, it is necessary to be clear about this here: Mary was neither created nor invested as Princess of Wales. In the sixteenth century (and at the time of writing this), a woman was not eligible to hold the title in her own right. The designation "Princess of Wales" was reserved only for the wife of the Prince of Wales. There are no official documents, generated by the crown, which refer to Mary holding the title of Princess of Wales or Prince of Wales.

The designation referring to "princes council" signifies only that spelling has changed over the intervening centuries. The modern word "princess" was often spelled with only one "s" in the sixteenth century. Moreover, the possessive was often not employed and rarely with the type of punctuation common to modern usage. The "princes council" is properly translated into modern idiom as "the princess' council" with the term princess indicating Mary's rank as "my lady princess" rather than as a female Prince (or Princess) of Wales.

Despite this, Mary's princely household in the Welsh Marches associated her very strongly with the Principality. As indicated earlier, this association was compelling enough to persuade foreign and domestic observers into assuming that Mary held the title. Mary was the unofficial Princess of Wales because her household was on such a scale that many observers assumed that she held the title. This association of Mary and the Welsh principality persisted long after Mary left the marches for good in 1527. Mary's Privy Purse accounts from 1536 until 1543 record regular presents of leeks, a popular symbol of Wales, presented to her by a yeoman of the king's guard every year on St. David's Day.[91] Jane Dormer, a privy chamber lady in Mary's later households, insisted to her biographer that Mary had held the title of "Princess of Wales."[92] One of the more remarkable instances of this continuing association of Mary and her princely establishment with Wales is contained in William Forrest's poem on Catherine of Aragon, whom he identifies in the title as Grisild the Second. In this poem, printed in the last year of Queen Mary's reign in 1558, Forrest pointed to Mary's princely household as the mechanism by which she acquired an aura of sovereignty at a young age:

> Suche complaynte (syttinge all solytarye)
> Goode Grysilde wolde ofte vnto herselfe make,
> Prayinge to God for her Doughter Marye,
> That hee of her the gouernement wolde take . . .
> Whoe at that season, as Pryncesse soueraigne,
> At Ludlowe kepte howseholde much honorablye . . . [93]

In view of Henry's ambivalence regarding Mary's succession in 1525, it likely that he later considered her viceregal household to have been too successful in elevating her political status. This was especially the case once Henry resolved his doubts about a female succession by instituting divorce proceedings against Catherine of Aragon in 1527 with the aim of disinheriting Mary. Henry now found himself in the awkward position of trying to undermine Mary's succession after he had just spent lavish sums to establish her as his viceregal representative in the Welsh Marches.

The elevation of Mary's political profile through her Welsh household may help to explain why, later, men such as Robert Aske were uneasy about the passage of the second Act of Succession in 1536, which disinherited the princess. According to the Imperial ambassador, Eustace Chapuys, the English and especially the Welsh exhibited great personal loyalty to Mary during the 1530s.[94] The king had presented Mary to the political nation as its one of two possible future rulers (the other being Fitzroy) by granting her a materially impressive household set in the Welsh Marches just as if she were a Princess of Wales. The polity had responded to this household image-making with a level of enthusiasm that became, by the mid-1530s, severely embarrassing to the king. By 1533, Henry had a new daughter, Elizabeth. Mary's household history as the unofficial Princess of Wales made her too great a threat to Elizabeth's succession rights. Having promoted Mary via the household, the king would demote her by the same means.

LEGITIMACY BY HOUSEHOLD: THE COMPETING SUCCESSION CLAIMS OF MARY AND ELIZABETH TUDOR WITHIN THEIR COMBINED HOUSEHOLD, 1533–1536

Henry VIII continued to exploit the household's ability to display status in order to publicize his own views of the succession. With Elizabeth's birth in September 1533, the king now had two daughters. According to common law, if the English crown was simply property, then both of his daughters would inherit equal shares of the country. But the crown was also an office and so could not be divided. There could be only one heir. The king signaled which daughter was his chosen successor through his direct regulation of the scale and splendor of their respective households.

In 1527, a few months before Mary returned from the Welsh Marches, Henry began divorce proceedings against her mother, Catherine of Aragon. The Pope rejected Henry's argument that the previous Pope had been in error when he granted a dispensation that allowed Henry to wed Catherine even though she was his dead brother's widow. In retaliation for the Pope's refusal to overrule the previous dispensation, Henry instigated a separation of the English church from the Roman Catholic Church via parliamentary legislation in 1533. The fine details of the king's "Great Matter" has already been treated at length and so will not be detailed here.[95] Furthermore, the king announced the he had married Anne Boleyn in the spring of that year. In May, Boleyn was crowned queen-consort of England and gave birth to Elizabeth in September. Throughout the divorce proceedings, from 1528 until 1533, Mary no longer presided over a viceregal household. Nevertheless, a favorable comment by an unknown Milanese envoy in England in the early 1530s suggests that scale of her household was still suitable to one of her rank as the king's only acknowledged, if increasingly, contested heir.[96]

After Elizabeth's birth, the king wasted little time in reducing Mary's status. Significantly, his first target was her household. According to the Imperial ambassador, Eustace Chapuys, within days of Elizabeth's christening, Henry commanded that Mary's servants cease to wear her liveries and, instead, wear the king's.[97] This was a telling move. It is not too much of an anachronistic distortion to claim that Mary's household was "downsized" both in terms of scale and status. Mary's household had reverted to its standing between 1516 and 1519: it was merely a dependent adjunct to the king's rather than the satellite court of the king's immediate successor. Henry had stripped Mary's household of its status both literally and symbolically. It was a clear forewarning of the king's later plan to subsume Mary's household into that of Elizabeth's.

Throughout these years, the king had showed a genuine personal affection for Mary even if his support for her as his successor was minimal at times.[98] Initially, therefore, he hoped to persuade her to accept the Boleyn marriage despite its inevitable implications for her own disinheritance. Henry determined that the strongest incentive he could offer to secure her acquiescence was the continuation of her household on nearly the same scale it enjoyed prior to Elizabeth's birth. A checkeroll listing of all Mary's household officers and department heads as well as her senior staff carries the date of October 1533, a month after Elizabeth's birth.[99] The list provides a snapshot of Mary's household on the eve before she was to experience considerable loss in status as a result of the imminent reduction of her household.

Indeed, the list initially presents something of a puzzle. The king had already announced plans to reduce Mary's household shortly after Elizabeth's birth in September. Yet the list contains exalted names apparently indicating that in October 1533 that Mary's household was still of sufficient status to attract the service and residency of Margaret, Countess of Salisbury and Lady Margaret Douglas (Henry VIII's niece). Did the October list represent Mary's household accurately or was it a fantasy household offered to Mary, via the checkeroll, as an inducement to accept her own disinheritance? There is not enough evidence for a definitive answer. Given the positive comment by the Milanese envoy around this time that Mary's household was appropriate to her (then) status as heir to the throne combined with the rarity of household lists taking the form of fantasy literature *and* the tradition of compiling such lists for accounting during October, this study will proceed on the assumption that the October list of 1533 was an accurate depiction of Mary's household.

This October list indicates that, as late as 1533, Mary continued to preside over an aristocratic privy chamber staff including Margaret, countess of Salisbury, Ladies Douglas, Maltravers, and Hussey, supported by eight gentlewomen.[100] Her household contained the full complement of departments found in aristocratic and princely households. Although it was not comparable to her viceregal household of 1525, it was similar in scale to the household she had enjoyed from 1519 until 1525.

In late October/early November, Mary apparently officially refused to acknowledge the validity of the Boleyn marriage and her own disinheritance.[101] Her refusal is the likely motive for Henry ordering his Privy Council, in late October/early November, to outline a plan for reducing her household but, according to Chapuys, demoting the status of Mary via her household was so politically charged that, after debating the various options, the council could not resolve upon a plan of action.[102] On December 2, the Privy Council finally obliged the king by resolving to reduce the scale of Mary's household while at the same time arranging for the conveying of Elizabeth to her new residence of Hatfield.[103] Later in the same month the council promised "to set order and establishment of the pryncesse dowagers [Catherine's] house with all celeryte and also of my lady Maryes house."[104] At the same meeting, the Privy Council also put on the agenda "a full conclusion and determynacion to be taken for my Lady prynces house [Elizabeth]."[105] Within a few days, the king ordered a Privy Council delegation to leave for Mary's residence and unveil the king's plan for her living arrangements in light of her refusal to cooperate. The delegation informed Mary that the king had decided to deprive her of her separate household.[106] From now on, she would share a single establishment with her younger half-sister and supplanter as heir to the throne, Elizabeth.

From December 1533, Mary had to share accommodation in Elizabeth's manors as part of a combined household in which she was very much the junior partner. The king allowed Mary to retain some of her servants such as Margaret, Countess of Salisbury, and transferred others, such as Lady Margaret Douglas, to Elizabeth's "side" of the household.[107] Technically, Henry did not entirely deprive Mary of her household but, rather subsumed it into a combined household more focused on Elizabeth. The combined household was intended specifically to contrast the princely "state"—that is, lifestyle—of Elizabeth with the diminished state of Mary, and to anticipate in dress, furnishings and staff that which the first Act of Succession would shortly make law: that Elizabeth, not Mary, was the heir to the throne. The king also intended that the new household manifest a point that this Act would fail to articulate: that Mary was illegitimate and therefore ineligible to inherit. (The Act confirmed that Henry's marriage to Catherine of Aragon was invalid but did not explicitly state that Mary was illegitimate.)[108]

The distinction between the sisters was made apparent from the beginning. At least, this was the impression fostered by the biased (in favor of Catherine and Mary) Imperial ambassador, Eutace Chapuys. Chapuys claimed that the material distinction observed in the combined household clearly was skewed to exalt Elizabeth at Mary's expense.[109] According to Eric Ives, Queen Anne wanted to drive home the distinction between her daughter, the real princess, and the now illegitimate Lady Mary. Anne Boleyn's accounts reveal that she personally selected the sumptuous materials—satin, velvet, damask, and so on—that would clothe her infant daughter. Elizabeth slept under a bedspread of russet damask.[110] She wore caps of purple satin and taffeta. She warmed her infant hands in a black fur muffler trimmed with a white satin ribbon. According to Ives, Anne was practicing "the politics of ostentation" in order to manifest Elizabeth's exalted status—questioned by Roman Catholics at home and abroad.[111] (This is not to discount the likelihood that in addition to furthering her political agenda Queen Anne was also indulging in the pleasure of a wealthy parent dressing up her only child.)

If Anne was trying to enhance her daughter's legitimacy through material consumption, she had good reason to do so. For years after Elizabeth's birth, Mary was still a legitimate heir to the throne even if she was clearly not the first choice of the royal couple. Mary was illegitimate according to the English Church that had declared her parents' marriage invalid in the spring of 1533. This was only partially confirmed by Parliament. The first Act of Succession in October 1534 gave the church's ruling statutory support but did not explicitly declare Mary illegitimate or deprive her of her succession rights.[112]

The actual details of Mary's clothing and chamber furnishings for these years do not survive. State documents do reveal that Mary's depleted coffers were seized and her remaining servants detained.[113] It is usually assumed that both Mary and Catherine of Aragon led a deprived existence after the birth of Elizabeth in 1533. Understandably, biographers of the two women have assumed that the Privy Council's orders to reduce the household of Catherine and to conflate Mary's into that of Elizabeth's resulted in considerable hardship for both Mary and Catherine.[114] Imposing hardship or penury on either woman, however, would have been counterproductive to Henry's political intent. His goal was to manifest through their households that both Catherine and Mary were royal, but they were not to be treated according to their former titles of queen-consort and lady princess. Henry claimed, and there is evidence to support his claims, that the households he granted both Catherine and Mary after Elizabeth's birth were entirely appropriate to their new status as princess-dowager of Wales (Catherine) and the king's "natural" or bastard daughter (Mary).

Catherine enjoyed revenues and an independent household as the dowager princess of Wales. Henry granted Catherine not only an extensive household commensurate with her royal status but also estates to generate enough revenue to fund her household. Catherine was invested as dowager Princess of Wales by Act of Parliament, giving her legal title to lands and revenues that amounted to an income of around £3,000 p.a.[115] Furthermore, Henry approved an act of Parliament declaring Catherine a *femme sole*, which meant that Catherine held her lands and manors in her own right.[116] If Catherine were to (re)marry, then her lands would not pass out of her control; her new husband could not dispose of them or draw revenues from them without Catherine's explicit permission. Because Catherine died without legitimate offspring (at least according to Parliament and the English church), her lands reverted to the crown on her death.

Similar provisions were not made for Mary. Unlike her mother, she was given no lands to support an independent household. This was consistent with her status as the king's natural or bastard daughter. Indeed, for an illegitimate royal, Mary enjoyed a level of household status that was generous and indicative of Henry's personal affection for her. Although her household was little more than a glorified Privy Chamber staff whose first loyalty, initially, was to the king the fact that she had a Privy Chamber staff at all was indicative of the still-high status she enjoyed. Her household existed at the generosity of the king's but that was fully consistent with her status as his natural daughter as the king's chief minister, Thomas Cromwell, was at pains to point out to Henry's critics.[117] She was not, as Eustace Chapuys claimed at times, a servant in Elizabeth's household. She is not listed as part of the Privy Chamber staff of Elizabeth's household. Rather Mary's household formed one half of a combined establishment funded by the crown.[118]

Although Catherine and Mary were not exactly living in penury, their households reflected their demoted status. No longer queen-consort, Catherine ceased to control the considerable patrimony granted to the king's wife. This patrimony now belonged to the new queen-consort, Anne Boleyn. Mary was no longer the king's only legitimate child, the acknowledged heir to the throne. She was now just the king's natural daughter. As such, she was similar footing to her cousin, Lady Margaret Douglas, except that as a legal bastard, Mary was technically a rung or two below her cousin on the legal ladder. As such, Mary was no longer entitled to an independent household or to estates to fund such a household. Henry stripped Mary of her independent household and installed her in the newly created combined household of his "children." There are no indications that Mary's staff was less numerous than Elizabeth's nor that her furnishings less elaborate. By contrast, it is hard to avoid the inference that Anne Boleyn's lavish spending on Elizabeth occurring at the same time as the seizure of Mary's coffers was anything other than symptomatic of an unequal scale of the two sisters' households. The point of the new combined household was to ensure that visitors to this establishment were left in no doubt as to which of the king's daughters was his legitimate heir and which was not.

That Henry was scrupulous in his household provision for both Catherine and Mary is clearly revealed in a surviving set of instructions that Henry issued to Sir Thomas Wyatt, English ambassador at the court of Charles V. In these instructions, written by Henry's chief minister, Thomas Cromwell, it is clear that

Henry was acutely sensitive about the allegations that he had unjustly reduced the households and "state" of Catherine and Mary. The Emperor Charles, as Catherine's nephew and Mary's cousin, evinced concern over the treatment of his relatives now that Henry had repudiated his first marriage. In 1534 Cromwell instructed Wyatt to allay Charles's fears and assure him that Catherine and Mary were being treated generously and no less than their new legal status warranted:

> And as touching that whiche is spoken thence that the saide lady Katherine shold not be honorablie and well intreated as to suche a p[er]sonage aperteyneth. To that both vnto the Emperor and his Counsaile or to any other that will also affirme ye may trulie allege that such reporte and brute [rumor] is untrue affirmynge that in all things belonging to the saide lady Katherine both in the honorable estab-lishinge of hir house wt hir officers and s[e]rv[a]ntes and in the allotting and apoynting vnto hir of londes tentes possessions and all other things condign for such an estate, it is donne in every thing to the best that can be deuised and the like also of or doughter the lady Mary which we do order and entertayne as we thinke most expedyent and also as to vs semyth pertynent ffor we thinke it not mete that any pson shold perscrybe vnto vs how we shold order or own dowghter we being her naturall ffather which thinges or plesure is that ye boldlie and assuredlie shall de-clare and defend.[119]

Because not many documents from Mary's household survive from this pe-riod, it is necessary to glean as much as is reasonable from what few there are. An account by the steward of the combined household, Sir John Shelton, indi-cates at least one thing: Mary insisted on special treatment within the new combined household. Shelton's account was intended to explain why the com-bined household was costing more than the crown anticipated. He placed some of the blame on Mary by claiming that Mary was insisting on the same diet she had enjoyed when she had her own autonomous household:

> Item, where the lady Mary, the King's daughter after she was restored to her health of her late infirmity, being in her own house, was much desirous to have meat immedi-ately after she was ready in the morning, or else she should be in danger eftsoons to return to her said infirmity . . . therefore the said lady Mary, whose appetite was to have meat in the morning according to her accustomed diet, desired to have her breakfast somewhat the larger, to the intent that she would eat little more meat unto supper for the continuance and preservation of her health.[120]

Although Mary was able to overawe Shelton into continuing to indulge in her expensive dietary preferences, this was probably one the few concessions allowed her. Anne Boleyn's accounts, Henry's instructions to his ambassador and Shelton's report makes it possible to infer the materiality of Mary's life in the combined household. Her "state" was respectable, royal, but carefully not that of a legitimate princess or a credible successor to the throne. Mary was not in rags, but it was the infant Elizabeth and not Mary who received guests beneath satin cloths of estate. The king likely reduced Mary's material "state" to a point at which the contrast between her furnishings and clothing and those of Elizabeth would have been obvious to even the most casual of observers. Contemporaries would have recognized that the sumptuousness of Princess Elizabeth's clothes and furnishings indicated where the real power was located and which daughter the crown supported.

In essence, Henry and Anne were attempting to "legitimize" Elizabeth through the household "politics of ostentation." Her clothing and state were intended to convey a birthright that the innovative nature of her parents' union could not by itself guarantee. This strategy, apparently, achieved some success. An indication of the importance of material signs in conveying political status is revealed in the diplomatic correspondence of French envoys visiting Henry's court. During the 1534 negotiations for a marriage between the Princess Elizabeth and the third son of the King of France, French diplomats were invited to examine the king's youngest daughter who had been brought to court especially for the occasion. The diplomats, familiar with court magnificence, were nevertheless impressed with little Elizabeth's very rich apparel, which they conceded gave her the appearance of an exalted royal princess.[121]

All of this suggests a strong contrast in the material existence of the two sisters even though they were living under the same roof. Elizabeth was dressed with conspicuous consumption by her mother, but it is highly unlikely that Anne Boleyn purchased anything like this for Mary. Elizabeth probably had the much larger staff. It is likely that Mary and her staff occupied rooms that were noticeably less well appointed than Elizabeth's.[122] Mary now lived a visibly reduced existence as part of a combined household with Elizabeth.

At first, the king's policy of reducing Mary's status appears to have had the desired effect. Some among her staff became convinced that continued service in her household was unlikely to offer career advancement. Her French tutor, Giles Duwes, with her since her time in the Welsh Marches, left her household in 1533 and wrote her a guilty little letter that he sheepishly noted was "written by your vnworthy seruant the nyght that he toke leue of your grace."[123] The reduction of Mary's household, evidently, eroded Duwes's faith in Mary's political future; as he confessed that his departure might be permanent, "nat knowing if I shall haue grace to retourne in your seruyce or no."[124]

Mary's diminished household dismayed others besides her servants such as Duwes. Chapuys was convinced Mary's status had fallen so low that she was herself a servant in Elizabeth's Privy Chamber, but this unlikely suggestion has not been confirmed by any other source.[125] His comment indicates that Mary's household reduction was such a startlingly public indication of her demotion as to make even such melodramatic developments seem possible. Catherine of Aragon worried that Mary would find herself completely bereft of all her household staff and "shall haue no body to be wt you of your acqwayntaunce."[126]

That people close to Mary were so worried indicates that Henry's strategy was enjoying some success. By depriving her of her independent household and conflating her establishment with that of Elizabeth, the king had signaled a dramatic change in Mary's status. Whatever personal views people may held, they understood that it was now dangerous to treat Mary in public as if she were still a royal heir, a princely figure. By stripping Mary of her "state"—her household with its staff of servants wearing her liveries, its ornate furnishings, and some aristocratic members from its Privy Chamber—Henry hoped to neutralize the threat that Mary posed to Elizabeth's status as heir.

Yet, ultimately, the strategy failed. The king intended the conflated household to anticipate parliamentary legislation that Henry hoped would declare, explicitly, that Mary was barred from inheriting the throne. Despite the household reduction in Mary's status, Parliament failed to oblige the king in the first Act of Succession (1534). The Act declared that Elizabeth was the heir to the throne but the Act failed to bar Mary, explicitly, from the succession on grounds of her illegitimacy. Worse yet for the king, the rebels, in the 1536 grassroots revolt, known as the "Pilgrimage of Grace," demanded that Mary's succession rights be safeguarded and even further, be advanced in preference to Elizabeth's.[127]

The question of why the Pilgrimage of Grace rebels were so invested in Mary's succession rights was one that preoccupied state interrogators of the one of the rebel ringleaders, Robert Aske.[128] When asked about the demand concerning Mary's succession rights, Aske claimed that he regarded Mary as the most credible successor able to forestall a Scottish succession to the English throne. Aske was referring to the claims of the Scottish king, James V, as a Tudor descendant who had a viable claim to the throne should Henry die without a legitimate son to succeed him. Aske's reasons for his conviction regarding Mary's credibility could be religiously motivated in that, if he was a Catholic, he could not accept that the English church had authority to rule on the invalidity of king's marriage to Catherine of Aragon. This would mean that, as far as Aske and other English Catholics were concerned, Mary was Henry's eldest legitimate offspring. This, combined with a prescient assessment of the "Scottish" claim (James V's grandson James VI would eventually inherit the English throne), resulted in the rebels' demand that Mary's succession rights be officially recognized by king and Parliament.

Another admittedly less tangible and quantifiable reason that may have played a role in the rebels' demand that Mary's succession rights be officially safeguarded could be that the political nation, the polity, had acquired the habit of regarding Mary as their next sovereign. For seventeen years, Mary had been the king's only legitimate offspring. Her probable future as the next sovereign of

England had been acknowledged in England and abroad since 1519. In 1525, she had presided over a viceregal household reminiscent of male heirs to the throne—of Princes of Wales—as if she were serving the apprenticeship customary to heirs to the throne. Mary's households had played a part, arguably a very significant part, in convincing the polity that Mary was the most credible heir and the best defense against a Scottish succession. An instance of this lingering habit of obedience to Mary concerns a member of this Welsh household. One of Mary's gentlewomen from the Welsh household, Anne Hussey, found herself imprisoned in 1536 because she referred to Mary, inadvertently, as "my lady Princess" when asking a servant to bring them both a drink. In her deposition, she readily admitted that she knew the second Act of Succession in 1536 had effectively deprived Mary of the title of "Princess" but said she thoughtlessly reverted to "custom" during the incident.[129] Lady Hussey's words were all the more worrying because her husband, Lord Hussey, had once been the Lord Chamberlain of Mary's household and was directly implicated in the 1536 Pilgrimage of Grace rebellion that called for Mary's restoration to the succession.[130]

That it was the scale of Mary's previous households that could have played a large role in conferring (rather than simply reflecting) status on Mary is a conclusion based on documents attesting to the lasting impact of Mary's viceregal household of 1525. The recurring gifts to her on St. David's Day, the continuation of the household itself and of the "princes council" after her departure in 1527, the invocation of Mary as a "princess sovereign" in Ludlow in 1558 all indicate that this household at least made a deep impression on Mary's contemporaries. It was this household that had proclaimed Mary as the female equivalent of a Prince of Wales. Her pre-1525 households had been enhanced when occasion demanded, as during her reception of the French envoys in 1521, that she be publicly presented as the future sovereign of England. In 1533, at the time when Mary's was deprived of her independent household, Giles Duwes published his French grammar book in which he represented Mary as young but absolute prince presiding authoritatively over her own court in Ludlow. There is no record that Aske or any of the other pilgrimage rebels met Mary. Although their loyalty to Mary, doubtless, contained elements of religious conviction and jingoistic fears of a Scottish succession, there is no reason to exclude the possibility that they had also absorbed and internalized the message that Henry had intended (to his regret later, perhaps) to broadcast through the material opulence and exalted staff of Mary's households from 1519 to 1533: Mary was the next ruler of England, a sovereign princess.

Anne Boleyn was executed in May 1536. Within two weeks, Henry wed Jane Seymour. He was now determined to cleanly rid the succession of his most credible heirs—his daughters—in order to make way for either his own offspring by Jane or for a male successor of his own choosing (probably either Richmond or James V of Scotland). In July 1536, Parliament confirmed in the second Act of

Succession that the king's second marriage was invalid and that therefore Elizabeth was illegitimate. It was this Act that finally and explicitly disinherited Mary. The rebels in the Pilgrimage of Grace revolted and called for Mary's restoration to the succession. Immediately after the suppression of the rebellion, Henry put pressure directly on Mary herself to acknowledge the validity of the stipulations in the second Act of Succession. The king felt he could no longer tolerate her passive resistance that might serve to encourage others to withhold recognition of the legitimacy of his future offspring. After Henry indicated that he was prepared to proceed even more harshly against her, Mary finally submitted in late July and sent the king a written statement acknowledging her own disinheritance.

Eventually and rather famously Mary would bow to the king's wishes. Three years after her household was reduced, and in the year in which both Anne Boleyn and Catherine of Aragon died, Mary acknowledged the legal validity of her own disinheritance in a written document to the king. A copy of this fascinating document is preserved in the Harley collection in British Library. It is a chilling indication of the level of pressure Henry was bringing to bear on his daughter. This document on which Mary was requested to copy out her submission to the king was document containing handwritten copies of two other documents: one, a letter from Reginald Pole protesting Henry's divorce from Catherine of Aragon and the other a description of Catherine's reaction on hearing that she must relinquish the title of Queen. Mary was forced to squeeze in her submission in the space between these two passages, both clearly intended to cause the greatest possible intimidation.[131]

After using such a stick to beat Mary with, Henry was swift in coming through with the carrot. He rewarded Mary for her submission by making her the senior partner in the conflated household. Conversely, he demoted three-year-old Elizabeth (who was still officially his heir after Anne Boleyn's death in May until the second Act of Succession in July 1533) to subordinate status. The king provided neither of his daughters with an independent household suitable to an heir to the throne.

A checkeroll drawn up in 1536 indicates that, following her submission, Mary now had a larger privy chamber staff than Elizabeth.[132] Mary employed twenty-five members of staff whereas only seventeen staffed Elizabeth's Privy Chamber. Apparently, more servants were on their way to Mary as evidenced by her letters to the king's new chief minister, Thomas Cromwell, during this period. She requested that certain named servants to be allowed to reenter her service.[133] Mary's Privy Chamber accounts first date from this period of her rehabilitation.[134] Her signature at the bottom of numerous pages and her frequent corrections and notations indicate that she took great personal interest in her material resources.[135] Mary appears to have been particularly interested in her jewels; she signed every page of their inventory, and also scrutinized and corrected the notations as to their current locations. These accounts indicate that Mary's somewhat recovered status found expression in a renewal of her material resources.

Courtiers once again sent her expensive New Year's gifts. The king, queen, Cromwell, the dukes of Norfolk and Suffolk (and their wives), along with leading magnates and royal officials of the realm all sent her gifts for New Years 1537. Just as importantly, Mary was now in a position to reciprocate. For example, Mary sent her longtime supporter, Sir Anthony Browne, a gold and ruby broach when he drew her name as his valentine, and the Duchess of Norfolk received a gold and garnet broach.[136] Mary gave similar broaches to Anne Seymour, Countess of Hertford and Jane Dudley, Lady Lisle.

From this period, Mary's household is conflated with Elizabeth's only in a technical sense. Both households appear in the king's accounts.[137] They also shared a few senior officers such as the steward. In general, however, Mary spent much of her time at court or in country residences on her own. She continued to share accommodation with Elizabeth over the next few years but these were for brief and intermittent periods. While Mary was at court in the aftermath of her submission to the king, Elizabeth's establishment was, quite literally, looking the worse for wear.

According to her governess, Margaret Bryan, Elizabeth's household now did not have the resources to properly clothe the growing toddler. In her letter to Cromwell between May and July 1536, Bryan claimed that the household was in such straits because Elizabeth's status was uncertain. From May until July— when Parliament passed the second Act of Succession—Elizabeth was, legally, the king's only heir. Yet, her mother had been executed for adultery and the English church declared that her parents' marriage was invalid. All that Bryan could figure out was that Elizabeth "es pot from that degre she was afor."[138]

Bryan's letter is undated, but her concern over Elizabeth's status indicates that it was written in the period following Anne Boleyn's execution and before the passage of the second Act of Succession a few months later. The Act formalized Elizabeth's status as the king's illegitimate daughter and, therefore, would have precluded any need for Bryan to seek clarification from Cromwell. This makes it a near certainty that Bryan's letter to Cromwell was written sometime from May but before July 1533.

Elizabeth's uncertain political standing was made visible in her ill-fitting clothes. Bryan pleaded with Cromwell "that she may haue som rayment" for the little girl had niether "gown nor kertel nor petecot."[139] Bryan begged Cromwell to intercede with the king so that Elizabeth might "haue that es nedful for har."[140] Just as Elizabeth's lavish clothing had previously given her the appearance of king's only legitimate heir, so now her outgrown wardrobe signified her diminished political importance.

Paradoxically, Bryan's letter reveals that Elizabeth's household, unable to clothe their young mistress properly, was still managing to entertain on a scale so lavish that Elizabeth's health and social development were at risk. Apparently, the steward of the combined household, John Shelton, insisted that Elizabeth preside over the main meal "euery day at the bord of astate" (board of estate or high table).[141] Bryan understood that, in this case, the politics of ostentation might be harmful to the three-year-old Elizabeth, who would be unable to resist the "dyvers metes" and other rich foods laid out in the great hall. As far as Bryan was concerned, Elizabeth was far too young to preside over such a display of gastronomic hospitality, to "kepe syche rewl yet." [142] Elizabeth's practical ability to operate as head of the household was clearly limited by her age. As will be discussed later, Elizabeth's minority would emerge as a perennial problem in maintaining the status and order of her household. For now, Bryan was mainly concerned about the ludicrous financial management in which the banquet table groaned with food, whereas its young mistress barely had enough to clothe herself appropriately.

Elizabeth's household was in crisis with the issue of display and hospitality at its focus. Bryan considered that Elizabeth should appear dressed in an appropriate manner as a king's daughter. Shelton evidently wished the household to continue much as it had done during the period when Elizabeth was the king's only acknowledged heir by presenting a lavish table over which the three-year-old princess formally presided. Bryan's depiction of Shelton accords with that found in other records. Shelton made repeated requests for money to Cromwell and other officials to help fund the household's increasingly inappropriate hospitality to the point that officials were becoming exasperated.[143] Either the money was not forthcoming soon enough for Shelton or was simply adequate for his ambitions, for he most likely authorized a Ralph Shelton (presumably a relative) to set up a poaching scheme involving several of the steward's servants in the parklands surrounding Hatfield.[144] No wonder Elizabeth's high table had such "dyvers metes."

Ralph Shelton spent a term in the Fleet prison for the poaching; John Shelton's punishment, if any, is unknown.[145] Indeed, in August 1536, Henry, against the advice of government officials, authorized a payment of four thousand pounds to Shelton as the "steward of our children's household" to fund the yearly expenses both of Mary and Elizabeth in the (technically) combined household.[146] Yet, by 1537, Shelton was no longer steward of Elizabeth's household. William Cholmely, Mary's steward/cofferer after her return from the Welsh Marches, took over these duties for the combined household.[147]

Taken together, Shelton's activities and Bryan's letter indicate that the degree to which Elizabeth's household could offer hospitality was a matter of heated debate and deep concern. Bryan directly linked Elizabeth's uncertain political status—was she a princess, the king's bastard, or the product of one of Anne Boleyn's alleged extramarital liaisons?—to the conflict and chaos in her household. Shelton's motives are harder to discern; he was willing to risk prison (at least on another's behalf) and dismissal in order to maintain the fiction through lavish hospitality that Elizabeth was still a princess, the heir to the throne. Perhaps his kinship to Elizabeth (his wife was Anne Boleyn's paternal aunt) created a personal investment for him in trying to maintain her princely status through the household. Perhaps he simply wanted to be a steward of a grand household rather than of the relatively self-effacing, if more economical, establishment that Bryan outlined in her letter to Cromwell.

As demonstrated by the events described earlier, the combined household of Mary and Elizabeth was a vehicle for Henry VIII to publicize his view of the succession. In 1533, Henry VIII publicly demoted Mary by depriving her of her separate household. After Anne Boleyn's death, the king's neglect of Elizabeth's household and wardrobe heralded a negative change in Elizabeth's status. Henry VIII's household policy toward his daughters anticipated their legal dis-inheritance, which was given statutory expression in the 1536 Act of Succession. This Act had merely put into statutory form what was already an a household reality, visibly symbolized by the changes in the combined household. By deny-ing both Mary and Elizabeth separate households after 1536, the king intimated that, given his own free choice, he would nominate neither of his daughters as his heir. Indeed, he exhibited a special concern to keep Mary's household within a certain prescribed limit and potential staff were turned away by the crown with the warning that "her grace shall have no more than her number."[148] From 1537 until 1547, the only one of Henry's children who would preside over a princely household was the king's chosen successor, Prince Edward. Before the prince's birth, when biology and Parliament were slow to accomplish the king's plans for the succession, Henry had relied upon the scale and splendor (or lack thereof) of his daughters' households to make visible who among his children was his chosen heir—and who was not.

FURNISHING POLITICAL STATUS: MARY'S AND ELIZABETH'S SELECTION OF HOUSEHOLD GOODS FROM HENRY VIII'S INVENTORY, 1547–1548

Henry VIII's last will and testament had specified that Mary and Elizabeth each were to receive £3,000 "to lyve on" in "money plate jewelz and household stuffe."[149] For reasons that I will discuss later, this stipulation was converted into property. Instead of receiving these household goods as bequests, the princesses received, as a loan, a selection of household goods from Henry VIII's store-houses.

Of all of the princesses' biographers, only David Starkey, in his biography of Elizabeth, has devoted any attention to this furniture loan. Starkey regards the loan as indicative only of "royal furnishings" and he views the Privy Council as the agent determining what goods the princesses received.[150] I argue that it is more likely that the princesses personally selected these furnishings rather than the Privy Council. I also demonstrate that their selections were more than royal decorative statements. Their selections reveal that the princesses fully appreci-ated the value of household display in relation to political status. Their selec-tions provide a rare glimpse of Mary's and Elizabeth's direct involvement in the creation of their public images. Through these selections, the princesses, as heads of households, were able to showcase their political ambitions and reli-gious preoccupations.

Because the crown palaces were bursting with furnishings, the government of Prince Edward, now King Edward VI, decided that a detailed inventory was in order. This was a considerable undertaking, as Henry VIII was the Citizen Kane of his day with vast stores of furnishings and "stuff" crammed in palatial storehouses at the various royal residences. At Greenwich, for instance, the Ed-wardian government recognized the necessity of appointing extra officials "for the salf keapynge and often ayerynge, beatyng, turnyng and brusshyng" of all the royal textiles.[151] Not surprisingly, the new government was only too happy to entrust some of the goods to the keeping of the princesses. This inventory of Henry VIII's household goods—hereafter referred to as the "Inventory"—pre-serves a description of those goods that Mary and Elizabeth received or, as the Inventory phrased it, "dothe remayne in the charge of her graces officers at the kinges majesties pleasure."[152]

It is likely that Mary and Elizabeth personally selected the items listed in the Inventory, but the Privy Council probably set limits on the number of items the princesses could select. That the Privy Council would set such limits is indi-cated by the concern it expressed during its first recorded meeting in February 1547 in the Tower of London—where the nine-year-old Edward lodged, as cus-tom dictated, before his coronation. In this meeting, the council claimed that the security of the realm depended on the preservation of the king's "juelles, plate or other riche hanginges."[153] These provided the young king with a quick means to raise cash should Emperor Charles V or the French king attack. The council considered the retention of these goods as necessary for the honorable "discharge [of] our selfes towardes God and the worlde."[154] Given these senti-ments, the councilors were unlikely to allow the princesses to select as much as they wanted from the royal storehouses; some limits would be set.

Another indication that the princesses did not have free rein in their selections was that the furniture was very unequally distributed between them. Mary received the lion's share. Mary received twenty-four large Persian rugs to Elizabeth's "Nyne small Carpettes of Turquy making" along with four others making Elizabeth's total of thirteen far less than Mary's. Not only did Elizabeth receive less overall but her list describes several items as "olde and worne." Unlike Mary, Elizabeth obtained no beds, no linens of Holland cloth, and no feather pillows. Mary had selected so many furnishings that she requested the government to supply her with new carts to transport them. Elizabeth received no new carts either because she did not obtain enough goods to warrant them or because her request was refused. It is unlikely that left solely to her own devices that Elizabeth would deliberately have selected so many less items than her sister or of such inferior quality. Clearly, the Privy Council had more severely restricted the range and number of items available for Elizabeth's selection.

Despite this, the nature of the selections suggest that the Privy Council did not itself choose specific items but, rather, allowed each princess to select whatever appealed to them from among a predetermined range. This would be in keeping with their property grants in the same year. Scholars are more than open to the idea that the princesses had some say in which manors they could take legal possession of in 1547.[155] It hardly seems credible that the council would allow the princesses to select which of the king's manors they would like to own themselves and then, at roughly the same time, not consult them about which of king's furniture they would like to decorate their new manors.

In 1547, Mary was thirty-one years old, more than old enough to decide for herself which furnishings she would like. Mary probably received her furnishings in September 1547, a few months after she obtained legal title to her estates in May. Evidence for a September delivery comes from stray reference in the Inventory, separate from the list of all the other goods allocated to Mary, referring to another tapestry from the king's storehouses: the "folowing are delyvered to the ladye marye her grace vse mense Septembr anno primo Regis Edwarde sexti."[156]

Some items listed for Mary are reminiscent of furnishings that she owned in the early 1520s, a coincidence that again argues for her personal involvement in the selection. A tapestry set depicting "a king riding in a chariott in a blewe gowne with starres" was likely the Alexander tapestry listed in her 1523 inventory.[157] The Inventory described the 1547 tapestry set as depicting a "fier in the middes," which separated two portrayals of a woman in the clouds. One of the cloud-dwelling women sat between another fire and a city and the other woman held "the worlde in thone hande and bunche of grapes in thother hande." Furthermore, there was a chariot drawn by two beasts and the tapestry also represented "the distruccion of the Children vnder herode."[158] This could well be the set listed in Mary's 1523 inventory as depicting the Old Law and the New.[159]

Some indications of previous possession also may be detected in the allocation of damaged goods to Mary in 1547. For instance, a tapestry set in which the "Lettre B" figured prominently is reminiscent of one that the duke of Buckingham gave her, listed in the 1523 inventory.[160] The 1547 Inventory noted that the set was "burned in one place."[161] It seems unlikely that Mary's household officers would have accepted the tapestry in this condition unless specifically instructed by their mistress to do so. It is also equally improbable that Mary would have issued such instructions unless the burned tapestry had some special meaning for her.

Elizabeth was fourteen when the selection of the goods was made and fifteen when her furnishings were delivered in December 1548.[162] Even assuming that Elizabeth solicited adult advice on her selection, she was certainly old and educated enough to have decided opinions. By the time that she was fourteen, Elizabeth could speak several languages, including Greek and Latin, and was fond of translating classical and modern philosophical and religious works from their original language such as Greek into languages such as Italian. Elizabeth's education and intellectual accomplishments as a teenager drew flattering commentary in her lifetime and has continued to draw admiration from her modern biographers.[163]

The concentration of chapel goods in Elizabeth's allocation alone argues that the Privy Council was not the only determining factor in both princesses' allocations. If the Privy Council was the determining agent in selecting the royal furnishings, why would the council award Elizabeth so many chapel goods and allow only one altar cloth to Mary? Even Starkey, who assigns agency to the Privy Council in the selection of these goods, admits that it is "curious" that Elizabeth received more chapel goods than Mary.[164] Elizabeth, however, had already demonstrated an interest in religion. She had already presented translations from French, Latin, and Italian of religious treatises as gifts to Henry VIII and Katherine Parr. Surely, the solution to the mystery is that Elizabeth, perhaps on the advice of her religiously inclined household officers, asked for these chapel goods herself.[165]

Another indication that Mary and Elizabeth themselves selected their furniture was that these and other items emphasized readily identifiable themes unique to each princess. Mary's furniture through their sumptuous material and figurative depictions highlighted her royal lineage and reinstatement as the next successor to the crown. Elizabeth's allocation also centered on her royal status and, as indicated earlier, her religious interests. It is unlikely that the Privy Council would have chosen items at random that so closely accorded with the ambitions and interests of each princess.

With the third Act of Succession (1544), Mary was the heir to the throne and she selected furnishings that reflected and proclaimed her status. One of the more interesting items she chose was a "sparver" or canopy that could be hung either over a bed or a throne. Not only was it made of ornate materials—cloth of gold tissue, black velvet, and purple and yellow silk—but it also contained an image of female sovereignty: it was "enbraidered with M crowned."[166]

Assuming that this sparver was not originally made for Mary herself, then how did this item find its way into Henry VIII's collection? Perhaps it originally belonged to Mary's great-grandmother, Margaret Beaufort or to Mary the French Queen, or Mary's great-aunt, Margaret, Duchess of Burgundy. It is possible that the initial does not refer to a mortal person but to the Virgin Mary, Mother of God, Queen of Heaven, hence the crowned letter "M." What can be said is that in all probability this tapestry represented female sovereignty and power whether it was initially intended for a mortal woman who shared the initial with the Virgin or was intended to grace the walls of a chapel and reference only the Virgin Mary herself. There were few masculine names that began with "M" who were exalted enough to commission their own tapestries. The point of most relevance here is not who originally owned or commissioned the tapestry with the crowned "M" but rather that Princess Mary, heir to the throne in 1547, was by her selection of it, "repurposing" it to proclaim the credibility of her future as the next sovereign of England.

Other items that indicated her special royal status were two very fine cloths of estate. They were much more lavish even than those Henry had provided for her in 1523.[167] They were made of crimson cloth of gold, red damask, silver tissue, and fringes of Venice gold and silk. Mary selected matching chairs to be placed beneath these cloths so that cloth and chair served as royal thrones. Both were crimson-colored and a third chair bore the king's arms. The combination of cloths of estate and chairs would have made especially impressive thrones as their materials such as cloth of gold and silk were very expensive and, consequently, highly prized.[168]

In addition to the cloths of estate, Mary selected tapestries that not only emphasized her current status as heir to the throne but also her royal lineage. Among the tapestries chosen by Mary was one that contained "borde[r]s of the kinges armes and lettres H E."[169] The initials and royal arms suggest that the set had belonged to King Henry VII and Elizabeth of York, Mary's grandparents. She also chose a tapestry "marked with letter K."[170] Catherine of Aragon spelled her name in English fashion with a "K" after she arrived in England.

Many of Mary's selections denoted her high status through their lavish materials and market value. For example, several of her cushions were made of cloth of gold, velvet and silk in various colors. Some contained elaborate embroidery, for example one cushion of cloth of gold "raised with gold and silver Tissue of rooses and Honnysuckles," and two of crimson satin "with a traile alover embrawdred with rooses" and matching silk tassels.[171]

These large rich cushions were typically used turn window seats into regal reception areas, and chests into royal benches from which Mary might grant an impromptu audience. Tudor houses did not contain a great deal of what we would call "furniture"—no sofas or upholstered chairs. Often there would be no more than one or two chairs in a room (many rooms containing no chairs at all) and these were universally understood to be reserved exclusively for the householder and a very important guest. Cushions made it possible to be seated comfortably on storage chests and window seats, which were generally the only other items of furniture.[172] Those permitted by their rank to be seated in the presence of the princess would have been fully sensible of the honor as they seated themselves on cushions of cloth of gold and satin.

Other high-status items in Mary's allocation were the Holland table and bed linens. She was allowed to choose twenty-four "turkey carpets" or Persian rugs that in this period were displayed as luxury items covering tables and cupboards. Fifteen sets of "verdours" or fauna tapestries lined her walls and partitioned her rooms. The princess' guests would have slept on kingly beds she chose from the royal storehouses. Beds were status items in this period as attested in wills in which beds are often the first item mentioned in order of importance. One of the more famous examples is Shakespeare's will in which he left his best bed to his eldest son whereas his wife received "my second best bed."[173] Mary selected four elaborate bedspreads or "counterpoyntes" from Henry VIII's collection.[174] Three were made from satin. Furthermore, her guests would have appreciated sleeping on any of the twenty feather mattresses, along with matching bolsters, and eight "pillowes of downe"; down was the most expensive and luxurious filler material.[175] Special beds reserved for visitors of the highest rank were hung with canopies or "trauerses" made of crimson, yellow, and blue silk. "Traverses" were the vertical portion of a bed or throne canopy while sparvers or "celers" were the horizontal, ceiling part of the canopy.

Mary used her household goods to proclaim her political ambitions, her royal lineage, and, most important, her reinstatement as heir to the throne. The tapestry with the crowned "M" especially embodies all these aims. This tapestry—with its overt association of sovereignty and the feminine gender—would have held compelling political resonances in the household of a female heir to the throne. The tapestries of Catherine of Aragon and Henry VII and Elizabeth of York emphasized her royal lineage. Mary's cloths of estate and royal tapestries unequivocally asserted her reclaimed position as heir to the throne. This recovery was given further expression in the actual recouping of her former household goods when she was the acknowledged heir during Henry's reign. A visitor to

any of Mary's manors from 1547 until her accession in 1553 would have understood through her household furnishings that this was an abode of the royal
heir to the throne who held the ancestral right and financial resources to make
good on the claim.

Elizabeth's selections, while relatively restricted in number, were no less
thematic. Probably with the guidance of her household officers, she chose furnishings that hinted at her possible future as a religious and educational patron.
Although Elizabeth was prevented from matching Mary in the quantity of
goods, she strove nevertheless to select items of the highest quality.

One of the altar cloths that she chose was made of cloth of gold, crimson,
and white velvet. Another consisted of cloth of yellow satin, "garnisshed in sundry places withe small pearles and fringed withe Silke." [176] Yet another cloth
bore a fringed edge of "blewe yellowe and grene silke." Elizabeth selected
matching vestments: cloth of gold, white, blue, crimson, and purple velvet, embroidered with "Trayles of golde." [177] Elizabeth's cushions were equally ornate.
Three cushions were made of cloth of gold. Others were tasseled in gold and
red silk, while another was entirely of gold damask. [178]

Although Elizabeth could not secure a cloth of estate, the princess laid claim
to her royal status through the selection of thrones. Like Mary's thrones, Elizabeth's chairs had Henry VIII's arms painted on them. [179] They were covered in
cloth of gold and crimson velvet fabric. The canopies that hung over them were
made of taffeta, cloth of silver, white, and crimson silk. [180] Sitting in her father's
chairs overhung with rich material, Elizabeth would have received important
visitors in a material setting that wordlessly attested to her royal lineage.

Elizabeth also chose items that reflected her humanist education. She selected an allegorical tapestry that most probably survives today in the royal collection as a set labeled The Triumph of the Gods. In Elizabeth's allocation, it is
called "Tapestrie of the Triumphes" and it depicted, as its modern title suggest,
the attributes and exploits of Greco-Roman gods. This was an elaborate and
avant-garde tapestry set, which, when originally ordered by Henry VIII in 1542,
"represented a complete acceptance of Italian Mannerist design." [181] As I indicate in the next chapter, this aesthetic would have fitted in well with the Italianate culture of Elizabeth's courtly household of the 1550s. Elizabeth selected
another famed tapestry set from the Inventory, this one illustrated Christine de
Pisan's "Citie of Ladies." [182]

Christine de Pisan (1364–1430) published *Livre de la cité des dames* (*The Book
of the City of Ladies*) in 1405, which contains sketches of praiseworthy women
from history and mythology. It was rare for a tapestry to depict relatively contemporary literary projects. Of all the tapestries in Henry VIII's inventory with
more conventional themes from the Bible or classical poetry, it is certainly

significant that Elizabeth chose a set that portrayed the work of female scholar. Moreover, it is likely that the panels depicted "six worthy ladies" mentioned in Pizan's work.[183] It would be difficult to find a more explicit statement of female leadership and intellectual abilities than this tapestry, especially as it hung in the halls of a formidably learned young woman who was second in line in succession to the throne.

Elizabeth's selections from her father's storehouses indicate her junior status relative to Mary, as well as her personal inclinations. Her focus on chapel goods clearly relates to her recent translations of religious works. Elizabeth furnished her houses as religious centers. Elizabeth, like Mary, understood the value and use of opulent display. Not entitled to the cloths of estate, Elizabeth would at least be able to sit upon lavish cushions and receive guests in former thrones of Henry VIII. The tapestries that would now adorn her manors, although not new, contained themes that touched on classical learning (The Triumphs) and female empowerment (City of Ladies). The visitor to Elizabeth's manors while she was in residence would have understood that this was the household of a royal, wealthy, and educated young woman who had the lineage, financial resources, and mental acumen to emerge as a figure in the religious life of the nation and if the opportunity arose, in its political life as well.

The theme of Elizabeth's selection of household goods is reminiscent of a famous early known portrait of her probably completed between 1546 and 1547.[184] It shows her standing against a backdrop of a bed hung with curtains. The bed is certainly not foregrounded or rendered in enough detail to provide the viewer with a clue as to its material. Nevertheless, its inclusion in the portrait is clearly intended to present the princess within a domestic (although not subordinate) context, just as the contemporaneous portrait of Prince Edward depicts him in a lavishly furnished domestic interior with a window overlooking his principal residence, Hunsdon.[185] The different scale and detail of the backgrounds— probably both painted by the same artist—indicate their unequal status. Elizabeth's household background may have been much more modest in her portrait than in Edward's, but it was deliberately present. In fact, the portrait also provides some corroboration to the notion that Elizabeth and her household sought actively to display her erudition. The elements that dominate the princess in this depiction are her books and the, apparently, windowless domestic interior. The princess prominently displays a broach in the form of a cross on her dress. The household as portrayed in this picture was a self-contained religious and educational center.

Throughout the period 1516–1547, Henry VIII chose the princely household as the most visible means to publicize his favored choice of successor. It was certainly quicker and perhaps even more effective, than relying on his fertility or on Parliament to resolve the issue the succession in the absence of a male heir of his own body. The king, a prolific builder of palaces and an avid collector of household furnishings, used the households of his children as the primary mechanism to display his hopes for the political future of his kingdom.

The king's clear reluctance to leave the kingdom to a female successor was first made manifest as early as 1516 in his refusal to grant Mary a household commensurate with her official status as his heir. Only briefly, in 1525 and again in 1533, did Henry bestow on Mary and Elizabeth, respectively, households that mirrored their legal status as his successors. After the birth of Prince Edward, the king ensured that Edward's household, as the king's chosen (and legal) successor, dwarfed those of his sisters. Edward's household materially eclipsed the combined household of sisters and indicated their subordinated political importance.

After Henry's death, Mary and Elizabeth, now presiding over their own independent establishments, could regulate for themselves (albeit with input from the Privy Council) the quality of their material furnishings. They demonstrated that they too understood the importance of the household practice of the "politics of ostentation." It is fitting that Mary and Elizabeth reclaimed their status as heirs to the crown through their display of Henry VIII's household goods, considering that he was the one who sought to deny each of them their birthrights by reducing the material quality of their childhood households.

The "material cultures" of these princely households—from Mary's early nursery households to the independent households the princesses received in 1547—served public notice of their political status. Mary only began to live in a style approaching that associated with a royal heir when her father loaned her his cloths of estate in 1523 and later when she presided over a viceregal household in the Welsh Marches. Elizabeth's wardrobe proclaimed her the king's heir in 1533 and the scale of her household emphasized her succession rights by absorbing the competing claims of Mary. Later, when Mary and Elizabeth were able to assume control over the construction of their public images, they used household furnishings to display their political ambitions, religious interests, and erudition. Their domestic material cultures publicly manifested to a patriarchal state that these female heirs were royal, wealthy, and politically viable.

The material display in their households indicated that these were no ordinary princesses. They were not themselves mere ornaments of the court, as previous princesses had been. Exceptionally for royal unmarried women, they were princely rulers over their own courts. Like the ducal courts of the Italian city-states as described by Castiglione in *The Courtier,* the households of the princesses served as stages on which they could display their "magnificence." This term conveyed a carefully constructed display designed to showcase the wealth and prestige of the ruler. A ruler's political reputation derived just as much from his ability to present himself and his court as "magnificent" as it derived from the size of his domain or the splendor of his military successes. When Mary and Eliza-beth furnished their post-Henrician households with goods from his storehouses, they were staking out claims for themselves as political operators and future rul-ers. They were displaying the credibility of female rule.

Furnishing a princely court was not simply a matter of scattering some or-nate cushions. In many ways, these material objects helped the princesses con-struct their political personas as potential sovereign or, at least, patron futures and aspirations. The objects did more than enhance or reflect their political status but, in a real sense, actually *constituted* their political identities as poten-tial heirs to the throne and religious leaders. Moreover, Mary's and Elizabeth's courts were also furnished with people: their resident staff and nonresident re-tainers and suppliers. In stating that their households functioned as courts, it becomes essential to examine their respective court cultures.

NOTES

1. S. Thurley, *The Royal Palaces of Tudor England: Architecture and Court Life 1460–1547* [Yale UP, 1993], *passim*

2. C.M. Woolgar, *The Great Household in Late Medieval England* [Yale UP, 1999], pp. 46–82

3. S. M. Levy, *An Elizabethan Inheritance: The Hardwick Hall Textiles* [London, 1999], p. 38

4. G. Beard, *Upholsters and Interior Furnishings in England, 1530–1840* [Yale UP, 1997], pp. 32–33; L. Jardine, *Worldly Goods: A New History of the Renaissance* [Lon-don, 1996], pp. 399–402

5. N. Korda, *Shakespeare's Domestic Economies: Gender and Property in Early Modern England* [Pennsylvania UP, 2002], p. 8

6. Levy, *An Elizabethan Inheritance . . .* , pp. 1–41

7. E. Ives, *Anne Boleyn* [Oxford, 1985], p. 273; Beard, *Upholsterers and Interior Furnishings*, p. 34; J. Thirsk, *Economic Policy and Projects: The Development of a Consumer Society in Early Modern England* [Oxford UP, 1978], pp. 8, 106; L. C. Or-lin, *Private Matters and Public Culture in Post-Reformation England* [Cornell UP, 1994], p. 255

8. W. Harrison's *Description of England*, ed. Georges Edelen [New York, 1968], p. 200

9. B. Harris, "Property, Power and Personal Relations: Elite Mothers and Sons in Yorkist and Early Tudor England," *Signs: Journal of Women in Culture and Society* (1990), 15/3, p. 611

10. This description of the household as a theater of hospitality derives from an early-seventeenth-century image of the household found in Sir Henry Wotton, *Elements of Architecture* [London, 1624], p. 82, Early English Books Online, Huntington Library

and Art Gallery, January 29, 2007, http://gateway.proquest.com.proxy.lib.utk.edu:90/openurl?ctx_ver=Z39.88-2003&res_id=xri:eebo&rft_id=xri:eebo:citation:99855523

11. N. Orme, *From Childhood to Chivalry: The Education of the English Kings and Aristocracy, 1066–1530* [London, 1984], pp. 18–23

12. F. Jones, *The Princes and Principality of Wales* [Wales UP, 1969], p. 98 and F. Hepburn, "Arthur, Prince of Wales and His Training and for Kingship." *The Historian*, 55, (1997), pp. 4–9

13. Although her proper title, as Brandon's wife, was Duchess of Suffolk, contemporaries referred to her as "the French Queen" out of courtesy to her former rank and probably, in part, to distinguish her from her niece and namesake, Princess Mary

14. B. J. Harris, "Power, Profit, and Passion: Mary Tudor, Charles Brandon and the Arranged Marriage in Early Tudor England," *Feminist Studies*, 15/1 (Spring, 1989), p. 63

15. Sebastian Guistinian, *Four Years at the Court of Henry VIII: Selection of Despatches . . .* , tr. Rawdon Brown, 2 vols. [London, 1854], p. 182

16. *LP*, II, 1621

17. There are two copies of Henry VIII's private expenses from 1509 until 1518. One copy is at the Public Records Office and the other used here, BL Additional 21481, is now at the British Library. Also, they are abstracted in *Letters and Papers*, commencing in April 1509 through December 1518

18. D. Loades, *Mary Tudor: A Life* [Oxford, 1989], p. 29

19. BL Additional 21481, f.236v; *LP*, II, pt.2, p. 1473; BL Additional 21481, ff.253r, 269v, 277r, 286v. f. 253v (*LP*, II, pt.2, 3429)

20. *LP*, II, p. 2, p. 1480. Also, see *LP*, Addenda, I, pt.1, 259 for list of expenses of Mary's household for the three years from its inception in 1516 until 1519, with Sydnor listed as one who was to receive wages, suggesting that he had been part of Mary's household from its formation

21. BL Additional 21481, f.238v; *LP*, II, pt.2, p. 1473

22. *LP*, vol.2, pt.2, App. 58 (3)

23. *CPR*, 1467–1477, p. 366; P. Williams *Council of the Marches*, p. 7

24. *LP*, VII, 440

25. *LP*, III, 3375

26. *LP*, II, pt.2, pp. 1441–1480; P. Williams, *Tudor Regime*, p. 59

27. *LP*, XIII, pt.1 1057

28. Williams, *Tudor Regime*, p. 59

29. *LP*, XIII, pt.1, 1057. BL Cotton Vitellius C., i., ff. 39r–44v [formerly 59r–64v]; printed in P. R. Roberts, "A Breviat of the Effectes Devised for Wales," *Camden Miscellany*, 1975

30. Loades, p. 28

31. *LP*, VI, pt.2, 1528

32. *LP*, XIII, pt.1, 459

33. BL Cotton Vitellieus C., i., ff.45v, 46v

34. Loades, p. 9

35. Loades, p. 12, fn.4 notes the difficulty in reconstructing the chronology of Catherine's pregnancies

36. Loades, p. 16

37. Guistinian, *Four Years* . . . , p. 240

38. *LP*, III, pt.1, 491

39. Loades, pp. 29–30

40. The source for the following description of Mary's household reception of the French envoys, a letter from the Privy Council to the king, simply refers to the envoys as the "gentilmen of ffraunce." BL Cotton Caligula D VII, ff. 238r, 239r

41. The French king was right to be suspicious, for Mary was recovering from a recent illness. The Privy Council wrote to Henry that they had visited Mary often recently "whoe god be thanked is in prosperous health and convalescence." BL Cotton Caligula D.VII, f.238v

42. *Ibid.*, f.240r

43. MSS has suffered fire damage, hence the bracketed interpolations. BL Cotton Caligula D. VII, ff.238v-239r; in *LP*, III, pt.1, 896 it is listed as f.231, according to an old numbering of the manuscript

44. *Ibid.*, ff.240v-241r

45. The notion of "furnishing" a chamber with people as well as inanimate objects was common in England in the sixteenth and seventeenth centuries. See *A Collection of Ordinances and Regulations for the Government of the Royal Household made in divers reigns from King Edward III to King William and Queen Mary* . . . [London, 1790], p. 341 for an early-seventeenth-century example

46. BL Cotton Caligula D. VII, f.238v

47. *Ibid*

48. *LP*, III, pt.2, p. 1533. The following description of her household goods also comes from this source

49. *LP*, III, pt. 2 ,2585 and 3375

50. BL Cotton Vespasian, C. XIV, f.273; *LP*, 3/2, 2585

51. *LP*, III, pt. 2, 2585

52. Harris, "Property," p. 611

53. *LP*, III, pt.2, 3375

54. *LP*, III, pt.2, 2585; not all gifts were of this lavish yet impractical kind; Sir Richard Weston gave her twelve pairs of shoes

55. *LP*, 3/2, 3375. The editor misdated these accounts as ending on September 1523, although he does acknowledge that the original manuscript list the accounts as ending in September, year fifteen of Henry VIII's reign. As Henry's reign began in April 1509, a September dated to the fifteenth year of the reign is 1524. Also, the accounts for the two previous years survive listed in *LP*, 3/2, 2285. The 3375 entry clearly refers to a separate account rather than a duplicate of 2285 and the only year it describes is 1524 as the manuscript itself indicates

56. *LP*, 3/2, 2585

57. The details of the 1523 Christmas are in *LP*, 3/2, 3375

58. For instance, 4 oz. of saffron cost her household in 1523 three shillings, whereas a pound of pepper cost only two shillings and a pound of almonds cost only twenty pence. *LP*, 3/2, 3375

59. *LP*, 3/2, 2585

60. *LP*, 3/2, 3375

61. For Buckingham, *LP*, III, pt. 1, p. 504; For Mary, *LP*, III, 3375

62. *LP*, IV, pt. 1, 1390, 1431; BL Harley 6807, ff. 29r–47v

63. *LP*, III, 1508, 1571

64. *LP*, IV, pt. 1, 528

65. *LP*, IV, pt. 1, 1577, nos.11 and 12

66. S. J. Gunn, "The Regime of Charles, Duke of Suffolk, in North Wales and the Reform of the Welsh Government, 1509–1525," *The Welsh History Review*, 12/4 (December 1985): pp. 461–495 and R.A. Griffiths, *Sir Rhys ap Thomas and his Family: A Study in the Wars of the Roses and Early Tudor Politics* [Wales UP, 1993]

67. P. Williams, *The Council in the Marches of Wales under Elizabeth I* [Wales UP, 1958], pp. 12–15 and C. Skeel, *The Council in the Marches of Wales* [London, 1904], pp. 49–52; Loades, p. 39

68. BL Cotton Vitellius, C.i., ff. 7r–18v [formerly 23r–35v], hereafter cited as "Instructions." This was a contemporary file copy made from the signed original which accompanied Mary to Wales but is no longer extant. MSS has been numbered by different archivists over the years. I will provide numbers counting from the first folio but also indicate older, numbering scheme of folios in brackets

69. "Instructions," f. 7v

70. For instance, after Mary's birth, Henry VIII's accounts for August 1516, July 1517, and February 1518 record payments to "the commissioners in the marches of Wales"; BL Additional, 21481, f. 267v for August 1517. For July 1518, see *LP*, II, pt. 2, p1480

71. Harris, *English Aristocratic Women* . . . , p. 29

72. "Instructions," f. 10r

73. BL Cotton Vespasian, F.XIII, vol. 2, art. 187, f. 240r [formerly f. 134]

74. See, e.g., Henry Parker's description of the Christmas festivities at Margaret Beaufort's household when her establishment at Collyweston was serving as the satellite royal court in the Midlands in 1501 as quoted in F. Kisby, "A Mirror of Monarchy: Music and Musicians at the Household Chapel of the Lady Margaret Beaufort , Mother of Henry VII," *Early Music History*, 16 (1997), p. 211

75. For Mary's expenses in 1525–1526, see BL Royal 14 B. XIX, 5324, unbound manuscript, no folio numbers; Loades, p. 41. Building repairs on some of the marcher residences accounted for some of the expenditure

76. "Instructions," f. 8r; T. P. Ellis, *The First Extent of Bromfield and Yale, Lordships A.D. 1315* [London, 1924], p. 4 for a description of how the medieval history of these counties became crown lordships. The significance of these grants for Mary's political profile receives fuller treatment in Chapter 3

77. This number is taken from the staff of the actual household departments, which was listed at 123 combined with the servants assigned to senior staff, about 90, who also wore Mary's livery. BL Harley 6807, ff.3r–6r

78. *LP*, IV, pt.1, 1577

79. *LP*, IV, pt.1, 1577

80. F. Watson, ed., *Vives and the Renaissance Education of Women* [London, 1912], p. 133

81. *CSP Spanish*, IV, pt.2, 1157

82. BL Cotton Vitellius, C.i., ff. 19r–20v [formerly 35r–36v]; originally "princes" council in MSS to add further confusion but this was clearly short for "princess" rather than "prince's"

83. BL Stowe 141, f.13r; Loades, pp. 46–74

84. S.J. Gunn, "The Regime of Charles, Duke of Suffolk, in North Wales and the Reform of the Welsh Government, 1509–1525," *The Welsh History Review*, 12/4 (December 1985): pp. 461–495 and R. A. Griffiths, *Sir Rhys ap Thomas and His Family: A Study in the Wars of the Roses and Early Tudor Politics* [Wales UP, 1993]

85. Wolffe, *Crown Lands* . . . , pp. 64, 84–85

86. For an extended treatment of the procedures and history of the title, see F. Jones, *The Princes and Principality of Wales* [Wales UP, 1969]

87. BL Cotton Vitellieus C., i., f. 45v

88. J. North, *England's Boy King: The Diary of Edward VI, 1547–1553* [Welwyn Garden City, UK, 2005], p. 16; best modern edition is in W. K. Jordan, ed., *The Chronicle and Political Papers of Edward VI* [London, 1966]

89. Henry's plans for sending the prince to the Welsh marches after his investiture are in *LP*, XIII, pt.1, 1057. BL Cotton Vitellius C., i., ff. 39r–44v [formerly 59r–64v]; printed in P. R. Roberts, "A Breviat of the Effectes Devised for Wales," *Camden Miscellany*, 1975

90. BL Cotton Vitellieus C., i., ff. 45v, 46v

91. Madden, pp. 19, 61, 152

92. H. Clifford, *The Life of Jane Dormer, Duchesss of Feria*, ed. Rev. Joseph Stevenson [London, 1887], p. 80

93. W. Forrest, *The History of Grisild the Second: A Narrative, In verse, of the Divorce of Queen Katharine of Aragon* (1558), ed. W. D. Macray [London, 1875], p. 86

94. For discussions of the persistent loyalty of the Welsh to Mary, see G. Williams, "Wales and the Reign of Queen Mary I," *The Welsh History Review*, 10/3 (June 1981): 334–358 and also his *Recovery, Reorientation, and Reformation Wales, c.1415–1642* [Oxford: 1987], p. 281; and Skeel, "Council," p. 74

95. The seminal treatment of the "Divorce" and the resulting Reformation legislation is in Elton, *Reform and Reformation*, pp. 103–273

96. Loades, p. 61

97. *CSP, Spanish*, IV, pt.2, 1127

98. *CSP, Spanish*, IV, pt.1, 633

99. BL Harley 6807, ff.7r–9r

100. *Ibid.*

101. *LP*, VI, 1186, 1249

102. *CSP Spanish*, IV, pt.2, 1144

103. Strype, I, pp. 153–155

104. BL Cleopatra, E. VI, ff.325r–328r

105. *Ibid.*

106. *CSP, Spanish*, 4/2, 1161; Loades, *Mary Tudor* . . . , p. 78

107. R. K. Marshall, *Mary I*, [London, 1993], p. 24

108. 25 Hen VIII, c.12, art. II in A. Luder, *The Statutes of the Realm* [Records Office, 1810–1828], vol. 3, p. 473

109. *CSP, Spanish*, 5/1, 1

110. E. W. Ives, *Life and Death of Anne Boleyn: The Most Happy* [Oxford 2004], pp. 253–254.

111. Ives, *Anne Boleyn*, p. 273

112. Luder, *Statutes of the Realm*, III, p. 471; 25 Hen. VIII, c.22

113. BL Cotton Otho C., X., f.265

114. Mattingly, *Catherine of Aragon*, p. 374; Prescott, *Mary Tudor*, p. 50; Marshall, *Mary*, p. 23. Loades, p. 79, rightly takes issue with this popular assumption and points out that Catherine's household was hardly that of a pauper

115. 25 Hen. VIII c. 28 in *Stat. Realm*, p. 484 and Loades, p. 79. Strype [1721], I, no. lxx

116. *Ibid.*

117. BL Cotton Nero, B. vi., ff.89r [formerly ff.86r]; Madden identified Cromwell's hand in the corrective gloss; Madden, p. lxiii

118. BL Arundel 97, *passim*

119. *Ibid.*

120. *LP*, VII, 440; quotation from editor's transcription, *not* the abstract

121. *LP*, VII, 191

122. *CSP, Spanish*, IV, pt.2, 1165; though this source must be treated with caution, as Chapuys habitually exaggerated the plight of Catherine and Mary probably in order to convince the Emperor to take stronger measures against Henry on their behalf

123. Duwes, U3r–v

124. *Ibid.*

125. Chapuys dispatch to Charles V as quoted in Prescott, p. 42

126. BL Arundel, 151, f.195v

127. Item no. 3 in Pontefract articles regarding Mary printed in N. Key and T. Bucholz, *Sources and Debates in English History 1485–1714* [Oxford, 2004], p. 63. For full treatment of rebellion, see M. Bush, *Pilgrimage of Grace: A Study of the Rebel Armies of October 1536* [Manchester UP, 1996] and R.W. Hoyle, *Pilgrimage of Grace and Politics of the 1530s* [Oxford UP, 2003]

128. Excerpted in M. Levine, *Tudor Dynastic Problems, 1460–1571*, [London, 1973], pp. 157–158

129. BL Cotton Otho X, f. 260v

130. A. Fletcher and D. MacCulloch, eds, *Tudor Rebellions*, 5th ed. [Harlow, UK, 2004], p. 44

131. BL Harley 283, ff.111v–112v

132. BL Cotton Vespasian, C. XIV, ff.274r–275v

133. For many of Mary's letters concerning the return of her servants in 1536, see BL Cotton Otho, C.X., ff.266r–291r

134. BL Royal MS. 17 B XXVIII; see also Madden. There is, however, quite a discrepancy in folio numbers from what is cited in Madden and the numbering system currently in place in the manuscript

135. It is possible that she also totaled the accounts herself on occasion. In the manuscript, the totals on ff. 6v, 19v–20r, 22r, 25r all match her handwriting and also indicate a change of ink

136. Dates of these gifts were not generally specified in her jewel inventory. BL Royal MS. 17 B XXVIII, ff. 112r–124r

137. BL Arundel 97, *passim*

138. BL Cotton Otho X, f.234r

139. *Ibid.*

140. *Ibid.*

141. *Ibid.*

142. *Ibid.*

143. *LP*, XI, 130, 104

144. *Ibid.*

145. *LP*, XI, p. 202

146. BL Additional Charter 67534 as cited in Loades, p. 111

147. He was listed as Mary's cofferer in the October 1533 checkeroll, BL Harley 6807, ff.7r–9r. In Henry VIII's privy purse expenses 1538–1541 in BL Arundel 97, f. 2r, Cholmely is referred to as the "late Cofferer," suggesting that he had died or had moved on to another post by 1538

148. This was Cromwell's reply to the countess of Sussex when she attempted to secure a place in Mary's household for Katherine Basset, daughter of Honor, Lady Lisle. *The Lisle Letters*, ed. M. St. Clare Byrne, IV, 167, 192

149. The transcription of Henry VIII's will is in *Fœdera*, III, p. 145

150. Starkey, pp. 97–98

151. *APC*, p. 305

152. From transcription of the Inventory in *The Inventory of King Henry VIII*, vol. 1, ed. David Starkey, [London, 1998]. The following descriptions of the allotted goods are on Starkey, pp. 376–380 for Mary and pp. 380–382 for Elizabeth

153. *APC*, II, p. 20

154. *Ibid.*

155. Loades, *Mary Tudor*, p. 138; Starkey, *Elizabeth: Apprenticeship*, p. 96

156. *Inventory*, f 356v

157. *LP*, III, pt. 2, 3375

158. Unless otherwise noted, all quotations regarding Mary's receipt of goods from Henry VIII's storehouse are from the printed edition of 1547 inventory taken of Henry VIII's "stuffe" in D. Starkey, ed. *The Inventory of Henry VIII*, pp. 376–380

159. *LP*, III, pt.2, 3375

160. *Ibid.*

161. *Inventory*, p. 377

162. Starkey, p. 97

163. For a refreshingly unpanegryrical assessment of Elizabeth's erudition, see Starkey, pp. 83–84.

164. Starkey, p. 98

165. Starkey admits that these chapel ornaments accorded with Elizabeth's later taste as queen in chapel decoration; Starkey, p. 98

166. *Inventory*, p. 378

167. *LP*, III, pt.2, 3375

168. Beard, *Upholsterers*, p. 319

169. *Inventory*, p. 377

170. *Inventory*, p. 378

171. *Ibid.*

172. Digby, *Elizabethan Embroidery*, p. 108

173. Quoted in Beard, *Upholsterers*, p. 33

174. *Inventory*, pp. 378–380

175. Beard, *Upholsterers*, p. 18

176. *Inventory*, p. 380

177. *Ibid.*

178. *Inventory*, p. 382

179. *Ibid.*

180. *Ibid.*

181. Thurley, *Royal Palaces*, p. 224

182. For full discussion of this set of tapestries, see S. G. Bell, *The Lost Tapestries of the City of Ladies: Christine de Pizan's Renaissance Legacy* [California UP, 2004], *passim*

183. Bell, *The Lost Tapestries . . .* , p. 148

184. An image of this portrait can be accessed at http://englishhistory.net/tudor/monarchs/eliz1-scrots.jpg

185. An image of this portrait can be accessed at http://www.tudorplace.com.ar/images/EdwardVI08.jpg

2. THE PRINCELY HOUSEHOLD

Patronage and Corporate Loyalties

I would live your servant still
And you my Saint unnamed
    —Thomas Campion, *Second Book of Ayres* [London, 1612],
                                                    XVIII

The last chapter examined how Mary and Elizabeth exploited one of the resources of the princely household—display—to enhance their political status.
Display also was a hallmark of court culture. Scholars have long employed the
term "court culture" to describe the habits of dialogue and ceremonial exchange that distinguished Renaissance courts throughout Europe.[1] The cultures that existed in the households of Mary and Elizabeth Tudor bore many
similarities to that of Continental courts. The courtly pastimes of poetry, lively
conversation, and platonic romance that feature in the classic articulation of
court culture, Castiglione's *Il Cortegiano* (1528) also were diversions in the preaccession households of Mary and Elizabeth Tudor. Although their households
were not based in urban areas as the royal courts were, their household accounts indicate that the princesses drew on city resources, like booksellers, to
furnish the basic elements of their domestic court cultures.

This chapter focuses on the divergent cultures that characterized the households of the princesses. An artistic and practical courtly culture of reverence

existed in Mary's household. The princess overawed her staff but also evinced a strong sense of *noblesse oblige* toward her servants. Elizabeth's household exhibited quite a different culture. Elizabeth's staff treated their underaged mistress with parental affection. Her household created a Protestant, erudite and, somewhat paradoxically, Italianate court culture whose existence was not dependent on the princess. Rather, Elizabeth was the product of this domestic culture and not the initiator of it.

Their surviving household accounts, state documents, and literary representations reveal a network of mutual obligations and a sense of corporate identity determining the nature of daily interaction between the princess and her staff. The relationship between householder and live-in servant could be intensely familiar. Senior officers and Privy Chamber servants especially were constant companions of the householder serving them at meal times, dressing them, functioning as companions and personal assistants.[2] This relationship of loyalty and obligation between princess and servant was initiated by the oath of service undertaken by each resident and non-resident servant. Both Mary and Elizabeth understood the responsibilities implied in accepting people into their service. The following discussion will show that these domestic relationships were not only social but also political. The political dimension of service and lordship defined the relationship between princess and servant while also setting the tone for the culture of the household. On occasion, this dimension of household service and obligation could be politically explosive as servants privileged their loyalty to their mistress or to the household culture over and above the loyalty the owed as subjects to their sovereign.

THE HOUSEHOLD COVENANT: SERVICE AND GOVERNANCE

Those who worked in Mary's and Elizabeth's households were not simply contract employees but members of a quasi-sacred corporation bound to serve and obey the head of household. This bond manifested itself in the ceremonial taking of an oath by which the servant entered a relationship of mutual obligation with the head of household; this relationship was, since late medieval times, known as the *conventio*.[3] The household oath was the formal invocation of the *conventio*. The servant was obligated by the oath to render honest service to the householder—they should not steal the household's goods or disrupt its "politique order."[4] By accepting the oath, the head of household, in turn, was obligated to be a 'good lord' or mistress to the servant.

The oath was usually little more than a straightforward promise to serve the head of household faithfully and that the oath-taker was honest. The oath was witnessed either by a senior staff member(s) or before the entire household.[5] Servants remained in the household for varying lengths depending on their skills and positions ranging from temporary laborers to Privy Chamber servants who spent much of their lives in service in one household. Long-term service was a special feature of royal households as such positions were highly coveted. Both Mary and Elizabeth retained individuals who served in their Privy Chambers throughout much of the period covered in this dissertation.[6] For example, Beatrice ap Rice joined Mary's household in 1519 and continued to serve, along with her family, up to and after Mary's accession in 1553. Katherine Champernon joined Elizabeth's household in 1536 and served (except for periods in which she was in prison) up to and after Elizabeth's accession in 1558. This was in keeping with late medieval practice in elite and royal households in which senior staff often served for many years. At the turn of the seventeenth century, it became more usual for servants to serve out seven year contracts.[7]

Although there are no accounts of either princess receiving the oath from a kneeling servant offering his hands—as medieval knights did when offering feudal service to their lords—this household oath was, nevertheless, a faint echo of feudal ideals of service and obligation.[8] Servants undertook not simply to perform their "offices" competently and honestly but bound themselves personally to obey the householder in all things. The servant was literally "subject" to the householder's authority just as subjects were under the authority of the crown.

The household oath's potential of creating political allegiances that could benefit the householder at the expense of the crown can be see seen in an incident related by John Foxe in the 1570 edition of *Book of Martyrs*. According to Foxe, a certain Laurence Sherrif, a grocer who supplied Princess Elizabeth's household, engaged in a fist-fight with his best friend over the friend's disparaging remarks about Elizabeth. At the time (early 1550s), Elizabeth was under house arrest and in political disgrace. Foxe justified Sherrif's violence merely by noting that as Sherrif was Elizabeth's grocer, he was "then servant unto the lady Elizabeth, and sworn unto her grace."[9] It is little wonder, therefore, that when a conflict arose between the householder and the monarch that the householder's staff found itself in an untenable position as subject to two mutually hostile authorities.

Some hint of this is just discernable in the "Instruction Book" for Mary's 1525 Welsh household. In common with royal and elite households, Mary's household was governed by a council.[10] Because Mary's was a royal, viceregal household, her councilors governed a region of land just as the monarch's household had governed England from medieval times to the sixteenth century. According to the oath her household councilors must take, their primary loyalty was to the king and his successors. Yet, in 1525, Mary was the king's heir. To whom, Henry or Mary, did they owe their primary loyalty? The Instruction Book indicates that the oath administered to those serving in her household owed a dual loyalty: one to Henry as sovereign and the other to Mary as titular head of household:

The Oathe for the Counsaylors

Ye shalbe true and faithful vnto the Kinge our Soveraigne lord kinge Henry the eight and vnto his heires . . . And ye shalbe faithfull and true vnto my lady princesse grace And ye shall according to yor iust discretion knowledge and oppenione give vnto her true and faithfull counsayle in all things as shalbe demaunded of yo" by way of good advise and counsayle . . . And also you shall perceaue [perceive] any thinge to be done or attempted contrary to her honor estate degree or suertie . . . so helpe you god and the holie Contents of this book.[11]

Although the oath stipulates that the councilors must be the king's loyal subjects, the oath also binds the councilors to Mary as their mistress. This sense of dual obligation embodied in the oath was certainly more theoretical than real in this instance. It was highly unlikely that the nine-year-old princess would stage a rebellion against her father and call on her councilors to support her against the king. Moreover, the councilors obtained their appointments through Henry's patronage not Mary's. The oath leaves no room for doubt that the councilors must retain their loyalty to the king even though they are swearing the customary oath of loyalty to Princess Mary as their mistress. The implication here is that those who composed and/or commissioned the "Instructions" understood that the customary oath taken by staff to the householder could, unless otherwise specified, could conflict with a subject's assumed loyalty to their monarch.

The household oath was the mechanism, the ceremonial (in a rather minimal sense) enactment of the concepts of service that bound the servant to the householder. Although the householder did not swear a reciprocal oath to the servant, both Mary and Elizabeth would, as the following discussion shows, exhibit a sense of obligation toward their household staff. The household oath manifested the household's existence as a corporate entity bound by a shared sense of identification with the householder. This corporate identity received reinforcement through various outward signs such as liveries and badges, communal dining and sleeping (except for the householder and his kin) and communal worship in the household chapel. Another source of corporate identity was the general expectation that the householder would utilize the material resources of the houschold to care for his servant, to be a "good lord" or mistress.

Evidence suggests that householders took the responsibilities of domestic authority seriously. It was routine for heads of households to provide health, educational, and retirement plans for their servants. It was not uncommon for lords to pay a stipend to faithful servants who had retired from service.[12] As this section later discusses, both Mary and Elizabeth provided for their servants' welfare in a manner comparable with "benefits packages" offered by some of the more enlightened modern businesses and governments. They paid for the medical, educational, travel and social expenses of their staff. In return, the princesses received corporate followings of faithful agents who were loyal to their mistress and to the religious and political ideologies she represented and espoused.

THE CULTURE OF REVERENCE AND PRINCELY PATRONAGE IN MARY'S HOUSEHOLD, 1519–1553

This section traces the development of a culture of reverence that characterized Mary's household court. Beginning with the implications of the French marriage negotiations in 1518 and expedited by the court culture of Mary's Welsh household in the mid-1520s, Mary grew used to receiving complete obedience and reverential treatment from her staff. In return, Mary's household accounts indicate that she not only provided for the physical and social welfare of her domestic staff, but she also dispensed political patronage via the "extraordinary" members of her Privy Chamber staff.

As discussed in the last chapter, Mary's household began to dramatically expand in scale and quality in the wake of the French marriage negotiations of 1518 and Catherine of Aragon's final miscarriage in November of that year. Another consequence of these events for Mary's household was that it began taking on aristocratic staff, albeit exclusively in the Privy Chamber. The appointment of Margaret Pole, countess of Salisbury as Mary's governess was the strongest manifestation of this trend. By early 1519, Salisbury was serving as Mary's governess and the Lady Mistress of the household.[13] Salisbury was royalty herself. She was the niece of Edward IV and a peer in her own right.[14] Generally speaking, only monarchs numbered aristocrats amongst their domestic staff, even then it was usually for ceremonial occasions. That Mary errantly employed someone like Salisbury as her governess indicated the high status that the politically elite (save, at times, Henry VIII) was prepared to accord her.

Salisbury remained with her until at least 1535. It was unusual for such a high-ranking, royal, aristocrat to serve permanently in the household of a royal offspring.[15] When Salisbury temporarily left Mary's service in 1521 because she fell under suspicion for helping her cousin, Edward Stafford, Duke of Buckingham (in the activities for which he would eventually be executed), Henry appointed a new governess for Mary drawn from the gentry class: Jane Calthorpe, wife to the courtier, Sir Philip Calthorpe. Calthorpe obtained the position when the Dowager Countess of Oxford turned down the appointment because of illness. Calthorpe's rank was much more in accordance with the social status found in previous and subsequent households of royal children. Jane Calthorpe's husband served in Mary's household, probably as chamberlain.[16] Although Salisbury had returned to Mary's service by 1525, the Calthorpes maintained their connection to the princess. Sir Philip's daughter would later serve in Mary's household and would wed one of Mary's most prominent supporters over the subsequent years, Henry Parker, Lord Morely.[17] Salisbury had returned to Mary's service when the Princess' household removed to the Welsh Marches as she is mentioned prominently in the documentation for the Welsh household.[18] The reason that Salisbury did not serve in Mary's household much beyond 1535 was a combination of Mary reaching her majority (she was nineteen in 1535) and Salisbury's arrest in 1539 and subsequent execution in 1541.

In 1525, Mary's Welsh household included a Privy Chamber headed by Salisbury and staffed with her relatives, Katherine, Elizabeth and Constance Pole. Among Mary's senior staff in the marches was Thomas Grey, Marquis of Dorset as Master of Horse in 1526.[19] Later, the 1533 October checkerroll indicates that such exalted persons as the Ladies Douglas, Maltravers and Hussey supported Salisbury in the Privy Chamber. Margaret Douglas was not only aristocratic but also royal. She was Henry VIII's niece and Mary's first cousin. Ladies Hussey, Maltravers, and Kingston, among others, were the wives and daughters of important magnates and courtly nobility.[20] A unique confluence of circumstances— Mary's childhood betrothals, her status as the king's only heir, her gender (even high-ranking women did not have places at court unless they served in a royal Privy Chamber), and her close age with other single royal ladies like Margaret Douglas—resulted in an unusually aristocratic Privy Chamber staff. The nobles of her childhood households "furnished" Mary's chamber to a high standard.

As the Privy Council account of Mary's reception of the French envoys in 1520 attests, the social rank of household servants directly reflected the sociopolitical rank of the householder. In order to make a good impression on the envoys, the Privy Council had ensured that the highest ranking women—who were not in attendance on Queen Catherine in Calais—were present in Mary's chamber during the reception. The presence of elite women conferred significant social status on Mary's household. It was the presence of these women of high rank that the Privy Council hoped would make an "honorable" impression on the French envoys. Elite women serving in Princess Mary's household sent a very important message to the French envoys. While the monarch was abroad, his daughter's household served as the royal court. Only the household of the ruler's consort or heir could serve this function in the absence of the monarch's household. Thus, the Privy Council, by packing Mary's household with the highest-ranking aristocracy remaining in England, were leaving the French envoys in no doubt of Mary's status as the next ruler of England.

Servants in Mary's childhood households would have understood that the princess was an important personage—one deserving of their reverence—not only from the aristocratic members of staff but also from the attention she received from the royal family, nobility and foreign ambassadors. During the French marriage negotiations, Mary, as the matrimonial prize, was at court fairly frequently during 1518. The significance of this for Mary's household was that her staff witnessed high-profile diplomatic occasions. Mary was usually in her nurse's arms when she was displayed during audiences with foreign ambassadors.[21] On these occasions, the household staff would have observed the deference, which was sometimes deliberately exaggerated, paid to the princess. During the French negotiations, the Venetian ambassador attended a carefully stage-managed presentation of Mary for his benefit. Sebastian Guistinian confessed himself impressed with the elaborate deference paid to the two-year-old Mary. Guistinian reported that Mary, unlike modern children, was not a child to be picked up and cuddled by indulgent adults. Dukes and cardinals had to bend low and touch only her hand, which the two-year-old Mary extended toward them for the reverential kiss. So strict was this observance that Guistinian was left with the (erroneous) impression that Mary commanded greater reverence than did her mother, Queen Catherine.[22]

These types of ceremonial exchange made a deep impression on contemporaries. As the example of Foxe's account of Elizabeth's grocer, Laurence Sheriff, illustrates, Mary's servants surely would have been similarly (although hopefully not quite so violently) impressed with Mary receiving the homage of dukes, cardinals and foreign ambassadors. When Salisbury joined Mary's household at the conclusion of the French negotiations, this would have considerably reinforced the impression that Mary was destined for great things. It most probably assumed great meaning for Mary's household staff. Helping to lavishly clothe their young mistress for the ceremonies surrounding her betrothal to the dauphin in 1518, her subsequent appearances during court festivals and her later betrothal to Charles V (in 1521), must have constantly reinforced the notion that Mary was more than a king's daughter, more even than the future monarch of England. It would have been odd if her household failed to regard her as someone very likely to also wear the crown of France or bear the title of Holy Roman Empress. That her staff were fully aware of these marriage negotiations and took them seriously can be seen in a work by Mary's later French tutor, Giles

Duwes. Duwes later attributed to one of her ladies the admonition that Mary should learn French herself rather than have to rely on a fair maiden to translate "To your husbande and lorde were he either kyng or emperour."[23]

THE PRINCELY COURT OF THE WELSH HOUSEHOLD, 1525–1528

Important as the French negotiations were in the development of Mary's household culture, evidence suggests that it was her Welsh household of 1525 that exercised a determinative influence on the household's evolving daily culture. Establishing a culture of reverence was, in fact, one of Henry VIII's goals for the Welsh household. His "Instructions" stipulated that her household servants treat the nine-year-old Mary with the reverence "as to so great a princess doeth appertaine."[24] Salisbury's job description, as specified in the "Instructions," was to regulate Mary's environment to ensure that she was always presented to the public via her household as a personage worthy of special reverence:

> thie that be lades gentlewomen and maydens being about her persone and also her chambers with others attendant vpon herr, vse themselves sadlei, honorable, vertuously and discreetly in words, countenance, gesture, behavior and deed wth humility, *reverence*, lowliness—due and requisite, so as of them proceed no manner of example of evill or vnfittinge manners or condicions, but rather all good and godly behauior.[25]

These orders also manifest another, more subtle, function of the household, which was to impress on Mary herself her exalted status. These stipulations appear in the section that deals with Mary's daily routine, her education, and permitted pastimes. That they appear among other orders concerning her upbringing argues that the servants' behavior also was intended to be part of her training. These orders would have the effect of instilling in Mary a sense of her own importance. Regulating the behavior of the servants toward Mary not only ensured that she was treated according to her rank but trained Mary to expect this kind of treatment as her due.

The Welsh household was a royal court. It even inspired a work modeled on Castiglione's *The Courtier*. Mary's French tutor Giles Duwes, printed in 1534, *An Introductory for to Learn to Read, to Pronounce, and to Speak French*.[26] Duwes's book was clearly a response to *The Courtier*.[27] In this work, Mary appears as a princely ruler participating in the courtly pastimes familiar to Castiglione's readers: lively conversation, artful service and platonic romance. The structure of the book is in dialogue form, as was Castiglione's. In Duwes's work, these dialogues appear in French with the English translation as a gloss. Throughout, Duwes presented Mary a princely ruler concerned that her staff fully participate in the artistic culture of the household. When a servant absented himself from dinner, thereby failing to contribute to the evening's diversion, preteen Mary threatened to withhold from him her royal patronage:

> Ah/ maister Amencr [Almoner] I had nat wend that ye had so forgotten me. . . . And touchyng the profyte/ ye knowe that whan I dyd prayse your frenche/ ye dyd warant me that within a yere I shulde speke as good or better than you/ wherefore by suche condycion that so myght be/ trustyng more of the power of the kyng my father/ & of the good lady my mother than of myn owne/ dyd promise you a good benefyce/ for the impetation of the whiche me thynketh that ye ought to do some by dylygence.[28]

A very young Mary is here chastising her much older servant for not fulfilling his role. His role is to entertain, instruct and advise his young mistress. In this account, Duwes emphasizes that Mary's servants are courtiers and that Mary's household on the Welsh Marches is a viceregal court. Duwes represents Mary as fully conversant with her own role. She was the presiding ruler of a court. She was the conduit of patronage in that she had direct access to the ultimate sources of royal patronage "the power of the kyng my father/ & of the good lady my mother." Moreover, Duwes depicted Mary as possessing a precocious grasp of the complex details of office holding and patronage when Mary threatened the almoner specifically with the denial of "a good benefyce" or church office that the old almoner had evidently been coveting. While the idea of a child threatening the career advancement of an adult may strike a modern reader as chilling and obnoxious, it was consistent with Duwes's overall depiction of Mary as a princely ruler presiding over a princely court.

According to Duwes, Mary's court very much conformed to the Castiglione model. Duwes described the culture of Mary's household/court as one characterized by erudition, gentle manners, lively conversations and a pervasive consciousness of Mary's status. He depicted the princess receiving messengers from foreign courts and discussing international politics, somewhat jokingly, with her Privy Chamber staff. As noted above, Duwes claimed that Mary was especially keen to enliven the dinner table with learned and elegant conversation. Repeatedly, Duwes depicted her servants as expressing sentiments to Mary that accorded with Duwes's own vow that "wherfore nothing to me shall be possible that having your commandement I do not fullfill to my power."[29] According to the French tutor, the princess' servants tendered her artful, flattering, and sincere service just as Castiglione had advised his Italian courtiers to behave toward the duke of Urbino.

According to Duwes, this court even had its own literary culture. Its courtly poems and letters, as in other royal courts, praised and flattered the ruler. Duwes himself dedicated a French poem to Mary as "most sovereign."[30] When servants excused their absences from her presence, they wrote her elegant and hyperbolic letters. Among the letters Duwes includes (or composes?) from Mary's servants, the following panegyrical address was typical: "To the right high, right excellent, & right magnamous, My right redouted Lady, my Lady Mary of England, my lady and mistress, greeting [you] with joy everlasting."[31] According to Duwes, Mary played her part as the princely patron by commissioning the book. Since she herself gave the order, her tutor, "durst nat" refuse "because of mine obedience that by any service or sacrifice that to her I may do, fullfilling her most noble and gracious comandement . . ."[32]

Duwes includes an episode of courtly love-play. Although only nine when the Welsh household was constituted, the tutor depicts Mary as participating in the drawing of names on Valentines Day. When Mary drew, as her valentine, her treasurer, Sir Ralph Egerton, a man old enough to suffer from gout, the young princess insisted on referring to him as her "husband adoptif." As his pretend wife, the princess took the treasurer to task for taking better care "of your goute . . . than ye do of your wyfe." She further laments that she can hardly believe "that the goute myght with holde a good husbande hauyng some loue to his wyfe" and begs Egerton to teach her what "a good husbande ought to teche his wyfe," that is, the full definition of love (intellectually speaking, one hopes). In true courtly fashion, the princess' "husband" then discourses at great length on the philosophical and moral definition of love.[33]

Space does not allow for an exploration of the implications of Mary—as a female child authority figure—assuming mock sexual submission to an old male (although knightly) servant. What is important here is that this episode places Duwes' depiction of Mary's Welsh household within an emerging tradition of court culture. According to the French tutor, the princess presided over a court no different from that of other royal monarchs. She received foreign ambassadors, royal messengers and engaged in courtly pastimes. Whether or not Duwes was presenting a realistic picture of her household throughout the mid-1520s is less important here than the fact that he depicted a court culture of reverence that anticipated the actual behavior of Mary's servants in subsequent years. Mary's servants would later risk their lives in the service of their "most sovereign" princess.

Mary's household on the Welsh Marches was clearly an impressive establishment. It would have a direct effect on Mary's subsequent households. A great proportion of her Welsh staff remained in her service right up to her accession in 1558. The October 1533 checkeroll of Mary's household reveals that more than two-thirds of her staff in 1533 derived from her 1525 household. This continuity existed in all levels of the household from Privy Chamber gentry attendants to kitchen staff.[34] Consequently, much of her 1533 household would have begun their service with her when she was the *de facto* princess of Wales. Indeed, many continued their association with Mary from her Welsh household right through to her household after her accession.[35]

Moreover, the senior officers of Mary's household continued to derive from the gentry and noble classes. Salisbury's long service in Mary's household has already been noted. After Salisbury's arrest in 1539, Mary would not find a "servant" of social rank that matched Salisbury's. Not surprisingly, Mary would have trouble recruiting aristocratic staff after her disinheritance in 1536. Yet, by the late 1540s, the high social rank of her household officers attracted notice. During Edward's reign when Mary was once again the next heir, her conflict with the Edwardian regime over religion made service in her household too politically sensitive to attract staff among the high nobility. Nevertheless, the social standing of her household could still elicit favorable comment from knowledgeable observers. The Imperial ambassador noted in 1551 that her senior staff were all wealthy and of ancient lineage.[36] The surviving household accounts and lists confirm the ambassador's assessment. Her chief officers, Robert Rochester, Francis Englefield, and Edward Waldegrave, were all knights from respected gentry families. From the death of Henry VIII, when Mary was once again heir to the throne and mistress of her own independent establishment, her Privy Chamber recruited staff mainly from gentry families who were associated with regions near her estates. Other gentry families such as the Dormers served in Mary's household out of personal loyalty to her and her political/religious agenda. The Dormers sent at least three women to serve in Mary's Privy Chamber including Jane Dormer, the future Duchess de Feria.

The Welsh household began and intensified other trends besides low staff turnover and recruitment. It also played a significant role in the development of Mary's political image. Duwes's depiction presented Mary to the literate English polity as a princely ruler. There is corroborating evidence that suggests that Duwes's representation of a culture of reverence in Mary's Welsh household was more than just a literary construct. As indicated in the last chapter, Anne Hussey, one of Mary's staff from the Welsh household was unable to break the habit of reverence toward Mary by 1536. Lady Hussey's inability to treat Mary as anything less than a sovereign princess was indicative that at least one servant, Anne Hussey, had treated Mary with the reverence specified Henry's "Instructions" for Mary's household on the Welsh Marches.

HOUSEHOLD PERKS: MARY'S PRACTICE
OF "GOOD LORDSHIP," 1536–1543

In return for this reverential service, Mary's Privy Chamber accounts reveal that she took seriously her responsibility to be a good mistress to her servants. The princess assumed responsibility for her household in 1532 when she was sixteen.[37] Her accounts as well as her correspondence indicates that she cared for her servants from birth through to marriage, retirement, and death. Moreover, these documents show that Mary identified her domestic staff as extensions of her public persona; what was done to them reflected on her and vice versa.

Mary served as godmother to a great many children of the aristocracy; indeed, it would be hard to find a noble or politically important family from 1536 until 1553, which did not have at least one child who claimed Mary as their godmother. Her financial support of her servants' children suggest that she also took on this function for many children of her senior staff. The accounts specifically list her as godmother to the son of one of her Privy Chamber grooms, Thomas Borough. Furthermore, she paid for the education of the children of her laundress Beatrice ap Rhys (spelled "Rice" in the accounts) and her husband David. There are frequent notations in the household accounts concerning their children, Henry and Mary. The April 1538 entry was typical: "Itm geuen to a prieste of Windesor who teacheth a Childe of Dauid ap Rice."[38]

When Mary ap Rhys reached the next stage in her life, marriage, the princess provided the taffeta wedding gown.[39] The ap Rhys children were not the only ones to receive Mary's attention on their marriage. Contracting a marriage while in the princess' service usually resulted in a gift of some kind from Mary. In April 1537, her accountant recorded an "Itm geuen to the mariage of one of the Ewry the xvth Daye of this mounth."[40] A Mistress Fynes received from the princess money "on her maryage to by her a kyrtell."[41] Mary gave her servant, John Scutt, two deer to grace his wedding feast.[42]

When her servants retired or left her service Mary continued to be their "good mistress." Her accounts record that David Candeland "my lades g[ra]ce olde sunte" received a small sum in July 1537.[43] Sums like this were also dispersed to Richard Baker, Humphrey Andrews and a Richard who was designated in the accounts as "a pore man and sõmetyme wodberer."[44] The princess supported her servants after their deaths. When William ap Richard and his wife died of plague while in her service in September 1537, Mary paid for their burial expenses.[45]

Mary's accounts suggest that her servants enjoyed something analogous to the modern concept of an expense account. The two Privy Chamber women,

Frances Elmer and Mary Brown, who usually conveyed her gifts to her noble godchildren and represented her at their christenings, were always reimbursed for their traveling expenses.[46] When her staff left the household to perform errands on her behalf, they were not expected to pay for traveling expenses out of their wages. Thomas Palmer and Thomas Borough, gentlemen of her Privy Chamber, appear regularly in her accounts as receiving reimbursement for expenses incurred while on purchasing expeditions.[47] When her Privy Chamber gentlewomen, Frideswide Knight and Mary Brown, accompanied her to court, the princess paid for their boat passage from Greenwich to London.[48] Also, when her servants had to lodge elsewhere, either on long trips on the princesses' business or because they had been in contact with people suffering from contagious diseases (and so were not allowed to return immediately to Mary's household), then their "extra hospitium" expenses were reimbursed.[49]

If her servants revered her, Mary, in return, conflated her interest with theirs. In 1533, when the Privy Council sent a delegation in mid-October to urge her to comply with the king's orders that she renounce the title of princess, Chapuys reported that she insisted on receiving the delegation in front of her assembled household staff—driving home the point that what happened to her would also have consequences for her staff.[50] In the wake of the 1533 loss of her separate household, Mary requested that the king find employment for the servants she would be unable to take with her to the new combined establishment.[51] Mary's interests and those of the household were so closely aligned that, according to Chapuys, the king blamed Mary's servants for encouraging her to persist in her refusal to acknowledge the validity of the Boleyn marriage and her own illegitimacy.[52] If true, then the household was supporting their mistress' political future even at the cost of the gainful employment of the individual members. It was, after all, Mary's noncompliance had played a role the king's decision to dissolve in Mary's independent establishment. The focus then of this particular corporate identity was Mary and her political future rather the collective economic interests of the household staff.

Perhaps in recognition of the economic sacrifices made on her behalf, Mary did her best to ensure that her servants were employed (whether in her household or elsewhere) and well treated. When, in 1536, Mary submitted to the Reformation legislation and, consequently, was partially restored to Henry's favor, she began immediately to write to Henry's minister, Thomas Cromwell, about her servants. Indeed, nearly all of her handwritten surviving correspondence from this year concerns her servants—which ones she wanted to take into service again, how they were being treated when on errands for her, and so on. Interestingly, she expressed gratitude to Cromwell for arranging for her reconciliation with the king following her submission; she was grateful not just on her behalf but also for "me and my seruants." She recognized the dependency of her staff on her own political fortunes. She acknowledged to Cromwell that her political rehabilitation had resulted in "benefite to my frendes and seruantes."[53]

These statements also indicate that Mary regarded her servants as an extension of herself. When Thomas Wriothlessly offered exceptional hospitality to one of Mary's servants, he received the rare compliment of a hand-written letter from Mary thanking him for the "intertaynyng [of] my seruant." [54] Her staff was part of her persona, like badges on livery. What was done to her would accrue to her staff and vice versa. This sense of obligation and identification extended even toward her mother's old servants. After thanking Wriothelesly for how he treated her servant, Mary then requested that Wriothelesly take Queen Catherine's old servant, Anthony Coke, into service and declared pointedly that "I do love hym well."[55] Mary continued to exert herself on behalf of her servants well after the 1530s. In April 1547, she wrote Anne Seymour, duchess of Somerset (Seymour herself had been a member of Catherine's Privy Chamber), on behalf of other of the old queen's servants, Richard Wood and George Brickhouse.[56] Indeed, except for Mary's letters to the monarch—Henry VIII or Edward VI—it is hard to find correspondence from her before her accession, which does not contain appeals from her on behalf of her household servants.

Mary's accounts indicate that the princess also funded her servants' in-house recreation and fully participated in it herself. The accounts from 1536 to 1543 indicate that the princess continued to preside over an artistic courtly culture that echoed that described by Duwes in reference to her Welsh household in the 1520s. Mary patronized scholars such as Henry, Lord Morley, and Sir Thomas Elyot.[57] She continued the tradition of drawing valentines and rewarding her pretend husbands with jewelry. The accounts contain frequent notations of payments to musicians. The princess herself was noted for her musical proficiency.[58] Something of the convivial atmosphere of her household court is suggested by the numerous entries concerning gambling. The princess was an avid card player and, in royal tradition, did not carry enough coin on her person to cover her debts. She therefore borrowed from her Privy Chamber servants, whom she later reimbursed. Another pastime was playing bowls and apparently, Mary's staff were happier risking their economic future on Mary's political potential than on her ability to win at bowling. On one occasion, the princess' staff refused to sponsor Mary as she bowled. The princess was forced to enter into the game by wagering her breakfast.[59] If her servants had doubted her ability to prevail then they were proved right when the princess lost her breakfast and went hungry that morning.

These household accounts reveal the unsurprising fact that Mary's patronage of her servants varied according to their social class. Those lower down the social scale were the most likely to receive cash payments and gifts for expenses and to mark social milestones. As noted above, Mary also sponsored the endeavors of her servants to obtain pensions and livings outside her household. These accounts do not preserve any indications that she reimbursed, in similar fashion, the noble ladies who sometimes served in her Privy Chamber during her frequent sojourns at court. They were not given gratuities the way staff of lower social classes were. Rather Mary bestowed on her high gentry and noble servants gifts of jewels and political patronage.

Mary may have scrutinized her Privy Chamber accounts and, occasionally, totaled the sums herself, but it was her jewelry inventory that received her most intense concentration. She signed every page and the inventory is liberally glossed with her handwritten corrections.[60] Mary kept this jewel list with her long after her Privy Chamber accounts ended in 1543. The inventory even preserves a present Queen Mary gave to Princess Elizabeth soon after Mary's accession in September 1553. The list does not specify why the jewels were given but the identity of the recipients and evidence from other sources, such as letters, suggest that many of the jewels were awarded to those ladies who had waited on Mary while she was at court. The recipients were all wives of prominent men at court or in the government during the reigns of Henry VIII and Edward VI. Because these women did not have places at court when Henry was between wives and not at all during Edward's reign, it is likely that their service in Mary's Privy Chamber occurred only when the princess was at court. None of the high-ranking women listed in Mary's jewel list appeared in her household accounts as part of her permanent Privy Chamber staff. This is not to preclude that some of the recipients were simply friends and relatives who never "served" in Mary's Privy Chamber such as Princess Elizabeth and Lady Jane Grey. With this caveat in mind, it is still possible to mine Mary's jewel list for clues as to who were part of her political as well as personal network.

Among those who received jewels from Mary was Margaret Douglas. Other recipients of jewels from Mary who also can be confirmed as having served in her Privy Chamber: the daughters of Sir John Shelton and Mary Kingston, wife of Sir William Kingston, the constable of the Tower.[61] There many prominent women who cannot be confirmed from another source as serving in Mary's Privy Chamber but who, likely, received jewels from her as partial payment for their service in her Privy Chamber while Mary was at court are Frances and Eleanor Brandon, Jane Dudley, and Anne Seymour. As already discussed, Seymour had served in Catherine of Aragon's household and there was a noticeable trend for Catherine's servants to transfer to Mary's service after Catherine's death in 1536. One of Mary's most informal and affectionate surviving letters is to Anne Seymour. [62] In the case of Jane Dudley, the present of a jewel may be related to Mary standing as godmother to Jane Dudley's son.

An obvious explanation for the jewel presentations is that Mary was simply reciprocating New Year's gifts from these women. There is a problem with this:

the list notes which women received jewels as New Year's gifts. For all other recipients, the occasion is unspecified. It is unlikely that *all* who received jewels
from Mary obtained them as New Year's gifts. Several of the aforementioned
women could have received jewels from Mary out of friendship. Mary's personal attention to the jewel list suggests that she did not give them out lightly.
Admittedly, there is no concrete evidence that Mary gave jewels in return for
extraordinary service in her Privy Chamber. There is, however, a curious confluence of circumstances that suggest strongly that there was political dimension to Mary's relationship with politically prominent women such as Anne
Seymour, duchess of Somerset, Frances Brandon, Duchess of Suffolk, Jane
Dudley, Duchess of Northumberland and Margaret Douglas, Countess of Lennox. Two of these women, Brandon and Douglas, were royal, whose claims to
the throne itself were inferior only to those of Henry's direct offspring. Dudley
and Seymour were married to men who ruled on behalf of the underaged monarch, Edward VI. Neither woman was regarded by contemporaries as apolitical.
It stretches the bonds of credulity to imagine that when Mary met these women
that politics was not an item for discussion.

The question is whether Mary's jewel list provides credible grounds for
speculating that these women regarded Mary as a political patron and/or client.
The jewel list certainly indicates a relationship of some kind and it is difficult to
imagine that there was not some political component to the relations among
such politically active and prominent women. Whether the jewels indicate
Mary was their client or their patron is the more thorny issue. Lines of patronage and clientage were not as simple as the terms might indicate. These women
may have served in Mary's Privy Chamber indicating that she served as their
patron but yet it was Mary who had ask a favor from Anne Seymour regarding
the employment of her servant.[63] It is entirely possible that these women served
in Mary's Privy Chamber when Mary was at court and there was no queen-
consort's chamber in which they could serve. Mary then might have sent them
jewels as a kind of payment for their service while at the same time cultivating
a relationship with someone like Anne Seymour, whose husband Edward Seymour, Earl of Hertford (future Duke of Somerset) was among the most powerful men at the court of Henry VIII (Seymour would later become the Lord
Protector for Edward VI).

The ambiguity of these relationships and how domestic accounts can raise
more questions than answers is demonstrated in the documents relating to the
relationship between Mary and Katherine Parr, Henry VIII's sixth and final
consort.

Katherine Parr served in Mary's Privy Chamber at court in 1546 as an "extraordinary" member. "Extraordinary" membership in royal Privy Chambers
was generally reserved for high-ranking nobility who did not need wages and

who could not be expected to serve permanently in another's household when they usually had their own large establishments to oversee and manage. Because there are household lists for Mary's household in this period and Parr was not a permanent member of Mary's Privy Chamber, Parr's service as "extraordinary" member in the princess' chamber at court must be inferred from two significant circumstances. Parr was resident at Henry's court in late 1542 and her residency at court can only be explained if she was serving in Mary's Privy Chamber.

Lodgings at court were not available to all noblewomen nor were they guaranteed for the wives of noblemen who themselves held official positions at court. The presence of women at the court of a male monarch meant they were serving in the "queen's side" of the royal household or in the households of one of the king's dependent female relations like a sister or daughter resident at the court.[64] When Henry was between wives, noblewomen had practically no place at court. Mary's frequent residency at court helped to alleviate the problem. Given the presence of Katherine Parr at court in 1542, the most logical inference is that she obtained her place there by serving in Mary's Privy Chamber.[65]

According to one of Parr's modern biographers, she began serving in Mary's Privy Chamber in 1542 during one of the periods when Henry VIII was between wives.[66] Parr had a claim on Mary's patronage because her mother, Maud Parr, had served in the Privy Chamber of Mary's mother, Catherine of Aragon. [67] As previously seen, Mary was sensitive to the claims of those who had served her mother. It is most likely her service in Mary's Privy Chamber that brought Parr to the notice of her future husband, Henry VIIII. Indeed, during this period, when Parr was court, the Imperial ambassador reported that Henry VII took to calling on his daughter nearly three times a day.[68] Parr's husband died in March 1543 during her term of service in Mary's chamber and in July Katherine Parr married Henry VIII and became queen-consort of England.

The point where Parr moves from serving in Mary's Privy Chamber to becoming queen-consort is where terms like "patron-client relationship" seem too rigid. Who was the patron and who the client? Parr first gained Henry's notice through her service in Mary's Privy Chamber yet, after her elevation to the consort's throne, Parr was the more socially and politically prominent. It was she who provided lodgings for Mary at court from now on. Susan James, Parr's most recent biographer, argues throughout that it was Mary who was Parr's client. She even credits Parr with being instrumental in getting Mary restored to the succession in the third Act of Succession (1544).[69]

Symptomatic of the problems involved is the evidence that James' cites. On her royal wedding day, Parr bestowed on Mary two unspecified sums of cash.[70] For James, this is evidence of a patron, Parr, lavishing gifts on her client, Mary.

Yet it could also be read as a client (Parr) paying off her patron (Mary). When the Imperial ambassador complimented Parr on the deference that she was paying to Mary even though Parr, as queen-consort, now outranked the still-illegitimate Mary, Parr demurred and claimed she it was her duty to defer to Mary.[71] For James, this is evidence of Parr condescending to show special treatment to the maladjusted Mary. Then, again, perhaps it was Parr exhibiting signs of obligation and deference to Mary. Parr took into her royal household one of Mary's former servants, the widowed Lady Kingston.[72] Perhaps she did so in fulfillment of Mary's request. Parr later presented Mary with an extravagant set of gold bracelets set with rubies, diamonds, and emeralds—more deference or condescension?[73] This study comes down firmly on the side of steering a middle course. Clearly Mary and Parr were friends. The political dimension to their relationship was complicated by their changing political fortunes. Parr was elevated to the consort's throne in 1543 but by late 1547 (after Henry VIII's death) she has to fight for precedence with Anne Seymour, duchess of Somerset. Meanwhile, Mary is once again the heir to throne in 1547 and the "second person" in the kingdom after the sovereign. Doubtless, the role of patron and client was always ambiguous between the two women and emphasized in different ways depending on each woman's political fortunes.

At times in their relationship, Parr appears to treat Mary as her patron and at others, she may be extending her patronage *to* Mary. Mary's political relationship with Parr with all its complexities and variations may have been similar to that she had with other politically prominent women like Frances Brandon, Jane Dudley, and Anne Seymour. Mary's jewel list indicates that these relationships, with their inevitable political resonances, existed even if it cannot always pinpoint from which direction the political patronage was flowing. Mary, with her frequent visits to court and her blood relationship to the monarch, would have been a particularly good patron. Serving in the princess's household while she was in residence at court would have provided more "career opportunities" for elite women who otherwise would not have had access to the court while Henry was between wives and Edward remained an unmarried minor.[74]

Another significant aspect of these relationships is that the jewel list provides documentation of an elite female network. Such a network was not unique to Princess Mary.[75] Although a victim of her father's complicated and contradictory view of women, Mary's jewel list demonstrates that she was able to plug herself into a female network that one can only hope provided much needed emotional and political support.

Mary's household was a court in which its courtiers depended on their princely ruler for their room, board, entertainment, and livelihood. Like the royal household/court of her father, Mary's household court was a center of political patronage. Mary was not only a generous employer to those members of staff most economically dependent on her but she also acted as a useful conduit for royal patronage for her more socially exalted "courtiers": her intermittent Privy Chamber ladies. Katherine Parr's elevation to the consort's throne attests to Mary's ability as a political patron. The princess had upheld her end of the *conventio* to all of those who served in her household and Privy Chamber. In return, Mary's servants—from the "extraordinary" like Katherine Parr to the less exalted but essential permanent staff like the ap Rice family—offered Mary loyal and dedicated service. The loyalty of Mary's servants would play a decisive role in the coming political crises that became a feature of Mary's life during her brother's reign. Indeed, as one contemporary observer noted, Mary would owe her eventual elevation to the sovereign's throne to the loyal service of her household/Privy Chamber staff.

Sitting on her ornate cushions beneath a rich cloth of estate or a canopy depicting her crowned initial, in a room lined with tapestries proclaiming her lineage, Mary appeared before her servants—some of whom had been with her for decades—as a quasi-sacred figure to which they had rendered homage as a "sovereign princess" since the 1520s. She cared for them, identified with them, promoted their interests and political ambitions and they, in turn, regarded her as their "most sovereign" mistress for whom they were willing to risk imprisonment and death. As the following discussion notes, there is evidence that Mary herself regarded her role as householder as analogous to that of a bishop's pastoral care of his congregation or flock.

As the immediate heir of Edward VI, Mary's actions from 1547 through 1553 were of national consequence. Her decision not to conform to the Protestant services mandated in the Act of Uniformity in 1549 was regarded by the young king and the Privy Council as deliberately provocative. Characteristically, Mary defied the new policies not just on her behalf but also on her household's. Even though the new legislation had specifically outlawed the traditional Latin mass, Mary ordered that mass be celebrated with special pomp in her residences.[76] This earned a swift reprimand from the Privy Council[77] and a summons sent to three of her household officers, including her comptroller Sir Robert Rochester, to appear before the council to answer for Mary's household defiance.[78] Mary immediately protested the summons and claimed that her household was at a standstill without Rochester "because the chief charge of my house resteth only on the travails of my said Comptroller."[79]

Later, on August 14, 1551, the Privy Council again summoned to London Rochester along with two other of Mary's senior officers, Sir Francis Englefield and Sir Edward Waldegrave.[80] The council ordered the officers to return to Mary's household. The council ordered them to inform Mary that her household must allow and attend the new Protestant service. Rochester, Englefield and

Waldegrave were then to proceed, by virtue of their household offices, to ensure that the household complied with the Act of Uniformity. Mary's officers were appalled. They informed the council that they could hardly presume to issue commands to their revered mistress in her own house. The Privy Council argued that their first loyalty was to the king and that should give them more than enough authority to follow the Privy Council's orders. Nevertheless, Rochester, Englefield, and Waldegrave duly returned to the princess' household. Mary refused to allow her senior officers to deliver their message to her let alone to regulate the household's religious observances.[81]

The Privy Council subsequently summoned the same officers before them yet again to report on their progress. On learning that the officers had refused to violate Mary's direct orders, the council again commanded them to return to Mary's house and carry out their commission:

> ... the which thing they all refused to do, albeit they were enjoyned to do the same in vertue of their allegeaunce and as commaunded from the Kinges Majestie, the said Rochester and Walgrave saying that they had rather endure whatsoever punisshement or emprisonment the Lordes shuld think mete for them, and Sir Fraunces Inglefeld alledging that he could neither fynde in his harte nor in his consyence to do it.[82]

This was an alarming development from the government's viewpoint. Mary's officers placed their obligation to her over their allegiance to the crown. An indication of the seriousness with which the councilors regarded it is their decision to commit Rochester, Waldegrave, and Englefield to the Tower of London.[83] The Tower was a prison reserved for high crimes against the state and prisoners rarely left it alive. King Edward himself wrote to the princess on the Privy Council's advice warning her that her household defiance posed a danger to "the commen tranquilytie of our realm."[84] The Privy Council dispatched a delegation to Mary on August 24. The delegation's mission was to deliver instructions to Mary's household staff to cease attending the forbidden mass. Anticipating resistance, the council ordered the delegation to give Mary's household a civics lesson: "in the whiche clause ye shall use the reasons of their naturall deuty and allegaeaunce that they owe as subjectes to their Sovereign Lorde, which derogateth all other erthly duetyes."[85] The council, in effect, was instructing the delegation to clarify to which corporate body—the body politic rather than the body domestic—the individual members of Mary's household owed its primary duty.

When the delegation arrived, Mary refused to surrender her household authority. She spoke confidently of both her servants' loyalty and her ability to maintain control over their actions no matter what the delegation threatened them with: "none of your nue Service (said she) shalbe used in my howse."[86]

According to the delegation's report, she openly scoffed at their attempts to use her servants to subvert her authority within her household:

> And after this we declared unto her Grace according to our instruccions for what causes the Lordes of the Kinges Majesties Counsell had appointed Rochester, Inglefeld, and Walgrave, being her servantes, to open the premisses [forbidding the Latin mass] unto her, and how yll and untruly they had used themselfes in the charge committed unto them, and besides that, how they had manifestly disobeyed the Kinges Majesties Counsell, &c. To this she sayd *it was not the wysest counsell to appoint her servantes to comptrolle her in her owne howse,* and that her servantes knew her mynde therin well ynough, for of all men she might wurst endure any of them to move her in any suche mattiers, and for their punyshment my Lordes may use them as they think good.[87]

This is quite a revealing exchange. Mary displayed serene confidence in her ability to suborn the allegiance of her officers away from the king. Her household was her private princedom and the council was foolish to send her own subjects to issue commands to her in her own domain. She considered that her senior officers did no more than their rightful duty in refusing to try and override her authority. Her statements make it plain that even if Rochester and his colleagues had attempted to regulate her household without her permission, they would have failed. Her writ, not the king's, was the only one that ran in her household.

It took a direct order from the king himself to persuade Mary to back down and cease to publicly celebrate the Latin mass in her manors.[88] Mary reported to the Imperial ambassador that Edward was considering dissolving her household and this may have also played a part in her decision to reach an unequal compromise with the king.[89] She refused to allow the new Protestant service to be celebrated in her manors but nor did she continue to celebrate the Latin mass. She continued to petition, unsuccessfully, for the privilege to hear the Latin mass in her Privy Chamber. In return for her partial submission, her officers were returned to her.[90] Although Mary had lost the battle, the actions of her household resulted in a widespread understanding that her establishment was a bastion of the "old religion," which the majority of English subjects still practiced (albeit now in private). According to the later recollection of one of her former Privy Chamber ladies, during this period, the princess' household was "the only harbour for honourable young gentlewomen, given any way to [Catholic] piety and devotion."[91]

Mary herself regarded her household as a congregation. Earlier, in 1550, when Mary toyed with the idea of seeking asylum at the court of Charles V (see Appendix B), she reportedly told the Imperial ambassador that what held her back and gave her the most pause was "the thought of leaving my household, which, though small, is composed of good Christians who may, in my absence, become lost sheep."[92] It needs to be emphasized at this point that this phrasing is that of the nineteenth-century editors of Imperial ambassador's dispatches. The phrasing is distinctive enough to suggest that the editors were probably replicating the pertinent of the original document. This abstract alone, however, cannot be regarded as conclusive evidence of Mary's attitude toward her household.

There is other evidence suggesting that Mary, in common with other secular heads of household, exercised thaumaturgical or priestly functions. A notation in her accounts for April 1537 indicates that Mary performed the sacerdotal function of christening a child.[93] In an age in which monarchs were considered to heal diseases by their touch, it is possible that, on occasion, the princess performed minor religious ceremonies for her neighbors, servants, and clients. The high-rate of infant mortality made secular christenings of dying infants somewhat commonplace. Midwives often performed a rudimentary christening ceremony for the all-too-many infants losing the fight for life soon after their birth.[94] Mary's status as a wealthy householder and a member of the royal family endowed her with significant thaumaturgical credentials, which easily qualified her to perform christening ceremonies.

Further evidence that Mary regarded herself as a religious authority figure and her household as her personal parish comes from her above-mentioned confrontation with the Privy Council. Mary's refusal to allow the Protestant service mandated by her brother's government to be observed in her own house represented a serious political challenge to the monarch's authority. Scholars often blame the supposed weakness of the Edwardian government as the primary reason why Mary's defiance was tolerated. In 1974, Lawrence Stone identified "the absence of charismatic leadership" during Edward VI's reign as one of the causes for political instability yet the behavior of Mary's household suggests that Catholics, in particular the Catholic dependents associated with Mary's household, had found in the princess householder a leader of sufficient thaumaturgical charisma that they were willing to risk death on her behalf.[95]

Much to the astonished dismay of the Privy Council, Mary's household staff placed their obligations to the princess above those to the government. The Privy Council was horrified. Mary exercised a religious authority over her household that her contemporaries likely regarded as not that dissimilar from that of a bishop over the souls in his episcopate. Mary's household staff were her "flock" in the sense that they were under her religious authority. Mary apparently felt herself charged not simply with the responsibility for ensuring the physical well-being of her household but also she was responsible for their spiritual welfare.

As head of household, Mary exercised a spiritual authority that was not shared by unmarried English princesses before her or after her, save for her half-sister Elizabeth. English princesses living in nursery households or at the royal court were not charged with the physical and spiritual welfare of their staff since their households were merely subsets of the monarch's. In a real sense, Mary and Elizabeth, by virtue of their positions as heads of households, served apprenticeships as religious leaders that their female predecessors and successors were unable to serve. By the time that Mary and Elizabeth acceded to the throne and assumed governance of the English church, they had already exercised authority as religious leaders over their household staff, tenants, and clients. When John Knox protested female headship of the English church in 1558, in his infamous *First Blast*, he was attempting to put the toothpaste back in the tube: Mary had been determining the religious policy of her household since 1547.

ELIZABETH TUDOR'S PROTESTANT FAMILY: 1533–1553

The culture of reverence and patronage in Mary's household may have found echoes in other elite households. It does not, however, appear as a feature of the household culture in Princess Elizabeth's establishment. Elizabeth's servants were certainly loyal, obedient, and conscious of their mistress' royal blood but they exhibited more of a parental feeling toward her. The household practiced a familial culture committed as much to reforming religion as to providing a stable, familial environment to its young mistress.

From 1533 until 1550, when she turned sixteen, Elizabeth was legally a minor. Elizabeth's account books, her correspondence, government depositions and the letters of her servants all suggest that her youth combined with her relative lack of status, after 1536, meant that the princess was not able to overawe her staff as Mary did hers. Instead of learning the habit of reverence, Elizabeth's servants assumed responsibility for her upbringing and education. It was the household and not its young mistress who dictated the household's agenda and established its artistic and practical culture. This culture was distinguished by erudition, Protestantism, and an interest in contemporary Italian artistic culture. It was a culture that forged such a strong corporate identity that, as will be demonstrated later, its corporate persona existed independently of its titular figurehead, Princess Elizabeth.

Whereas it was true to a certain extent that in all royal nursery households, including Mary's and Prince Edward's, servants "raised" the royal child rather than the parents, this feature was emphasized in Elizabeth's household. Her birth order in the royal family meant that she was less important than both Mary and Prince Edward so that the king, on occasion, had to be forcibly reminded of her existence.[96] Indeed, there is no evidence to suggest that Henry even saw his younger daughter from January 1536 until September 1542.[97] Thereafter, they encountered each other only during Elizabeth's infrequent and short visits to court from 1543 until Henry's death in 1547. This paternal neglect combined with her mother's early death resulted in Elizabeth experiencing very little interaction with her biological parents. As will be detailed later, it was her household staff that supervised her development and arranged for her education—with the king's approval.

Elizabeth's household from the beginning employed many of the princess' maternal kin. The first steward of her household was Sir John Shelton whose wife, Anne Shelton was the chief gentlewoman of her Privy Chamber. Lady Anne Shelton was Anne Boleyn's paternal aunt. Elizabeth's first governess, Margaret Bryan, was distantly related to the Boleyns (Bryan was the half-sister of Anne Boleyn's mother). John Ashley, a Boleyn relative by the marriage of an aunt, joined the household sometime before 1540. Although these blood ties might strike a modern reader as rather weak, Elizabeth herself took them seriously. When John Ashley was arrested during the Seymour crisis of 1549, Elizabeth asked for his release "for he is my kinsman" even though his relation to her derived from no more than his maternal aunt having married the brother of Elizabeth's maternal grandfather![98]

The presence of these Boleyn relations and the evidence of Queen Anne's interest in the material splendor of her daughter's environment indicates that Anne, before her death, was an important, if indirect, early influence on the development of her daughter's household's culture. Henry VIII funded the household and had the final say in all important aspects of his daughter's upbringing, such as when she was weaned, but it was Anne who was guiding the routine behavior and agenda of the household.[99] She instructed her relative, Anne Shelton, to ensure that Mary—when living in the conflated household in 1534—did not attempt to usurp Elizabeth's status by claiming the princely title.[100] By installing her relatives and supplementing Henry's expenditure on the household with her own purchases of lavish clothing for Elizabeth, Anne was attempting to ensure that Elizabeth would receive the treatment due to a princess and heir to the throne. The queen also may have begun to draw up plans for Elizabeth to receive a Protestant humanist education.[101]

Anne Boleyn's death in 1536 effectively removed almost all direct parental authority from Elizabeth's household. During the summer of 1536, the king concentrated all his paternal attention on Mary. His only interest (other than financial) in the combined household of his daughters was to enlist the staff to help ensure Mary's submission to the Reformation legislation.[102] At this point, Elizabeth's household, which had benefited from a familial atmosphere, now suffered because of it. With hardly any parental authority in evidence, the staff jockeyed for position like squabbling family members. As already mentioned, Sir John Shelton, the steward, and Elizabeth's governess Margaret Bryan came into open conflict over the level of hospitality the household could offer. A central point in the conflict was the issue over who had seniority within the household—Shelton or Bryan.

According to Bryan's 1536 letter to Cromwell, Shelton "sayth he es master of thys hows."[103] Affronted by this challenge to her position, Bryan sniffed "what fashion that shal be, I cannot tel. For I have not sen et afor." She pointedly reminded Cromwell that the king had created her a baroness in her own right, and that it was she who had been entrusted with the initial upbringing of the king's two elder children, Mary and Richmond. She closed the letter with the complaint that Shelton "wel not be content" to be ruled by her. Cromwell's response, which presumably contained the king's decision on what was to be done about the situation, has not survived. In any case, events such as the birth of Henry's son, prince Edward in 1537, changed the situation as Bryan left Elizabeth's household to become Edward's governess.

The Bryan/Shelton conflict could have resulted from personal investment in the status of Elizabeth and her household. Both were related to her, albeit tangentially. What is beyond doubt was that there was a crisis of authority within the establishment. Clearly, three-year-old Elizabeth was too young to assert her authority over the household or as Bryan put it, "to kepe syche rewl yet." There was a power vacuum at the top of the establishment due to the Elizabeth's age, her uncertain status as both illegitimate and yet the king's acknowledged daughter, and a lack of parental interest. As the Bryan/Shelton conflict suggests, it was the household staff who would themselves would attempt establish the chain of command until the princess was old enough to assume responsibility for the household. Neither Bryan nor Shelton referred the matter to the three-year-old Elizabeth for obvious reasons.

The Bryan/Shelton conflict presaged the division of authority along gender lines that persisted in Elizabeth's household. Bryan's replacement, Katherine Champernon, became Elizabeth's governess in 1536 but is unclear whether she was the "Lady Mistress" of the entire household as Margaret Salisbury had been in Mary's childhood households.[104] Elizabeth later refereed to Champernon as "her mistress," that is, her governess, but not as the mistress of the household.[105] Elizabeth would also later award sole credit to Champernon for how she was brought up suggesting that Champernon, like Salisbury, was responsible for regulating Elizabeth's Privy Chamber environment. Evidence suggests, however, that Champernon did not overrule the steward or the "cofferer" (treasurer).

Judging from Champernon's and the cofferer Thomas Parry's later testimony, they divided household authority between them. Parry administered household accounts and, later, Elizabeth's property, while Champernon was in charge of the princess' Privy Chamber.[106] In the absence of young Elizabeth's leadership, her household divided authority among themselves and along gender lines.

Champernon's 1536 entrance into Elizabeth's household not only ushered in a more smooth *modus operandi* but it also reinforced the familial atmosphere in the household and brought the household some important connections at court (see Table 1). Sometime around 1540, Champernon married a member of Elizabeth's staff, John Ashley, the aforementioned kinsman to the princess. This meant that Elizabeth was literally being raised by her relatives. Champernon's sister, Joan, married the important Henrician courtier, Sir Anthony Denny. This reinforced a preexisting Denny connection to Elizabeth via Denny's sister, Joyce. Joyce married John Cary, a brother of William Cary who had married Elizabeth's maternal aunt, Mary Boleyn.[107]

It is unclear exactly when Thomas Parry joined Elizabeth's household but he was certainly in place before 1547 (probably well before then) when he was fielding enquiries as her cofferer.[108] When he joined, he brought in another Boleyn connection. His wife, Anne, married as her first husband Adrian Fortescue who was the son of Alice Boleyn, an aunt of Queen Anne's.[109] Parry also

Table 1. Elizabeth's Household Staff and Maternal Relatives

Source: J. L. McIntosh

Table 1. Elizabeth's Household Staff and Maternal Relatives	
Name	**Relationship**
Katherine Champernon Ashley (governess)	Married Elizabeth's relative John Ashley
John Ashley	Blood Relation through Ashley's maternal aunt marrying Anne Boleyn's grandfather
John Shelton (steward)	Married Elizabeth's relative Anne Shelton
Lady Anne Shelton	Sister of Anne Boleyn's father
Thomas Parry (treasurer)	Married Anne Fortescue, widow of Elizabeth's relative Adrian Fortescue
Adrian Fortescue (first husband of Anne Parry)	Son of Alice Boleyn, the sister of Anne Boleyn's father
William Cecil (surveyor)	Cecil and Parry families related by marriage
Sir Anthony Denny (Henrician patron and courtier)	Married to Joan Champernon, sister Katherine Ashley

connected the household to an important political ally, William Cecil, later Elizabeth's chief minister and already an rising official at Edward VI's court. Parry was from the Vaughn family who were, in turn, related by marriage to the Cecil family.[110] It was a connection that both Cecil and Parry acknowledged as their frequent correspondence during the 1550s attests.[111] The connection to the Cecils, specifically William Cecil, would also have significant repercussions for Elizabeth and her princely household.

Reinforcing this familial context in Elizabeth's household was the frequent presence of her half-siblings. For accounting purposes, she shared a household with Mary. Although Mary refused to accept that Elizabeth outranked her from 1533 until 1536, she publicly acknowledged the familial relationship even during this period. Her letter to Henry VIII in 1536 commending Elizabeth to him and Mary's later household accounts suggest that she was fond of her younger half-sister.[112] Later, Edward would frequently share accommodation with his sisters, especially with Elizabeth, as Mary spent her time increasingly at court. Elizabeth matured within a household environment that was overtly familial with the intermittent presence of her sister and brother and the constant comfort of her maternal kin serving on her staff.

EDUCATING ELIZABETH

It is unclear if anyone other than Champernon educated Elizabeth from 1536 until 1544.[113] In 1544, however, the king decided that Prince Edward would no longer habitually share accommodation with his sisters but preside over an expanded establishment of his own. Although the Prince and Elizabeth would still share residences from time to time, the separation of their establishments was more clearly delineated. One mark of this was that it was no longer possible for Elizabeth and Edward to share lessons, even assuming that they had done so previously.[114] John Cheke, a famous scholar of St. John's College, Cambridge now supervised the Prince's lessons. A colleague of Cheke's, William Grindal became Elizabeth's tutor at this time.[115]

Cheke and Grindal were part of a humanist, Protestant circle at Cambridge that included another of Elizabeth's future tutors, Roger Ascham. They advocated a combination of humane, but thorough, education in the classics with an overtly Protestant outlook. Three other scholar-politicians were associated with this group of St. Johns and Cambridge in general: Sir Anthony Denny, William Cecil, and John Ashley.[116] All three were associated, in varying degrees, with Elizabeth's household in 1544. Denny and Cecil were related by either marriage or blood to senior officers in the princess' establishment and Ashley was a member of staff.

It was this household nexus that resulted in the appointments of both Cheke and Grindal as tutors to the younger royal children. Denny was among the leading advocates of Cheke's appointment as Prince Edward's tutor.[117] Henry VIII was known to rely on Denny's advice in such matters since Denny and the king's physician, William Butts, had became the leading patrons of humanist learning at court in the early 1540s. Once Denny had secured Cheke's appointment, he then asked Cheke (probably at the request of his sister-in-law, Katherine Champernon) to recommend a tutor for Elizabeth. Cheke solicited his mentor, Roger Ascham, for a suggestion. Ashcam forwarded Grindal's name as a suitable candidate for the princess' tutor. This was not the first instance in which Ascham interested himself in Elizabeth's education. When his old college friend, John Ashley, married Katherine Champernon c.1540, Ascham began corresponding with the governess as to what methodology Champernon should employ when instructing her pupil.[118] Ascham would eventually emerge from behind the tutorial throne and formally become Elizabeth's tutor in 1549 after Grindal died.[119]

It was her household, then, which directed Elizabeth's education and shaped her religious agenda. The efforts of Denny, Champernon, Ashley, and Ascham had ensured that Elizabeth would receive her education as the hands of Protestant champions of the "new learning," William Grindal and Roger Ascham. As far as her education was concerned, Elizabeth's household had acted *in loco parentis*.

THE SEYMOUR CRISIS, 1549

The January 1549 arrest of Thomas Seymour, brother to Protector Somerset and fourth husband of Katherine Parr, resulted in serious political ramifications for Elizabeth. The princess was interrogated by a crown agent on suspicion that she had been involved in Seymour's treasonous plots to overthrow his brother's government. The behavior of her household during the Seymour crisis was highly revealing of how Elizabeth interacted with her senior staff, particularly with Katherine Champernon-Ashley. The crisis also revealed the various ties that bound the household staff; they were loyal not just to their mistress but to her future potential, to each other, and to their shared ideals. The depositions that Champernon-Ashley and Thomas Parry gave to government investigators also revealed the extent (or lack thereof) of the underaged Elizabeth's authority in her own establishment.

Other than members of her household staff, the person who came closest to acting as a mother for Elizabeth was Henry VIII's last wife, Katherine Parr. One of their shared interests was the promotion of the Protestant religion. After Henry VIII's death, both Mary and Elizabeth remained with Parr until April 1547. Mary left Parr's household around the time she obtained legal title to her estates and Elizabeth continued to visit Parr off and on throughout 1547 until mid-1548. In late April/early May 1547, Parr married Thomas Seymour, Lord Admiral of England. While Elizabeth shuttled between her own estates and Denny's manor at Cheshunt, she also frequently visited the Parr/Seymour establishment probably soliciting advice on how to administer her princely endowment of estates and manors that she received in May 1547. Parr removed northward to Sudeley Castle in Gloucestershire in May 1548 to await the birth of her child. She died from complications from childbirth in September 1548.

Thomas Seymour was arrested in January 1549 on charges of treason. Among the charges was the allegation that he had tried to lure Elizabeth into a matrimonial alliance after Parr's death without first obtaining the permission of the Privy Council as stipulated in Henry VIII's will.[120] Shortly after his arrest, Sir Anthony Denny, now an Edwardian Privy Councillor, along with William Paulet, chief steward of the royal household, came to arrest Thomas Parry and Katherine Champernon-Ashley. Parry and Champernon-Ashley faced questioning on their (and Elizabeth's) possible implication in Seymour's alleged matrimonial schemes involving the princess. They were taken to the Tower, threatened with charges of treason and "made their confession."[121] Based on the information they gave, the Privy Council dispatched Sir Robert Tyrwhitt with his wife to Elizabeth's residence of Hatfield to place her under house arrest. Lady Tyrwhitt now became Elizabeth governess.[122]

Tyrwhitt arrived at Hatfield by the end of January, less than two weeks after Seymour's arrest. He quickly concluded that Elizabeth and her staff had prepared themselves for this and agreed on the testimony they would give.[123] This became clear to him when he read the "confessions" of Champernon-Ashley and Parry. These depositions related little more than some earthy horseplay involving Seymour, Parr, and Elizabeth. The investigators, eager to add to their case against Seymour, pressed them to reveal details that would directly implicate the princess and Seymour as plotting a marriage with the aim of usurping the throne. Elizabeth's servants, however, steadfastly depicted their mistress as always refusing to contribute to any talk of marriage with Seymour. Under questioning by Tyrwhitt, Elizabeth herself failed to add anything substantive to the accounts of her servants. Tyrwhitt was suspicious and wrote to Protector Somerset of his conviction that they must all have agreed on the story beforehand: "they all sing the same song."[124]

Elizabeth's household was working as a unit. Tyrwhitt's assessment that Elizabeth, Parry and Champernon-Ashley had anticipated their interrogations and agreed on what they would state in their depositions is supported by the evidence. As Tyrwhitt noticed, there is considerable uniformity in all three depositions. There is only one significant deviation when Thomas Parry, gave a confused account of an embrace between Seymour and Elizabeth. When Tyrwhitt showed Elizabeth this deposition, she immediately seized on this anomaly by Parry and her cofferer of being a "false wretch."[125] Perhaps Elizabeth's outrage over Parry's deposition was due to her belief that he lied or that, any rate, she wished to convey the impression that he had done so. The uniformity of the depositions, however, raises the distinct possibility that Elizabeth's expostulation resulted from her irritation that Parry had strayed from the agreed testimony. If Elizabeth and her staff deliberately represented events in a formulaic manner to avoid suspicion, they would hardly have been alone in so doing as it was fairly common practice amongst those called on to give depositions.[126]

Moreover, Elizabeth and her household officers had more at stake than just protecting Elizabeth from coming under more intense scrutiny by the Edwardian government. Seymour was a committed Protestant. His Protestant sympathies had been one of his attractions for Katherine Parr.[127] This is significant as Parr and Elizabeth were very close.[128] True, Seymour was a mercurial Protestant who managed to alienate other leading Protestant leaders like the preacher Hugh Latimer.[129] Nevertheless, Elizabeth and her household had spent much of 1547 in his company and knew his Protestant views were sincere, if not deep. Champernon-Ashley's statements appear to distance the household as whole from Seymour while refusing to provide any further evidence against him. According to the governess, Seymour behaved inappropriately toward Elizabeth but Champernon-Ashley claims she never witnessed anything overtly romantic pass between them. All mention of marriage, Champernon-Ashley attributes to herself. According to all three depositions, not only was Elizabeth innocent of plotting any treasonous marriage alliance but so was Seymour. Furthermore, Tyrwhitt noted that Elizabeth openly defended Seymour and would "not hear anything said against him."[130] The princess, and her household, were ensuring that Elizabeth fulfilled a pledge she had made earlier to Seymour in a letter that she was a friend "not wonne with trifels, nor lost with the like."[131]

Primarily, the corporate household worked to shield the princess from the damage her reputation could suffer as a result of this crisis. Champernon-Ashley's strategy for protecting Elizabeth's reputation was to assume the blame herself. In her testimony, she portrayed herself as teasing the princess about her future marriage prospects, especially regarding Thomas Seymour.

The governess claimed that she constantly introduced the topic of Thomas Seymour to Elizabeth despite noticing that the princess was embarrassed about it. Immediately after Parr died in September 1548, Champernon-Ashley stated that it was she who urged the princess to write a condolence letter to Seymour.

The princess refused but the governess claimed that she pressed Elizabeth and gave up only after the princess refused to discuss it any more.

Understandably, this has motivated historians to dismiss Champernon-Ashley as a rather silly gossip.[132] Yet this could have been a deliberate strategy by the governess to rescue Elizabeth's personal and political reputation. The governess was, arguably, at pains to take the burden of guilt on herself.

The stakes were high. As Elizabeth herself made clear, her public reputation— and by implication her political one as well—were put at risk by this scandal. The princess requested that Protector Somerset safeguard her reputation from the damage that would inevitably result from the Seymour investigation. In her letter to Somerset, Elizabeth pointed out that the treatment of her household officers directly affected the public perception of her as a credible politician. She justified her request that Lady Tyrwitt be replaced as her governess "bicause . . . the people wil say that I deserved throwgh my lewde demenure" to have a new governess.[133] In this same letter, she thanked Somerset for authorizing the Privy Council to issue orders that the "ivel reportes" about her be quelled. She, however, refused to name the rumor-mongers and explained in the letter that, if she did name names, people would then label her a tattletale: "that shulde be but a briding of a ivel name of me . . . and so get the ivel wil of the people, wiche thinge I wolde be lothe to have."[134]

There is yet another significant insight to be gained from these depositions. Champernon-Ashley's and Parry's depositions indicate that the fourteen-year-old Elizabeth was not fully in control of her household; she was still the child who needed their guidance. Elizabeth herself acknowledged this. In the letter mentioned earlier, Elizabeth assured the Protector that she did not object to the idea of having a governess; she was not requesting "that I tak upon me to rule my selfe."[135] Champernon-Ashley's deposition fosters the impression (perhaps deliberately) that Elizabeth was still too immature emotionally to take charge of the household staff. She still needed a governess. When Seymour cut Elizabeth's gown "in a hundred pieces," Champernon-Ashley admitted that she disciplined the princess: "I chid with her grace when she came up that she was so trimmed."[136] On another occasion, Parry deposed that the governess had reduced Elizabeth—the nominal head of household—to tears.[137]

Not only was Champernon-Ashley able to intimidate Henry VIII's youngest daughter, but she had clearly not yet turned over to Elizabeth the power of decision regarding Elizabeth's own financial assets. Champernon-Ashley deposed that she and Parry had corresponded regarding Seymour's 1548 offer to loan the princess his London townhouse. (This loan was to offset the requisitioning by Somerset of Elizabeth's London residence, Durham Place.) The governess strongly urged Elizabeth not to accept Seymour's offer without first consulting Sir Anthony Denny. The governess then wrote to Parry informing him that she would soon come to London herself to "tell him her mind" regarding the Seymour offer of a London townhouse. It was Champernon-Ashley's decision to make, not Elizabeth's.[138]

As Champernon-Ashley continued her narrative of this proposed lease from Seymour, her tale begins to reveal the tension inherit in the relationship of an underaged (but precocious) householder attempting to establish her authority over people who do not fully trust her yet. As Champernon-Ashley prepared to go to London, Elizabeth did at least demand to know "what she [Champernon-Ashley] would do there."[139] When Champernon-Ashley told her that she intended to speak to Parry and to Seymour, Elizabeth was forced to issue a direct order to the governess not to do so "for it would be said that she [Elizabeth] did send her."[140] The governess obeyed the princess.

These incidents are very much what one would expect in the association of a governess and her pupil. They do not, however, conform to that of a servant and her mistress. Champernon-Ashley may have deliberately exaggerated her dominance in order to take most of the blame away from Elizabeth. Yet the governess was evidently in a position to discipline the princess; she ignored Elizabeth's requests not to mention Seymour; she persisted with unwanted advice; and she considered that she had sufficient authority to take charge of Elizabeth's property dealings regarding Durham Place. It is little wonder that Elizabeth referred to Champernon-Ashley as her mistress rather than the other way around.[141] Tyrwhit observed that Elizabeth's affection for her governess was unusually strong.[142]

Perhaps what Tyrwhit was struck by was Elizabeth's emotional dependence on Champernon-Ashley. Elizabeth readily acknowledged this dependence, albeit in characteristically pedantic fashion. In a letter to Somerset, Elizabeth indicated how much she felt she owed to her governess and to her household in general:

> . . . she hathe bene with me alonge time, and manye years, and hathe taken great labor, and paine in brinkinge of me up in lerninge and honestie, and therfore I ought of very dewtye speke for her, for Saint Gregorie sayeth that we ar more bounde the them that bringeth us up wel than to our parents, for our parents do that wiche is natural for them, that is bringeth us into this worlde but our brinkers up ar a cause to make us live wel in it.[143]

I am not suggesting that, at this juncture, Champernon-Ashley exercised more authority in the household than did the princess. Although only fourteen, Elizabeth was evidently beginning to assert her authority. The governess could advise her to write a condolence letter to Seymour but she could not force her. When the princess expressly forbade Champernon-Ashley from meddling in the Durham Place matter, the governess obeyed. The governess' testimony argues that from 1547 through 1548, Elizabeth was transitioning from child/pupil to adult/householder. Her governess could discipline her and attempt to strong-arm her without fear of punishment but she also had to obey Elizabeth's direct orders. During these years, 1547–1553, the princess and her staff were in the midst of realigning their roles. Elizabeth was learning how to establish her authority and her staff was allowing her to assume more responsibility. Nevertheless, the Champernon-Ashley testimony, Tyrwhit's and Elizabeth's letters to Protector Somerset indicate that Elizabeth continued to rely on her staff. They were still her "bringers-up" to whom she owed filial loyalty.

THE ITALIANATE CULTURE OF PROTESTANTISM IN ELIZABETH'S HOUSEHOLD, 1548–1553

Katherine Champernon-Ashley (and probably Parry) had returned to the household probably within a few months after Seymour's execution in March 1549.[144] By September 1549, Elizabeth was finalizing plans to visit the court.[145] The crisis was over with Elizabeth and her household escaping relatively unscathed. It is likely that the household culture that the governess had helped to create also survived intact; certainly it continued to develop.

Any description of the "household culture" of Elizabeth's establishment must necessarily be impressionistic. There are far fewer records from Elizabeth's household when compared to the documentation of Mary's household. There is almost no surviving correspondence between Elizabeth and her household staff nor little mention of Elizabeth's household before 1553 in state papers. Certainly there is no representation of Elizabeth's household comparable to Giles Duwes contribution to *The Courtier* genre for Mary's household. What follows can only be described as tentative conclusions based on a documented congruence of the beliefs, tastes and association of some of Elizabeth's most important household staff: the Ashley's, Roger Ascham, Balthasar Castiglioni (not Baldassare, author of *The Courtier*), and the Cecils and their extra-household links to figures such as Robert Morrison and William Thomas.

With these caveats in mind, it would appear that the household culture of Elizabeth's preaccession households comprised two seemingly contradictory elements: Protestant erudition and an appreciation for Italian artistic forms. Elizabeth's education had continued in a decidedly Protestant vein from the 1540s. When Grindal died in early 1548, Elizabeth appointed Roger Ascham as her tutor, overriding the advice of her close friends and frequent hosts, Katherine Parr and Thomas Seymour, who wanted to appoint their own Protestant client.[146] The princess' determination in this regard evidences her commitment, at the age of fourteen, to continuing her humanist education and Cambridge connections. Ascham was a leading proponent of the virtues of a classical education. He advocated learning Latin and Greek straight from ancient texts rather than through modern grammar books.[147]

Ascham was also a fan of Italian Renaissance culture. His correspondence was full of his desire to travel someday to Italy that he eventually did in the mid-1550s.[148] He taught both Elizabeth and Prince Edward, now King Edward VI, to write in the italic script fashionable in Italy.[149] Ascham was only one among many Protestant intellectuals in England who were fascinated by contemporary Italian culture.

Although many English Protestant humanists had rejected Roman Catholicism, they embraced the ideals embodied in *The Courtier*. Although it would not be printed in English until 1560, it was already very popular in manuscript with many pedagogues—both Catholic and Protestant—preferring to read it in the original Italian.[150] The popularity of this book, specifically its model of courtly behavior and the ideal of the civilized life, helped to fuel the vogue for all things Italian that was sweeping the elite and erudite of England. Even the young king was connected to this Italian craze through his tutor in political thought, William Thomas, who printed in 1549 his popular *History of Italy*.[151]

Elizabeth absorbed this interest in Italianate culture. She employed an Italian, Balthasar Castiglione (perhaps a relation to the author of *The Courtier*?) to tutor her in his native language.[152] Ascham claimed that she spoke Italian as if it were her native language. During this period, she sent Edward her translation from the Latin of Bernadino Ochino's "Sermon on the Nature of Christ," which she chose to render into Italian.[153] Her letters to friends were peppered with Italian phrases and references to Greco-Roman mythology. An example of this comes from an undated (c. 1559) letter to her maternal cousin, Catherine Knolles, Elizabeth signed herself "cor rotto" ["broken hearted" over Knolles voluntary exile to the Continent].[154] As noted in the previous chapter, the tapestries she chose from Henry VIII's inventory depicting Greco-Roman gods. Even her account books were decorated with pictorial initials in this style.

Elizabeth's household accounts indicate that this Italianate—and decidedly Protestant—culture was mannerist in its aesthetic but not baroque. Rather, it practiced an austerity now fashionable among Protestants. The princess' accounts are extant for only one year, from October 1, 1551, until September 1552. Although they contain elaborate decoration they do not contain the kind of detailed information for Privy Chamber expenditure as Mary's accounts from 1536 until 1543 do.[155] There are no references in the accounts to valentines, card games, or entertainments. It is possible that the household did not engage in these pastimes. As will be emphasized later in this study, Elizabeth's revenues did not cover her household expenses so there may not have been enough funds to allow for these diversions.[156] What discretionary income Elizabeth possessed, she used to sponsor the spread of Protestantism and humanist education. She patronized London booksellers, specifically those who sold bibles. She gave money to "Skollars of Cambridge" and, even-handedly, "to a pore Skollar of Oxforde." She was godmother to John Cheke's child (Cheke was Edward VI's tutor) and sent an obligatory present.[157]

Another possible reason for the absence of such of the kind of entertainments that pepper Mary's household accounts could be that it was becoming fashionable among Protestants to eschew "frivolous" pastimes such as dancing, gaming, and feasting. An example of this was the government's announcement that people should refrain from giving gifts to the king at New Year's in 1549 because it was reminiscent of the Catholic festivities that had formerly marked the occasion.[158] That this Protestant austerity may have influenced Elizabeth's household culture is suggested by the style of dress she affected during this period. John Alymer, a tutor to Elizabeth's cousin Jane Grey, and later Queen Elizabeth's bishop of London, wrote that in these years, 1548–1553, the princess refused to wear "the rich jewels and clothes left her by her father" and preferred simple apparel. This marked Elizabeth out as a Protestant. Aylmer also related a story that around this time, Princess Mary presented Jane Grey with an ornate gown that the Protestant Grey rejected claiming it would be morally wrong to accept such a gift and desert the example of "my lady Elizabeth, which followeth God's word."[159] Grey had made her choice—she was a follower of Protestant and simply dressed Elizabeth rather than of Catholic and ornately appareled Mary.

Lack of funds and an austere aesthetic did not absolve Elizabeth of the attendant responsibilities of being a head of household. Like Mary, Elizabeth practiced "good lordship" over her staff. For instance, she paid for the burial expenses of her servants. When Robert Arden fell ill in November 1550, Elizabeth covered his expenses during his recovery until March 1551.[160] The accounts are full of notations of her reimbursing her staff for their traveling expenses.[161] As indicated earlier, Elizabeth's accounts are not as extensive or detailed as Mary's but what little survives indicates that the princess practiced good lordship with a Protestant orientation. She provided for the burial, travel, and health expenses of her servants. She subsidized scholars and booksellers. Like Mary, Elizabeth kept a careful eye on expenditure and signed every page of the accounts herself.[162]

Taken together, these admittedly stray bits of evidence suggest that the culture in Elizabeth's household was quite distinct from that which characterized Mary's. Elizabeth's household was overtly Protestant in its employment and patronage of reformist scholars. Economic realities and religious fashion dictated the style of the household: plain and therefore symbolically Protestant. There were seemingly paradoxical hints that this ostensibly Protestant and frugal household paid tribute to the Catholic artistic culture of Italy. This cannot be pushed too far because the evidence is, at best, impressionistic. The altar cloths, however, that Elizabeth inherited from her father's storehouses were decidedly ornate perhaps approaching the Catholic mannerist style then currently in fashion. Elizabeth personally would retain a preference for ornate chapel furnishings. This preference of hers was so strongly associated with Catholicism that some of her subjects would later question the sincerity of Elizabeth's profession of the Protestant faith because of her fondness for sumptuous "papist" altar cloths.[163]

These chapel furnishings, contrasted against Elizabeth's simple apparel and bookish interests, would have made a striking appearance on a visitor to the princess' establishment. The tapestries—one at least showcasing Greco-Roman myths and another depicting strong and learned women from the *City of Ladies*—and ornate chapel goods would, amid all the Protestant simplicity in dress and pastimes, have possibly emphasized the complexities and abilities of the young woman who stood second in line to the throne from 1547 to 1553 and who was already the nominal head of her own princely household.

ELIZABETH'S SELF-DETERMINED HOUSEHOLD, 1553–1558

There are indications from other sources that her household was as loyal to its own culture as it was to the princess herself. An important aspect of the culture of Elizabeth's household was that it was not dependent on her leadership. As the Seymour crisis indicated, Elizabeth was emotionally dependent on her senior staff. Moreover, it was her governess and cofferer who had helped to arrange for her humanist Protestant education through their connections to Roger Ascham, Anthony Denny, and William Cecil. As the subsequent discussion illustrates, these endeavors by her senior staff were not solely motivated by benevolent disinterest in nurturing Elizabeth's mental and social development. Elizabeth's senior staff were committed to the furtherance of the Protestant and humanist agenda. They would actively campaign on behalf of this agenda even if it caused political embarrassment to their mistress, Elizabeth.

That Elizabeth's household staff depended on each other for their sense of corporate household identity more than on their underaged mistress is suggested in John Ashley's later account of the scholarly fellowship he enjoyed with Roger Ascham. Ashley harkens back to a time when Ascham was Elizabeth's tutor and traveled with her as part her household throughout 1547–1548 as she visited Katherine Parr at Chelsea and Sir Anthony Denny at Cheshunt:

> . . . our friendly fellowship together at Cheshunt, Chelsea and here at Hatfield, her grace's house; our pleasant studies in reading together Aristotle's *Rhetoric*, Cicero, Livy; our free talk mingled always with honest mirth; our trim conferences of the present world, and too true judgments of the troublesome time that followed.[164]

It is telling that in this account Elizabeth is *not* mentioned as part of this "friendly fellowship." Indeed, the emphasis on "free talk" suggests a relaxed atmosphere that the princess' presence would likely have inhibited. Ashley's account hints that, at least some, possibly a great deal of the household's culture existed independently of Elizabeth. It was her household officers, not the princess exclusively, who had fostered the household's Protestant and scholarly interests during the period when the princess was too young to assume authority over the establishment. Her style of dress and purchases of bibles indicate that, once she was old enough, she fully participated in this Protestant culture. Indeed, she was the product of it. Elizabeth fully participated and contributed to this Protestant erudite culture but she had not created it and it was not dependent on her leadership.

As Ashley's account hints, this shared culture created a bond among the household members and a sense of corporate loyalty. This culture reinforced a cohesion built during the years when Elizabeth was too young to assume control of the household. The household was forced to be self-reliant and had created a culture that reflected interests and preoccupations of its senior staff rather than focusing almost exclusively on the princess as Mary's household culture did.

An example of this internal cohesion and independence of Elizabeth is fund in a letter that the household wrote to Queen Mary's Privy Council in 1554. It was a letter written by the household officers as a corporate body independent of Elizabeth's nominal headship. In February 1554, a rebellion led by Sir Thomas Wyatt aimed to place Princess Elizabeth on the throne and overthrow Queen Mary. The government, suspecting Elizabeth's complicity, had "invited" her to court.[165] She declined the invitation and pleaded illness. Perhaps, Elizabeth's senior household officers considered this to be an obviously ambivalent ploy by the princess. In any case, the household staff felt it necessary to send a letter of unequivocal loyalty to Mary's Privy Council and to its president, Bishop Stephen Gardiner:

> May it please your good Lordship, That albeit we attend here on my Lady Elizabeth's Grace, our Mistress . . . we do not forget our most bounden Duty, nor yet our Readi-

ness in Words and Deeds to serve her Highness [Queen Mary] by all the Ways and
Means that may stand in Us, both from her Grace, our Mistress, and of our own
Parts also . . . [166]

Perhaps Elizabeth had suggested or had at least encouraged the letter.
Whether Elizabeth knew of and authorized the letter is less important than the
fact that she did not sign it and it was not in her name. The letter is a compelling demonstration of the corporate persona the princess' household had created and adopted. It was a corporate body irrespective of Elizabeth's nominal
leadership.

This mixture of parental concern and autonomy exhibited by Elizabeth's
household in this letter was also a feature of contemporary depictions detailing
the princess' activities and those of her household during the years 1553–1558.
The princess spent from early 1554 until mid-1555 in prison either in the Tower
or under house arrest. As John Foxe's *Book of Martyrs* and Sir Henry Bedingfield's correspondence with Privy Council make clear, the formidable group
identity, revealed in this letter, was both a source of strength (emotionally and
politically) for the princess and a source of worry.

Foxe's narrative of Elizabeth's incarceration, in his famous account of the
implementation Marian religious policy in *Book of Martyrs* (1563), is as much
about Elizabeth's servants as it is about the princess. This most likely resulted
from Foxe relying on the servants' testimony. Foxe's methodology favored eyewitness accounts and studies of state papers to which he could gain access. The
likelihood that Foxe based his narrative on the statements of Elizabeth's staff
presents some problems. Foxe's sources may have led him to exaggerate the role
of Elizabeth's servants. Moreover, Foxe's narrative did not appear until, at the
earliest, almost a decade after the alleged incidents took place. Some of the incidents only appeared in the 1583 edition, nearly thirty years later. This increases
the likelihood of distortion, inaccuracy, and manipulation to suit later agendas.
Although there is evidence that Foxe's narrative of Elizabeth's tribulations did
include exaggerations (which are detailed in the footnotes), his account does at
least preserve the impressions and ideals of Elizabeth's servants of the period. [167]

Throughout, Foxe presents Elizabeth's servants as tireless advocates committed to maintaining her status as heir to the throne and leader of the Protestant opposition. This begins immediately for Foxe when Elizabeth is arrested.[168]
In Foxe's melodramatic depiction, Queen Mary's commissioners arrived at
Elizabeth's residence in the middle of the night, barged their way past the
"aghast" servants and told the princess that they had orders to bring her to court
"either quick or dead."[169] Foxe here is representing Queen Mary's commissioners as deliberately rude and forgetful of Elizabeth's status as the Queen's successor. Foxe proceeds to highlight this rudeness by representing Elizabeth's
staff as scrupulously observant of good hospitality. According to Foxe, Elizabeth's

servants "entertained and cheered" the commissioners "as appertained to their honors."[170] In this way, Elizabeth's household, by observing the conventions of hospitality incumbent on an elite household, was upholding Elizabeth's status, which the commissioners' behavior had undermined. The commissioners had, according to Foxe, treated her as a criminal but her household continued to offer a deliberate and princely hospitality.

Given the strength of her household's corporate identity and the role Elizabeth's staff had played in her development, it is hardly surprising that the princess turned, in difficult moments, to her household much as a child seeks parental comfort. According to Foxe, when Elizabeth first arrived at the Tower in February 1554, Elizabeth refused to enter, whereupon one of her gentlemen ushers burst into tears. At this point, Elizabeth remonstrated with him that he was failing in his duty to her: "shee demaunding of hym what he mente so vncomfortably to vse her, seeing shee tooke hym to be her comfortour and not dismayor."[171] Perhaps the most dramatic instance Foxe relates of Elizabeth relying on her staff to be her "comforters" concerns the night, much later, that Sir Henry Bedingfield removed her from the Tower and lodged her at Richmond in preparation for her journey to house arrest at Woodstock Manor in April 1554. As it is illustrative of Foxe's overall depiction of the relationship between Elizabeth and her servants, it is worth quoting at length:

> [At Richmond] she . . . called her gentleman usher, and desired him, with the reaste of hys company to pray for her. For this night (quod shee) I thinke to dye. Wherewith he being striken to the hart, sayde: God forbid that any such wickednes should be pretended agaynst youre grace. So côforting her as well as he could, at laste burst oute in teares, and wente from her downe into the court, wher wer walking the Lord of Tame [Sir John Williams], and Sir Henry Benifield: and he staieng asyde the Lord of Tame . . . he spake on this wise: . . . Why I come to you at this tyme, is to desire your honour unfainedly to delcare vnto me, whether anye daunger is ment towards my maistres this night or no that I and my poore fellowes maye take such part as shal please god to appoint. For certenly we will rather dye, then she should secretely and innocently miscary . . . [172]

Foxe related that Lord Thame assured the servant that Elizabeth was no danger. The servant conveyed as much to the princess but Elizabeth was not comforted. The next day, according to Foxe, she again presented herself to her servants as, figuratively, a lamb being led to slaughter. As she traveled by barge down the river Thames from Richmond, she spotted some of her servants gathered together at the quayside to watch her dock. She sent a messenger to them with the words "tamquam ovis," that is, like a sheep, trusting that her erudite staff would be able to finish the rest of the Latin phrase. Later after her release from house arrest, Foxe claims that when she was brought to court she feared for life and, again, turned to her servants: she "desyred her gentlemen and gentlewomen to praye for her, for that shee could not tell whether euer shee should see them againe or no."[173]

Foxe's depiction of Elizabeth's emotional dependence on her servants is also a feature of Bedingfield's correspondence with the Privy Council. At Woodstock, Elizabeth was surrounded mostly by Privy Chamber servants whose first loyalty was to Mary. One of her few servants of her choosing was Elizabeth Sands. Sands, as the queen quickly learned, was an outspoken Protestant. Mary wrote to Bedingfield that Sands was "a pson off an evyll opinion, and not fyt to remayne aboute or sayde systers p[er]son."[174] Apparently, Queen Mary was aware of Elizabeth's emotional attachment to her servants and warned Bedingfield that separating Sands from Elizabeth would be difficult. Mary urged Bedingfield to "by the best meanes ye can p[er]swade hir to be contented to have the sayde Sands removed from hyr."[175] Foxe claimed Sands had little choice but to depart from Princess Elizabeth's household and then subsequently leave the country to join the English Protestant ex-patriot community on the Continent.[176] According to Bedingfield, this brought about "great mourning" in Elizabeth.[177]

The princess' emotional dependence on her servants indicates that the psychological bonds between Elizabeth and her servants was of a more intense nature than those that had existed between Mary and her servants. Where Mary could practically shrug off the incarceration of her most trusted household officer, Sir Robert Rochester, Elizabeth constantly sought the comfort and strength of her gentlemen ushers and Privy Chamber ladies—at least according to the depictions of Foxe and Bedingfield. This intense bond between Elizabeth and her servants found further expression in the refusal of her household to abandon the princess even when they were forbidden to serve in her household.

Queen Mary could dismiss one or two servants from Woodstock but she could not prevent Elizabeth's household from stubbornly maintaining its corporate cohesion. Just before Bedingfield removed the princess from the Tower, he wrote to the Marian Privy Council about what to do about "my ladyes gracs s'v[au]nts lieng about" the Tower gates despite having no official reason to do so now that the princess was in prison and no longer needed their services.[178] Once Bedingfield took Elizabeth to Woodstock, the princess' household took advantage of a nearby inn to reconstitute itself and thus complicated Bedingfield's ability to isolate Elizabeth.

This situation was, in part, a result of the common practice of forcing state prisoners to bear the financial burden of their own imprisonment. Elizabeth, therefore, perforce retained possession of her estates so that she could pay for the wages and living expenses of Sir Henry Bedingfield and his servants as well as the servants that the queen placed in Elizabeth's Privy Chamber. Not surprisingly, this situation caused friction between Elizabeth's cofferer Thomas Parry and Bedingfield. Parry refused to provide the necessary sums until he received official warrant from the queen that Elizabeth's household was responsible for Bedingfield and his staff.[179] This necessitated that Elizabeth regularly consult with some of her senior household officers to oversee the provisioning of the Woodstock staff.

This was all the opening tht her household needed. Although actual numbers are hard to come by, apparently a substantial portion of Elizabeth's household established themselves at the near-by Bull's Inn. Bedingfield claimed that there were far more at the Inn than the one or two officers the government originally envisioned would be necessary to ensure that Woodstock received its necessary provisions. Elizabeth's cofferer, Thomas Parry, led the way in Champernon-Ashley's absence (at this time, she was imprisoned in the home of Sir Roger Cholmley for suspected complicity in the Wyatt rebellion).[180] Initially, Parry had campaigned to reconstitute the household at Woodstock manor itself but Bedingfield complained to the Privy Council. The Privy Council responded by claiming that the resident clerk of the kitchen, rather than Parry, could disperse the necessary sums to pay for supplies and the wages of the Woodstock establishment.[181] Parry then set up his headquarters at Bull's Inn much to Bedingfield's consternation who described it, in June 1554, as "a m'velous coularbyll place to practise" subversion. It was not just Parry who resided there:

> . . . that syns hys com[m]yng hyther wth thoose that remayneth wth hym, daylie there hath repared unto hym to the nomber off xlti psons In hys owen lyverie, besydes the daylie repare off my ladys gracs s'vnts, beeng mannye more then have cause to repare hyther for any p[ro]vision.[182]

Bedingfield's emphasis on the servants in Parry's livery suggests that he suspected that the cofferer had circumvented the official restriction of Elizabeth's household by putting some of her servants in his own livery. It worked only to a limited degree because, as this passage indicates, Bedingfield still considered that there were more of the princess' household at the inn than was strictly necessary to ensure the household's adequate provision.

Bedingfield again wrote the Privy Council about the political danger of allowing such a crush of servants to reside at the Bull's Inn: "Even as I adv'tised yor l[ordships] longe agooe: the house also beeng a common Inne, wherin thei dooe lye, and thei so politicque as thei bee, I can gette no knowledge off there doengs by eny espiall."[183] An indication of what Bedingfield had to contend with is contained in his October report of Parry's continuing presence at the Bull:

> Mr Parry, thys great ladies coferer, dothe Intende to kepe hys awdyte here in Thys towne at the Inne where he lyethe, & auppon that colour theys viij or x dayes laste

paste divers of hys s'vaunts hathe repayred to thys the quenes highnes howse [Wood-
stock], seking occasion to speke wt their fellowes, whych beynge answered that they
myght not dooe, dep[ar]ted Imediatelye; and thereuppo[n] I sent incontynentlye to
the same Mr Parry, declaryrynge their repayer to this howse. And he answered him
that wente of that message, that he hadd warnyd all hir gracs s'vaunts, not beinge appointed to wayte dayly, uppon there alegiuance not to come eny nerer thys howse
then hys lodginge, and was, as he saide, for hys owne p[ar]te sorye theye should sooe
mysuse them selfes, p[ro]mysinge to dooe as much as lyeth in hym that yt shall nooe
nmore be sooe. I praye yor L[ordships] lette me know yor plesures how to use them
yf the happen to make the lyke attempte, After thys my second warnynge.[184]

It would be interesting to know whose allegiance Parry was invoking in
this passage—that which the servants owed to the Queen Mary or to Elizabeth?
Perhaps Bedingfield himself was uncertain for he was not mollified by Parry's
disingenuous protestations. He begged the Queen and the Privy Council to be
relieved of the impossible task of guarding a prisoner whose household refused
to be disbanded. As Bedingfield pointed out, the situation of Elizabeth needing
a household in order to pay for her own imprisonment meant that, as her goaler,
he could not completely isolate her: "there ys an evident waye that I cannot
avoyde by enye possible mense, butte that daylye & howerlye the sayde Parye
maye have & gyve intelligence" to the princess.[185] It is little wonder that Bedingfield begged to be relieved of the impossible task. He confessed that the end
of his guardianship of Elizabeth would be "the Joyfulleste tydyngs that ever
came to me."[186]

Bedingfield did not have to wait long. The experiment of guarding a state
prisoner whose household was determined to remain constituted and near her
ended in April 1555. It had lasted a year and Bedingfield's constant problems in
containing Elizabeth's household had exhausted the government as attested in
an October 1554 letter from Queen Mary to Bedingfield. Attempting to stem
the torrent of correspondence from Bedingfield to the Privy Council, the queen
asserted that that she had complete confidence in whatever steps he deemed
necessary to take to restrain the princess' servants "wherin ye shall dooe us acceptable s'vice" so there was no need for Bedingfield to seek advice for every
little thing relating to the princess and her truculent household.[187] Limiting the
access of Elizabeth's servants to their mistress had been practically an impossible task. Elizabeth would, technically, still be under house arrest (under a new
"governor," Sir Thomas Pope), but there were no more attempts to separate her
from her own household or to keep her under strict house arrest.

Although Elizabeth's household had displayed an impressive corporate loyalty to itself and to the point of frustrating Bedingfield's efforts to isolate the
princess, this autonomous persona of Elizabeth's household did not always
work in the princess' favor. From late 1553, Elizabeth had decided that it was

politically expedient to attend the reinstated Latin mass and to give no outward sign of her own Protestant beliefs. Her household did not follow suit. Foxe detailed the outlawed Protestant activities of some of her servants.[188] A groom of her chamber refused to hear mass. Her chaplain residing with her in the Tower claimed not to know how to perform mass properly. One of her gentlewomen lent the princess her a copy of her own contraband English bible.[189] Throughout Mary's reign, Elizabeth's servants were regularly summoned before the Privy Council for questions about their nonattendance at Mass.[190] Although Elizabeth scrupulously conformed from 1553 onward, her servants kept forbidden books and absented themselves from Mass.

It is tempting to interpret her servant's religious nonconformance as a ploy approved by Elizabeth to maintain her credibility with her Protestant supporters at a time when she felt constrained to conform to Catholicism. There is, however, no evidence to support this view. Indeed, a 1554 letter from Elizabeth to William Paulet, marquis of Winchester (and confidant of Queen Mary) suggests that the princess regarded her household's public defiance as an unwelcome frustration of her efforts to ally the government's suspicions concerning her political and religious intentions. She begged Paulet and his colleagues on the Privy Council not to associate her with the subversive activities of her household family. She asked that "of my owne things and doeings [that] myne owne words may stand in most creditt with you." Elizabeth sought to distance herself from "them of my nowne family [household]" whose nonconformity, she claimed, did not reflect her own intentions.[191]

Perhaps Elizabeth was being disingenuous here. However, it is equally possible, if not more so, that she meant exactly what she wrote. Although personally committed to the Protestant faith, as Queen Elizabeth would demonstrate an acute awareness of the strength of Catholic practices and belief still remaining in the kingdom; she would later alienate many of her Protestant supporters by not authorizing a radically Protestant realignment of the church after her accession.[192] As the heir to the throne, the princess understood the political threat she posed to her sister's regime as a focus for the disaffected. When she wrote the letter to Paulet, she was under house arrest at Woodstock because she had been the figurehead (perhaps unwillingly) of a rebellion, which had come very close indeed to overthrowing Mary. Elizabeth had every reason to cultivate an image of obedience at this time, which the actions of her servants threatened to undermine. The princess' letter achieved partial success. Later, when a few of her servants were implicated in another conspiracy in 1556, the government did not automatically assume Elizabeth's complicity.[193]

Nevertheless, the continued subversive activities of the princess' servants resulted in Elizabeth remaining politically estranged from her sister throughout the rest of Mary's reign. The autonomy of Elizabeth's household provided the princess with both a crutch and a problem during this period. Her household rallied in force to support her during her imprisonment but their subsequent activities meant that Elizabeth, whether she wished it or not, could be viewed as the Protestant alternative to the queen's Catholic regime. Elizabeth's household—with its unusually strong sense of corporate identity—could ensure that she did not suffer complete political neutralization. However, this same household persona meant that Elizabeth's staff did not feel itself limited purely by her own directives. Elizabeth's household had its own agenda that it could pursue, when necessary, without the benefit of the princess' leadership or, even at times, without her approval.

The loyalty of Elizabeth's household to the princess is certainly evident in the letter it wrote early in 1554. This same letter, however, also strongly demonstrated the corporate independence of her household. The princess was the focus, figurehead, and symbol of her household. Elizabeth's household, as demonstrated in the above letter and in its ability to reconstitute itself at the Bull's Inn, possessed its own internal cohesion and an identity that was only partly dependent on the princess. This was a Protestant, collegiate, household committed to the new religion and education. It was capable of taking unilateral action to protect not only its mistress but also its own existence and agenda. It had achieved this corporate cohesion during the period in which the princess' youth precluded her from assuming full authority over her staff. Rather she was dependent on her servants; as she put it, they were her "bringers-up." It is little wonder that John Strype, the seventeenth-century antiquarian, whose transcription remains the only source of the letter written by princess' household in 1554, referred to Elizabeth's servants as her "Governors" who had the "Care and Government" of the princess.[194]

This is not to suggest that Elizabeth failed to grasp the implications of her lineage or to assert her authority over her staff. Champernon-Ashley's testimony during the Seymour crisis indicates that as early as 1548, Elizabeth was, at least, beginning to take the household reins of power into her own hands. Yet, clearly, Elizabeth's household worked as a unit whether she was able to physically preside over it or not. This was a feature not found in Mary's household. When Mary lost her household in 1533, there is no record of her staff remaining stubbornly together, constituted as a household in exile. In the 1554 letter, Elizabeth's staff functioned as a corporate entity to the extent of corresponding on its own behalf, independent of its mistress. Even Foxe's narrative of Elizabeth's servant asking Lord Thame if there were any sinister designs on his mistress depicts the same servant as declaring what action the household as a whole— "I and my fellows"—will take to defend her. Almost always, Elizabeth's servants are represented as a group, working with their "fellows" toward the common goals of protecting Elizabeth's interests and pursuing their own.

Elizabeth's household functioned quite literally as a family both in the early modern and contemporary sense. It was a household bound by the *conventio* and by blood. This situation brought to the establishment its own rewards and problems. On the positive side, the household's function, in light of Anne Boleyn's early death and Henry VIII's neglect, to raise the princess was aided by the Boleyn familial connections amongst the staff to each other and to Elizabeth. Negatively, the household was subject to tensions that often characterize families. The Bryan/Shelton conflict over the scale of hospitality in Elizabeth's household had no correspondence in the records relating to Mary's preaccession household. Elizabeth's youth and her uncertain political future combined with a lack of parental authority meant that Elizabeth's preaccession household was forced to construct its own *modus vivendi*. It was her household that determined its own identity and agenda, setting its own policies rather than the underaged princess.

Unlike princesses before them, Mary and Elizabeth did not live at court or in dependent establishments in the country until marriage. Mary from 1525 until 1528 and both she and Elizabeth from 1547 until 1553 lived at their own courts. During these years, they were not royal dependents. Their main function was not to serve as disposable assets used in cementing diplomatic alliances. Rather, they were leaders of corporate followings. Their households—which probably employed, on average, between seventy-five and a hundred individuals throughout the period—were bound to the princesses in various ways. Initially, the oath, the *conventio*, bound the servant to the royal householder. The princesses' servants were their sworn men and women. As good householders, Mary and Elizabeth each fulfilled their part of the *conventio* by providing for the welfare of their servants and dispensing patronage to their noble staff (e.g., Katherine Parr) and scholars (e.g., Roger Ascham).

These ceremonial and patronage ties were reinforced by the artistic and practical cultures that each household manifested. Although each establishment adhered to a distinct aesthetic, they both reflected different interpretations of Castiglione's courtly ideal. Mary's household was an expression of her will. Her household culture revolved around her and her tastes and, like the court of Urbino in *The Courtier*, engaged in the courtly pastimes of intellectualized love-play, witty conversation, and scholarship along with less exalted but common pastimes such as gambling. Elizabeth was the product of her household's interests and its mission to raise and educate her. Elizabeth absorbed and contributed to the Protestant, Italianate, and academic culture her household had created.

These formal, economical, and cultural bonds forged strong group identities amongst the men and women who served in the households of Mary and Elizabeth. In addition to the daily benefits of convivial socializing and emotional support, Mary and Elizabeth also reaped political rewards from their corporate households. The culture of reverence in Mary's establishment resulted in her servants supporting her religious defiance of the government's Protestant edicts even at the risk of their own lives. This unquestioning obedience to her directives, even when it entailed a treasonous disregard of royal commands, bolstered Mary's public reputation as a determined leader of the Catholic opposition. Based on the behavior of her household staff, few of Mary's future subjects could have been left in any doubt of her religious views or her determination and ability to stand by them.

Elizabeth's parental household shielded the princess from the political fallout of Thomas Seymour's arrest. Its autonomous identity, independent from the princess, allowed her household to unilaterally reconstitute itself when she was under house arrest at Woodstock. This not only undermined the government's efforts to isolate the princess but it also maintained her princely status. Elizabeth might be a political prisoner but she still had a royal household even if she herself could not personally preside over it. By contrast, her household's loyalty to the Protestant culture it had created meant that Elizabeth herself was not always the primary focus of the household's allegiance. Yet even this sometimes politically dangerous household independence ensured that Elizabeth continued to be identified as a leader of the Protestant resistance.

As elite women, Mary and Elizabeth were not alone in reaping the beneficial political capital of managing and heading their own households. Other aristocratic women acquired *de facto* authority over their kin, neighbors, servants, and clients by virtue of their positions as widows heading their own households or wives managing the households, technically, headed by their husbands.[195] Not only did Mary and Elizabeth head their own households in their own name, but (again) in common with other noble and gentry women, they also owned property. One of the major functions of their households, as with the household of other elite women and men, was to serve as administrative centers for the management of properties. It is to the estates that the princesses received after Henry VIII's death that this study will now turn.

NOTES

1. To list but a few out of many: A. G. Dickens, ed., *The Courts of Europe: Politics, Patronage and Royalty* [London, 1977]; N. Elias, *The Court Society* [Oxford, 1983]; R. G. Asch, ed., *Princes, Patronage and the Nobility: The Court at the Beginning of the Modern Age* [Oxford UP, 1991], and J. Adamson, ed., *The Princely Courts of*

Europe: Ritual, Politics and Culture under the Ancien Regime, 1500–1700, [London, 1999]

2. Harris, *English Aristocratic Women*, p. 76

3. Woolgar, *The Great Household*, p. 30

4. Taken from a phrase found in a set of instructions issued by the crown for Mary's 1525 household urging Mary's household officers to maintain the "good politique profitable and substantiall order of the householde"; BL Cotton Vitellius, C.i., f. 9v

5. BL Harley 479, f. 7r as cited in Woolgar, *Great Household*, p. 30

6. Woolgar, *Great Household*, p. 37

7. Fletcher, *Gender, Sex . . .* , p. 212

8. E. G. Kimball, *Serjeanty Tenure in Medieval England* [Yale UP, 1936], pp. 18–68

9. Bk.12, p. 2296, accessed at http://www.hrionline.ac.uk/johnfoxe/main/12_1570_2296.jsp

10. Wolffe, *Crown Lands . . .* , pp. 54–55

11. BL Cotton Vitellius, C.i., f.7r

12. Woolgar, *Great Household*, p. 39

13. Initial evidence for Salisbury's appointment comes from *LP*, III, pt.1, 805; on May 13, 1520, Salisbury received as Mary's governess the revenues of a wardship, presumably as wages. Before 1520, Mary's governess was Margaret Bryan, who would later serve in the same capacity in both Elizabeth's and Edward's households. Before Bryan, Elizabeth Denton held the post but she may not have served. It seems most likely that Bryan was Denton's deputy and held the office in reversion until Denton's death. See *LP*, II, pt. 1, 454 and pt. 2, 3802

14. For full treatment of Pole, see H. Pierce, *Margaret Pole, Countess of Salisbury 1473–1541: Loyalty, Lineage, and Leadership* [Wales UP, 2003]

15. Mertes, *English Noble Households*, p. 65

16. Loades, p. 30

17. Madden, p. 277

18. *LP*, III, 1673

19. Loades, p. 41 questions whether Dorset ever actually served in this capacity but not the actual appointment itself

20. Lady Kingston (Mary Scrope Jerningham) had previously served in Katherine of Aragon's household and, as a nonresident member of Mary's household from 1536 to 1538. Harris, *English Aristocratic Women*, p. 17, fn. 37

21. *CSP Venetian*, II, 1287

22. *CSP Venetian*, vol. II, 1010, 1287

23. Giles, Du Wes, *An Introductory for to Learn to Read, to Pronounce, and to Speak French* [1532?], ed. R. C. Alston, Facsimile [Menston, UK, 1972], sig. T3v

24. "Instructions," f. 24v

25. "Instructions," ff. 8v–9r. My italics. There is a blank space in the manuscript between the two words of the phrase "vnfitting manners"

26. Although printed in 1534, scholars have persuasively argued that the scale of the household described by the French tutor as well as the named personnel were more reflective of the Welsh household than of Mary's later 1530s households. Loades,

p. 43 and G. Walker, *Persuasive Fictions: Faction, Faith and Political Culture in the Reign of Henry VIII*, [Scolar Press, 1996], p. 203

27. Printed in Italy in 1528, *The Courtier* did not appear in a printed English translation until 1560 but was, apparently, widely read at Henry's court by the early 1530s. See Starkey, *Reign of Henry VIII*, p. 33

28. Duwes, sigs. Aa4r–Bb1r

29. Duwes, sig.A4r

30. Duwes, sig.Aa2v

31. Duwes, sig.U4r

32. Duwes, sig. A4r

33. Duwes, sig. Bb2r

34. Loades, pp. 346–357 provides a detailed chart tracing the service of many of Mary's staff throughout her households from 1516 until her death in 1558. For continuous service of kitchen servants like Oliver Hunt from 1519 to 1533, see *LP*, III, 970; BL Harley 6807, f.5r, f.8v and Madden, pp. 12, 40, 56, 65, 71, 75, 89, 104, 113, 161.

35. Madden, pp. 205–276 and Loades, pp. 358–369

36. *CSP Spanish*, X, Jan.14, 1550, p. 5

37. BL Stowe 141, f. 13r–v

38. Madden, p. 67

39. Madden, p. 17

40. Madden, p. 25

41. *Ibid*.

42. Madden, p. 144

43. Madden, p. 30

44. Madden, pp. 20, 39, 55, 69

45. Madden, p. 39

46. Madden, pp. 9, 21, 28, 53, 70, 121

47. Both of these men appear too frequently in the accounts to list here; see index entries in Madden, pp. 213 and 254.

48. Madden, p. 28

49. *LP*, III, pt. 2, 3375

50. *CSP, Spanish*, IV, pt. 2, 1137

51. *CSP, Spanish*, IV, pt. 2, 1161

52. *CSP, Spanish*, IV, pt. 2, 1144. November 3, 1533

53. BL Cotton Otho, C.X., ff. 266r–v

54. BL Cotton Otho, C.X., f. 276r

55. *Ibid*.

56. PRO SP 10/1, no. 30; abstracted in *CSP Edward, Domestic*, 36

57. For Elyot, see Madden, p. 82; for Morley, see Dowling, *Humanism in the Court of Henry VIII* [Kent UK, 1986], p. 228

58. R. K. Marshall, *Mary I* [London, 1993], p. 6

59. Madden, p. 88

60. It was, apparently, common practice for householders or household managers (usually women) to sign the household accounts and inventories, e.g., Margaret

Beaufort (mother of Henry VII) signed her accounts, Jones and Underwood, *The King's Mother* . . . , p. 159

61. Ives, *Anne Boleyn*, p. 246; Loades, p. 115

62. TNA SP 10/1, no.38 abstracted in *CSP Domestic Edward VI*, 36.

63. *CSP Domestic Edward* 36

64. C. I. Merton, "The women who served Queen Mary and Queen Elizabeth: Ladies, Gentlewomen and Maids of the Privy Chamber, 1553–1603" [Cambridge, unpublished PhD, 1992], pp. 38–40

65. S. E. James, *Kateryn Parr: The Making of a Queen*, [Aldershot, UK, 1999], p. 90

66. *Ibid.*

67. *Ibid.*

68. Loades, p. 117

69. S. James, *Kateryn Parr* [Aldershot, UK, 1999], pp. 130–134

70. BL Royal MS. 17 B XXVIII, f. 61v

71. *CSP, Spanish*, VIII, p. 2 as quoted in James, *Kateryn Parr*, pp. 130–131

72. Harris, *English Aristocratic Women*, p. 222

73. Madden, p. 185

74. Harris, *English Aristocratic Women* . . . , p. 211

75. Harris, *English Aristocratic Women*, p. 10

76. Loades, p. 143

77. Mary protested the legislative changes in religion pushed through by the Edwardian government in 1547. See BL Cotton Faustina C. ii; f. 66r–67v for Protector Somerset's reply to Mary's letter of protest (which does not survive) concerning the 1547 repeal of the Act of Six Articles

78. APC, II, p. 238

79. Quoted from an unidentified source in Prescott, p. 123

80. APC, III, pp. 333–36

81. *Ibid.*

82. APC, III, p. 341

83. APC, III, p. 352.

84. APC, III, p. 341

85. APC, III, p. 345

86. APC, III, p. 350

87. *Ibid.* My italics

88. *CSP, Spanish*, X, pp. 350, 359

89. *CSP, Spanish*, IX, p. 257; X, pp. 362–364, 410

90. APC, III, p. 503 gives the date for their release from the Tower as March 1551 but this does not make sense since they were not committed to the Tower until August 1551. The more likely date is March 1552

91. H. Clifford, *The Life of Jane Dormer, Duchess of Feria*, ed. Rev. Joseph Stevenson [London, 1887], p. 61.

92. As abstracted in *CSP Spanish*, X, pp. 124–135

93. Madden, p. 26

94. J. Eales, *Women in Early Modern England, 1500–1700* [London, 1998], p. 87

95. Lawrence Stone, "Patriarchy and Paternalism in Tudor England: The Earl of Arundel and the Peasants Revolt of 1549," *Journal of British Studies*, 13/2 (May 1974), pp. 20–21

96. As attested in Margaret Bryan's letter to Cromwell in 1536 and Mary's letter to Henry VIII already cited; BL Cotton Otho X, f.234r

97. LP, XIX, pt.1, 780 for 1542 encounter

98. BL Lansdowne 1236, f. 35; CW, p. 35. For Ashley's descent, see Collins, *Jewels and Plate*, p. 199.

99. *LP*, IX, 568

100. Ives, *Anne Boleyn*, p. 247

101. Ives, *Anne Boleyn*, p. 272; Dowling, *Humanism*, pp. 233–234

102. Prescott, *Mary Tudor*, p. 79

103. BL Cotton Otho X, f. 234r. Source of all subsequent quotations from this letter.

104. *LP*, X, pp. 494–495 and XI, Oct.10, 1536

105. *CSP, Edward, Domestic*, 181

106. Haynes, *State Papers*, p. 96

107. R. Clutterbuck, *The History and Antiquities of the County of Hertford . . .*, London, 1815], vol. II, p. 107.

108. Haynes, *A Collection of State Papers . . .*, p. 96

109. *Dictionary of National Biography*, entries under "Fortescue" and "Parry"

110. Thomas Parry and William Cecil had a shared ancestor, their great-grandmother Maud Vaughan; Clutterbuck, II, p. 340

111. *CSP Edward Domestic*, 362, 363, 445, 468, 727, 735

112. *LP*, IX, 132

113. For discussion of who may or may not have initially educated Elizabeth see Dowling, *Humanism . . .* , p. 63; Ryan, *Roger Ascham*, p. 104; Johnson, *Elizabeth I*, p. 16

114. Most of Elizabeth's biographers have assumed that she and Edward shared their lessons but Maria Dowling argues that the princess' gender would have resulted in a different educational program. See Dowling, *Humanism*, p. 211

115. Starkey, p. 27

116. Dowling, *Humanism*, pp. 62–3, 106, 212, 234; Starkey, pp. 26–7; Ryan, *Roger Ascham*, p. 16

117. *Ibid.*

118. Ryan, *Roger Ascham*, p. 104

119. Ryan, *Roger Ascham*, pp. 102–118

120. *CSP Edward Domestic*, 191

121. Haynes, *State Papers*, p. 96. All subsequent references to Katherine Champernon-Ashley's testimony can be found in *CW*, pp. 25–30

122. Haynes, *A Collection of State Papers*, pp. 107–108

123. Haynes, *A Collection of State Papers*, p. 89

124. *Ibid.*

125. Haynes, *A Collection of State Papers*, p. 88

126. N.Z. Davis, *Fiction in the Archives: Pardon Tales and their Tellers in Sixteenth-Century France* [Stanford UP, 1990], *passim*

127. James, *Kateryn Parr*, p. 92

128. See letters 1, 2, 4, 8, and 10 from Elizabeth to Parr printed in *Collected Works*, pp. 5–7, 10–13, 17, 20

129. H. Latimer, *Sermons and Remains*, ed. G. Corrie [Cambridge, 1844], I, pp. 161–165, 228–229

130. Haynes, *A Collection of State Papers*, p. 108

131. CW, p. 19

132. Starkey, p. 73

133. BL Lansdowne 1236, f.33; CW, p. 32

134. *Ibid.*

135. *Ibid.*

136. CW, p. 28

137. Haynes, *A Collection of State Papers*, pp. 99–100

138. CW, p. 26

139. *Ibid.*

140. *Ibid.*

141. *CSP Edward VI, Domestic*, 181

142. *Ibid.*

143. BL Cotton Vespasian MS, F. III, f.48; CW, pp. 25–30

144. Collins, *Jewels and Plate*, pp. 201–202

145. *CSP Edward, Domestic*, 362

146. Ryan, *Roger Ascham*, p. 102

147. R. Ascham, *The Schoolmaster* (1570), ed. E. Arber [Birmingham 1870], pp. 25–31

148. Ryan, *Roger Ascham*, p. 135

149. Ryan, *Roger Ascham*, p. 107

150. Dowling, *Humanism*, p. 200

151. *The History of Italy* (1549) by William Thomas, ed. George B. Parks [Cornell UP, 1963], see Parks's introduction for discussion of the English interest in Italian culture

152. *CSP Mary*, 456

153. M. Perry, *The Word of a Prince* [Woodbridge, UK, 1990], pp. 49–50

154. BL Lansdowne 94, art. 10, f. 21

155. All quotations are from "The Household Account of the Princess Elizabeth, 1551-2," ed. Viscount Strangford, *The Camden Miscellany*, 2, [Camden Society, 1853], hereafter cited as "Accounts"

156. On the eve of her accession, Elizabeth claimed that her landed revenues had never been adequate to her expenses; M. J. Rodríguez-Salgado and S. Adams, "The Count of Feria's Dispatch to Philip II of 14 November 1558," *Camden Miscellany*, 4th ser., vol. 28 [London, 1984]. Hereafter "FD" for Feria Dispatch

157. "Accounts," pp. 80, 81, 85, 89

158. Bodleian Smith 68, f.44

159. Quoted in J. Strype, *Historical Collections of the Life and Acts of the Right Reverend Father in God, John Aylmer, Lord Bishop of London in the Reign of Queen Elizabeth* (Oxford, 1821), pp. 195–196

160. "Accounts," p. 84

161. "Accounts," *e.g.* pp. 86, 89–90

162. "Accounts," pp. 49–50, 94

163. S. Brigden, *New Worlds, Lost Worlds: The Rule of the Tudors, 1485–1603* [New York, 2000], p. 216

164. As quoted in Starkey, p. 81. Ashley's account prefaced Ascham's *Report and Discourse of the Affaires and State of Germany* [1555]

165. Strype, *Ecclesiastical memorials*, [1816] IV, pp. 130–132

166. Strype, *Historical Memorials*, 1781, Vol. III, p. 82

167. B. Usher, "Backing Protestantism: the London Godly, the Exchequer and the Foxe Circle" from *John Foxe: An Historical Perspective*, ed. D. Loades [Aldershot, UK, 1999], pp. 105–134

168. John Foxe, *Acts and Monuments of These Latter and Perillous Dayes . . .* [London, John Day, March 20, 1563], sig. 1710v

169. This is, likely, an example of a Foxian exaggeration; *CSP Mary*, 86

170. Foxe, 1563, sigs. 1711r–v

171. Foxe, sig. 1712r

172. Foxe, (1563) sig. 1713v

173. Foxe, sig. 1715r

174. C. R. Manning, "State Papers relating to the custody of the Princess Elizabeth at Woodstock, in 1554 . . .", *Norfolk Archaeology . . .*, 4 (1855), p. 166; hereafter these Bedingfield Papers will be cited as "BP"

175. *Ibid.*

176. Foxe, [1583 ed.], p. 580

177. BP, pp. 166–171

178. BP, p. 141

179. BP, p. 176

180. Collins, *Jewels and Plate*, p. 206; *CSP Mary*, 87, 426

181. BP, p. 155

182. BP, p. 194

183. BP, pp. 194, 196, 211

184. BP, p. 220

185. BP, p. 176

186. BP, p. 221

187. BP, p. 214

188. Foxe, 1583, p. 580

189. Foxe, 1583, pp. 580, 610; 1563, sig.1712r

190. BP, p. 219

191. BL Harley 37, f.14v; late-seventeenth-century copy. I am grateful to Janel Mueller for allowing me to quote from her original transcript. This letter does not appear in her modernized edition of Elizabeth's letters in *CW*

192. N.L. Jones, *Faith by Statute* [London, 1982], pp. 114–115; C. Haigh, *English Reformations* [Oxford, 1993], pp. 235–250

193. Starkey, *Elizabeth*, p. 193

194. Strype, *Ecclesiastical Memorials . . .* , [1781], III, p. 82

195. B. J. Harris, *English Aristocratic Women 1450–1550: Marriage and Family, Property and Careers* [Oxford UP, 2002], p. 6

3. PROPERTY AND POLITICS

Land Acquisition and Political Status

Why, cousin, wert thou regent of the world
It were a shame to let this land by lease.
But, for thy world, enjoying but this land,
Is it not more than shame to shame it so?
Landlord of England art thou now, not king.
— William Shakespeare, *Richard II*, 2.1

As significant as the material and daily culture were in conferring and enhancing Mary's and Elizabeth's political credibility, their households possessed another crucial function. These households (staff and the manors, which served as residences for the princesses) were the administrative centers from which Mary and Elizabeth controlled their landed estates. The princesses were not only heads of household but also holders of considerable properties. The revenues from these properties allowed them to use their households for the purposes of display and authority. It also endowed them with legal and political status. In this period, politicians reinforced their status through land acquisition. Property testified to a politician's ability to dispense patronage. For the nobility and upper gentry, land was a measure of her or his standing in society and in the political arena.[1]

A detailed examination of Mary's and Elizabeth's preaccession career as landowners can yield new insights into their preaccession political activities.

Indeed, I argue that the Edwardian political context as whole benefits from a thorough analysis of property grants to the princesses. An example of the connection between political status and land is detailed below in the discussion of the dispersal, location, and value of Mary's and Elizabeth's patrimonies. It shows the unequal political status of the sisters with respect to each other.

LAND OWNERSHIP, VASSALAGE, AND THE AFFINITY

Political loyalty in the sixteenth century, as during the medieval period, was expressed in England in terms of service and good lordship. During the Middle Ages, kings and nobles "retained" local knights, via the household, to act as reserve military recruiters. In return for this service, householders and kings practiced good lordship either by annuities or by sponsoring the knight's extramilitary activities.[2] Other knights were required to serve the lord or king directly in the household with various lengths in residency. This system was known as bastard feudalism and was largely on the wane by the time Mary and Elizabeth were presiding over their households.[3] Kings were more interested in recruiting judges than knights into service and aristocratic military retinues were too reminiscent of the overmighty nobles of the wars of the roses to be tolerated by the Tudor monarchs.[4]

Nevertheless, political loyalty was still expressed in terms of service within an economic context. It was this dimension that enabled Mary and Elizabeth to articulate their political ambitions through material culture and hospitality. Moreover, this economic function of the household—processing and distributing landed revenues—enabled the princesses to recruit political clients both within and without the household. Servants, tenants, and neighbors were dependant on the local elite household for economic employment and political patronage.[5]

Regional offices such as church livings and rural offices were usually in the gift of the local magnate. Royal commissions were invariably conferred, first, on the major landholders in each region and then to lesser-ranked gentry. Although scholars sometimes draw a distinction between the Justices of the Peace, as crown agents drafted primarily from the gentry class, and the nobility, they were, in fact, often one and the same person with regional magnates invariably heading the list of JPs.[6] In essence, the one with the most land in a particular area was also likely the person with the most political clout both on a national and regional level. This sphere of influence was expanded by the practice of vassalage/clientage.

Often, the nobility allowed their clients to enjoy the revenues of specific estates and stipulated that these clients were entitled to inherit these estates after the death of the original landowner. This was known as a *reversionary* grant. This was a legal device naming a successor (holder of the reversionary interest) to a designated property. On the death of original holder of the property, the land held in reversion would "revert" to whomsoever held the reversionary interest. In practice, the reversionary holder often already controlled the revenues from the specified lands from the time of the recording of the reversionary grant, so well before the death of the original landowner. The grant, by its nature, indicated a patron/client relationship between the landowner and reversionary holder since the property owner's consent was usually necessary in order for the recipient to obtain the reversionary interest. This was an effective means for property owners to patronize servants, clients, and colleagues. The landowner still retained legal title to the property and could even sue to revoke the reversion should the designated recipient prove unsatisfactory.

As will be discussed later, Mary and Elizabeth practiced this form of clientage in that they consented to reversionary grants to some of their estates. These land grants, however, were often small and were a recognition of a patron/client relationship already in existence rather than heralding the initial stages of it. Often, their gentry clients were either already tenants or neighbors.

This study has emphasized how Mary and Elizabeth functioned, in their capacity as landowners and householders, very much as other elite women did. There is one (possible) crucial difference that served to provide an advantage to the princesses that was not widely shared among their elite female contemporaries: Mary and Elizabeth could read Latin. Their royal education ensured that they could read conveyancing documents, accounts, and other state documents for themselves—all of which were in Latin. Barbara Harris's study of English aristocratic women from this period suggests that the princesses had acquired a useful and uncommon skill.[7] Few elite women knew Latin, which resulted in them being dependent on their more formally educated male relatives and clerics/servants.

Tenants and neighbors were an important part of the princess' affinity and would play a role in ensuring that the princess in question was able to pursue successfully her claim to the throne. Such clients, in fact, were instrumental for all elite householders in establishing their political patronage level both at the local and national levels. The tenants of noble landowners were usually gentry and other well-to-do people who leased or enjoyed reversionary interests in the magnates' estates and manors. In many cases, the gentry clients' family had been leasing manors and pastures for generations from an elite or royal family. Gentry, whose estates bordered those of an elite or royal magnate, sought to maintain good relations with their powerful neighbors in order to obtain political patronage and to ensure smooth cooperation in routine matters such as informal pasturage rights. In return, such gentry clients often formed the back bone of a noble's affinity. If the crown commissioned a magnate to draw up musters then the noble would invariably call on their affinity—their dependent neighbors and tenants—to bring in men and equipment.

This was part of the service rendered by the tenants and neighbors to their noble patron. These landed clients were not resident members of the elite household nor did they wear the householder's livery. Yet their economic and political dependence on the magnate meant that, when called on to do so, they functioned as if they were household retainers sworn to the service of the noble. This was not a matter of legal, formal, or official obligatory service owed to the elite householder. Such obligations, had they existed in a formal sense, would pose political and legal dilemmas when elite householders attracted the displeasure of the crown. Under such circumstances, clients were not required, in any formal sense, to support the elite householder/ local magnate. Yet the consistently rapid response that nobles received from their regional clients indicate that the latter took their informal obligations in this regard quite seriously.[8] As will be discussed later, some gentry clients were prepared, on occasion, to answer the call to musters from a local magnate even if it meant contributing to an army that intended to meet government forces in battle as was the case with Mary's clients in 1553 and Elizabeth's in 1558.

It should be emphasized that the affinity was not always defined in terms of land or proximity. Those who supplied or worked for the household like grocers and tailors but did not reside within the household were also part of the affinity. The householder also used these landless members of the affinity for political purposes. They served as messengers and rumor-mongerers when necessity arose. For instance, Mary received unofficial news of Edward VI's death by her goldsmith and later deployed her nonresident affinity to spread rumors that her military forces were overwhelmingly numerous.[9]

LANDED MAGNATES: MARY AND ELIZABETH ASSUMING LEGAL TITLE TO THEIR ESTATES, 1525 AND 1550

How and when Mary and Elizabeth first became landowners and official heads of princely households is germane to an understanding of how the princesses were able to establish themselves as authority figures *before* their accessions.

Their ability to form political networks was the direct result of their role as land-owners. As heads of household and regional magnates, Mary and Elizabeth exercised economic and political authority over their servants, neighbors and clients in much the same way as did elite male householders and widows.[10] By the time they acceded to the throne, both princesses had already established themselves as politicians with identifiable agendas and dedicated followings. In detailing how Mary and Elizabeth formally assumed headship of their households and acquired legal title to their estates, the discussion must, perforce, focus on abstruse and complicated notions of legal procedure and chaotic political machinations.

A caveat is in order here. The following discussion centers on the political benefits that Mary and Elizabeth reaped as landowners before their accessions but it must be emphasized that they did not technically "own" any land before their accessions. They enjoyed the revenues from these lands and lived in the manors granted to them but, ultimately, the crown retained ownership of them. The princesses could not transmit these lands to their heirs.[11] Nor could the princesses sell these lands to others. They could and did sponsor petitions to obtain reversionary interests in their estates but the monarch's permission was necessary before the petition could be granted.

Neither Mary nor Elizabeth enjoyed the legal status as *femme sole* as did their mothers and their paternal great-grandmother, Margaret Beufort. A *femme sole* could administer and dispose of properties granted to her, even by the crown, independent of the masculine oversight of husband, father, brother or son. Princess Mary and Princess Elizabeth held their lands at the pleasure of the monarch. Mary's first land grant was courtesy of her father and her second one, courtesy of her brother and his male advisors. Elizabeth, too, enjoyed landed revenues from estates that legally belonged to her brother, King Edward VI. The landed revenues Mary and Elizabeth enjoyed from 1547 derived from crown lands that were not permanently alienated from the crown.

MARY'S FIRST LAND GRANT, 1525

Mary's biographers concur that she did not enjoy any grants of lands before Henry VIII's death in 1547.[12] There is evidence, however, that Henry VIII granted Mary lands in 1525 when she was nine years old.[13] It is not surprising that Mary's biographers have not highlighted this grant as the evidence for the grant does not appear in the standard calendar listing land grants, the *Calendar of Patent*

Rolls. Furthermore, because the original patent for this grant has not survived (or was never issued as a patent), it is nearly impossible to determine how long Mary retained possession of the estates granted to her in 1525.

That Mary received a grant from Henry VIII of lands in 1525 between March and August (when she left for the Welsh Marches) is clearly stated in the "Instructions" drawn up for her household. The "Instructions" contain two references to Mary as having charge of her own estates. The preamble of the "Instructions" contains a list of the commissions the king granted to her household council. The fourth commission was "for surveyeng orderinge letting to farme and approvenge of all such lordshippes lands and seigmiencies, as be assigned to the supportacōn and maintenance of the chardgs for thestate and houseold of the said Princess . . ."[14] The second reference in "Instructions" make clear that the lands were granted to Mary personally rather than just placed at her disposal to fund her princely household. The "Instructions" order the surveyors to assess the value of: "the kings possessions and hereditaunces whatsoever they bene in the countrys palentyne of Chester, Wales and the Marches of the same and also Bromfielde Yale and Chirckland or elsewhere nowe assigned to the Princesse."[15]

The term "assigned" leaves little room for misunderstanding. Contemporaries, including Mary and Elizabeth, usually referred to grants of lands as "assignments."[16] Also, this statement refers exclusively to revenues from lands assigned to a specific individual for their exclusive use. To reassign these revenues, the crown would have to initiate another legal conveyancing process. The most obvious conclusion based on the text is that Henry VIII granted Mary revenues from these lands so that she could draw on the revenues to help defray the considerable expenses of her viceregal establishment.

Another reason to accept the phrasing of the "Instructions" at face value is that the lands assigned to Mary—the counties of Bromfield, Yale, and Chirkland— were those usually granted to the viceregal representative of the crown in the Welsh Marches counties. In 1525, Mary was serving exactly in that capacity in the marcher counties. It was customary for Bromfield, Yale, and Chirkland to form part of the patrimony granted to English princes when they were formally invested with the title Prince of Wales.[17]

In the early sixteenth century, the English crown had no male heir. Until July 1525 when Mary assumed the mantle (though not the title) of Princess of Wales, Henry had placed the governance of Wales and the Marches counties in the hands of Charles Brandon, Duke of Suffolk. In order to help him fund his Marches household and hold court as the crown representative in Wales, Henry VIII granted the counties of Bromfield, Chirkland, and Yale to Brandon. In March 1525, Brandon surrendered these counties back to the crown when he was recalled from his duties as the crown representative in North Wales.[18] That the "Instructions" specified that these counties had been assigned to Mary was

consistent with the reality in mid-1525 of her serving as the new crown representative in the marcher counties, replacing Brandon.

Indeed, a household on the scale that Mary received in 1525 almost required
that its nominal head, Mary, have landed revenues at her disposal in order to
help defray the costs of maintaining such a large establishment. It was customary
that crown representatives, from princes to nonroyal administrators like Brandon, were given a local source of landed revenues to fund what was, in effect, a
satellite, regional court. This custom was certainly in place in 1525. King Henry's
viceregal representative in York in 1525 was his illegitimate son, Henry Fitzroy,
Duke of Richmond. The king conferred vast estates and numerous manors on
Richmond in order to fund the young duke's viceregal establishment.[19] The "Instructions" indicate that in 1525, Mary like Richmond, received revenues assigned
for her exclusive use from specific estates to support her viceregal household.

Although Mary, like Richmond, was a minor, the conference of a grand
household supported by landed revenues meant that the king's children were
true viceregal governors of these border regions. In a decentralized state such
as Tudor England, governance traditionally devolved to regional landowners.[20]
One method of establishing authority of a monarch's viceregal representatives
was to embed crown representatives in preexisting ties of loyalty, patronage,
clientage, and overlordship by granting them estates in the regions they were
administer on behalf of the crown.[21] The crown would rely on local magnates
to carry out crown policy by acting as judges, calling musters, and networking
with local gentry and urban officials.

In particular, by having charge of specific lands in the area she was governing on behalf of the crown, Mary could function, at least figuratively, within
the feudal tradition of government through good lordship. Some of the "straun-
gers" who flocked to her household court in the Welsh Marches would likely
have been her tenant farmers, clerics, and landed gentry via the grant of Bromfield, Chirkland, and Yale. These clients owed Mary loyalty not just because
she was the king's daughter and her household Privy Council had judicial authority over them but also because the young princess was their titular landlord
and overlord.

Mary's household would be responsible for settling any disputes that arose
among those under her direct authority in Bromfield, Chirkland, and Yale, as
well as those under her viceregal authority in the Welsh principality in general.[22] At the tender age of nine, Mary, via her household and landed interests,
was a governor as contemporaries understood the term. As a landholder and
nominal head of a viceregal household, Mary was a significant authority figure
in her own right.

It is somewhat unclear when Mary surrendered the counties of Chirkland,
Bromfield, and Yale. Certainly they were no longer in her possession in 1534

when Henry granted them to his bastard son, Richmond.[23] After Richmond's death in 1536, the revenues from these lands would have reverted to the crown. As they were customarily part of the landed endowment of the Prince of Wales, it is likely that Henry granted them to his son Edward shortly after Edward's birth in 1537. In this, Prince Edward was more fortunate than his sisters. From 1534 until Henry's death in 1547, there is no record of either princess holding land in their own right.

All this changed in 1547. After the death of Henry VIII in January 1547 and ostensibly "in fulfilment" of his will, Mary and Elizabeth received lands worth between £3,000 and £4,000 per annum (see Appendix A for further discussion of Henry's will).[24] These lands were granted by patent letters that then had to be "sealed" or confirmed and entered into the patent rolls. Until the patents were sealed neither princess enjoyed official legal possession of her estates. Mary received her sealed patents by May 1547, four months after Henry VIII's death.

ELIZABETH'S DELAYED PATENT LETTERS, 1550

Elizabeth did not receive her patents until March 1550. Historians have attributed the delay for Elizabeth to the shifting political alliances between her and the head of the Edwardian Privy Council. Scholars have assumed that Elizabeth's patent letters were deliberately withheld by Edward Seymour, duke of Somerset.[25] These same historians have assumed that Somerset harbored lingering enmity toward Elizabeth over her alleged involvement in the treasonous activities of Thomas Seymour. Scholars have noted that Elizabeth received her patents after Somerset was removed from power by his rival, John Dudley, Earl of Warwick (later Duke of Northumberland). Based on the timing and the conclusions of the ill-informed Imperial ambassador, scholars have argued that Northumberland removed the obstacles placed by Somerset to prevent Elizabeth from obtaining her patent letters.[26] Elizabeth's receipt of her patents in March 1550 is, therefore, regarded as a testament of the special alliance that existed between Northumberland and Elizabeth.

Although this scenario has dramatic appeal, there is little evidence to support it. It has the further disadvantage of failing to consider the most obvious, if also the most prosaic, explanation for the delay in Elizabeth's receipt of her patents in comparison to Mary. Elizabeth did not obtain official title to her land in 1547, as Mary did, because, at the time, Elizabeth was legally a minor. Elizabeth was only thirteen years old in April 1547 whereas Mary was thirty-one. As a female, Elizabeth would not attain her legal majority until she turned sixteen in September 1549.[27]

A landowner's age was an important issue to contemporaries. A minor could succeed to a title but could not administer the associated estates, especially if they were held as "knight-service," until he or she came of age.[28] Hence, the practice of wardship whereby an underage heir became the ward of the crown with their estates reverting to the crown during the heir's minority. Even if a minor did not hold lands in knight-service, his or her legal title was a vexed question. Indeed, the famous articulation of the king's two bodies in "Calvins Case" as reported in 1608 by Sir Edward Coke turned precisely on the issue of whether Edward VI had the legal right to lease lands in the Duchy of Lancaster during his minority. The famous ruling was that Edward could lease these lands only because he was a king. Had he been just a royal boy then he would not have possessed legal title to his lands. His kingship, however, endowed him with a fully mature "body politic," which legally corrected the underaged deficiencies (in a legal sense) of his "body natural."[29] Therefore, Edward VI leased these lands as king not as a legal minor.

Of course, minors, especially royal children, did receive land grants. The crucial point is that they usually did not receive them by patent letters while still underage. As noted earlier, Mary received revenues from lands when she was nine but she probably did not have full legal title to them. The same would have been true of the lands "granted" to Henry's illegitimate son, Richmond. Kings often invested their infant sons with the Welsh principality or at least the lands associated with the title of Duke of Cornwall and Earl of Chester. Usually in these cases, however, the royal offspring received the *revenues* from the lands rather than *legal title* to them.

A similar arrangement was made for Elizabeth before she attained her legal majority.[30] The Privy Council allowed Elizabeth to draw on the revenues of her lands having already decided roughly the distribution of her estates. Elizabeth enjoyed the revenues from her estates but could not obtain legal title to them, via patent letters, until she attained her legal majority in September 1549.

The delay to be accounted for is not between April 1547 and September 1549 when Elizabeth was too young to take legal possession of her lands through patent letters but rather from September 1549 and March 1550 after she had attained her legal majority. Six months elapsed after September 1549, when she turned sixteen, and March 1550 when she finally received her patent letters officially conveying legal title to her of her estates. The mystery concerns this particular delay.

Elizabeth's sixteenth birthday in September 1549 would hardly have been a surprise so the letters should have been drawn up well before hand and then "sealed" or entered into the official court records. In fact, circumstantial evidence suggest that the patents indeed had been drawn up much earlier and that Elizabeth expected to receive them in September 1549. The circumstantial evidence is that Elizabeth planned to visit the court at exactly the time she should have been receiving her patents.[31] Perhaps this was a coincidence or perhaps Elizabeth's visit was intended to mark her receipt of her patent letters. The timing of this visit is highly suggestive. Elizabeth did not often visit her brother's court. Judging from her correspondence, Elizabeth usually confined her visits to special occasions such as Christmas and Twelfth Night. Her projected visit in September 1549 was unusual in that it did not coincide with a holiday. It did, however, coincide with her important sixteenth birthday. There is a certain logic in speculating that Elizabeth expected to receive her sealed patent letters as part of special planned celebrations to mark her attaining her legal majority. The question is: What caused the six-month delay from September 1549 to March 1550 in Elizabeth obtaining her patents?

In September 1549, when Elizabeth attained her legal majority, her relations with Protector Somerset were cordial rather than hostile.[32] It was Somerset who allowed Elizabeth to receive revenues from lands she technically did not yet have title to. Parry's testimony during the Seymour scandal and Privy Council records concerning the cessation of her pension from July 1547 indicate that Elizabeth was already receiving the revenues from her estates even though she did not yet have legal title to them. Elizabeth's patent letters had, apparently, been drawn up as early as 1548. During the Seymour crisis in January 1549, Parry testified that Elizabeth's patent letters had been drawn up for some time and this was common enough knowledge for Thomas Seymour to enquire in November 1548 as to whether Elizabeth's patent letters had "been sealed or no?"[33] Seymour's question indicates that estates and manors had been "assigned" or put aside for Elizabeth's use but she did not, as yet, possess formal legal title to them.

That the princess already had taken informal, unofficial possession of her manors and estates is confirmed by Elizabeth's correspondence before 1550, which indicates that she was in residence at her manors before obtaining legal possession of them.[34] Her informal possession of her estates was secure enough for the government to interfere in 1548 on her behalf when a royal official inadvertently ordered that a forest, which, evidently, had been awarded to Elizabeth in the unsealed patent letters, be sold to raise revenue. The unfortunate official was informed by no less than William Cecil—secretary to Protector Somerset and Elizabeth's surveyor—that the forest was part of Elizabeth's "settlement." Cecil peremptorily instructed the official to turn over the proceeds from the sale to the miffed princess.[35] Because Elizabeth was drawing the revenues from her estates, Somerset authorized the crown to cease paying for her expenses in September 1547.[36]

Unfortunately for Elizabeth, she attained her legal majority at exactly the same time as Somerset found himself engaged in a power struggle with Northumberland for control of the young king and leadership of the ruling Privy Council. Somerset suddenly removed the king (and the court) from London to Windsor as he struggled to maintain his hold on power.[37] The court and the government were in turmoil. Plans for Elizabeth's visit were scrapped and the formal issuance of her patents were shelved. Somerset was removed from his position as leader of the Privy Council and guardian of the king in late 1549. By Christmas, Northumberland was in firm control of the Privy Council and had earned the trust of Edward VI.[38] The situation was now stable enough for Elizabeth to be invited to court, perhaps for Christmas, and for her receive her patent letters that needed only to be "sealed" and entered into the patent rolls to become official. Yet Elizabeth would have to wait for a further three months.

The delay in the issuance of Elizabeth's patents has diminished from the original three years—from April 1547 to March 1550—to six months. From April 1547 until September 1549, Elizabeth had not yet attained her legal majority and so could not take legal title to her manors and estates. The six-month delay has itself been reduced by addressing the political context of the autumn of 1549 when Elizabeth should have received her patents. In the summer and autumn of 1549, the Edwardian regime was destabilized by rebellion and a power struggle between Somerset and Northumberland for leadership of the ruling Privy Council. By Christmas 1549, however, Elizabeth was old enough to obtain legal title to her estates and Northumberland was firmly in control of the government. Therefore, the delay to be explained is: Why did Elizabeth not receive her patent letters in the period between Christmas 1549 and March 1550?

Some clue to this additional delay can be seen in the wrangling between Elizabeth and Northumberland over Hatfield. In the patent letters that Elizabeth finally received in March 1550, there was no mention of what had been her principal residence, Hatfield. This must have been a shock as Elizabeth had occupied Hatfield since early 1547. [39] Most of the year she spent under house-arrest during the Seymour crisis in 1549 had been spent at Hatfield. That Elizabeth fully expected Hatfield to be included in her patent letters is suggested by her immediate reaction when she did eventually obtain her patents in March 1550. She protested.[40] She had been living there for much of the last two years.[41] Yet in January 1550 Hatfield was granted to Northumberland.[42] By June 1550, the Privy Council granted Elizabeth's petition to have "the house, parkes and lands of Hatfield" removed from Northumberland's keeping so that she could obtain full legal title to Hatfield.[43]

Elizabeth's ability to wrest Hatfield away from the most powerful man in the kingdom suggests a very different scenario from that canvassed by scholars. Elizabeth lived almost exclusively at Hatfield from 1548 until early 1550 because she understood it was to be part of her assignment that Parry had referred to in late 1547. Moreover, Hatfield had familial associations, her paternal grand-mother, Lady Margaret Beaufort, had occupied it at the turn of the sixteenth century.[44] In 1547, Elizabeth furnished it from household goods lent to her from Henry VIII's storehouses. She had thoroughly moved in. Yet just weeks after consolidating his control over the Privy Council, Northumberland seized it for himself in January 1550.

All this suggests a highly plausible explanation for the delay in Elizabeth's patent letters from Christmas 1549 to March 1550. Although the political situa-tion had stabilized, Elizabeth did not obtain formal legal title her estates be-cause Northumberland coveted Hatfield for himself. As this had been infor-mally assigned to Elizabeth since 1547 and so was, doubtless, already included the text of the patents drawn up two years before (but not yet sealed or entered into the patent rolls), a new set of patents needed to be drawn up excluding Hatfield from her "assignment." Drawing up new patent letters for Elizabeth that excluded Hatfield, and issuing patents that granted Hatfield to Northum-berland, was the likely cause for the Christmas 1549 to March 1550 delay in Elizabeth obtaining her patent letters.

The swiftness with which Elizabeth was able to regain Hatfield (she ap-pointed her own keeper to Hatfield by June 1550) after its exclusion from her patents in March 1550 argues that Elizabeth had a strong case for obtaining le-gal title Hatfield as her due.[45] The most plausible explanation for how Elizabeth was able to prevail against the new head of the government, was that Hatfield had been included in her original, though unofficial, patent letters. As if in ac-knowledgment of the original timetable and content regarding her legal title to Hatfield, it was granted to her on her seventeenth birthday, September 7, 1550, exactly a year later than she had probably expected it to come into her formal possession.[46]

The wrangling over Hatfield reveals that, initially, Elizabeth suffered from Somerset's removal from power in preference to Northumberland. It also re-veals the significance of Elizabeth's underaged status. Until she attained her legal majority and could receive formal legal title to her estates, her ability to control her lands and stabilize her estate was far from assured. Northumberland was able to make a play for Hatfield because it had *not* been formally and legally conveyed to the princess while she was still a minor.

The history of Elizabeth's ownership of Durham Place also illustrates how much Elizabeth gained both politically and legally by receiving her patent let-ters in 1550. Northumberland was not the first to exploit Elizabeth's legal inabil-ity to obtain formal legal title to her properties before September 1549. Although Elizabeth enjoyed good relations with Somerset, he did not hesitate to requisi-tion Durham Place in 1548, which was earmarked to serve as Elizabeth's London residence.[47] Somerset converted it to a mint. Durham Place was included as part of Elizabeth's "assignment" in March 1550. At this point Somerset was no longer head of the government. His replacement, Northumberland, also had designs on Durham Place. Having failed in his bid to obtain Hatfield, Northumberland attempted to poach Durham Place for himself in 1553. By this date, however, Elizabeth held legal title to it; therefore, Northumberland had to gain her consent. By the time Northumberland applied to her, she had already heard of his plans and expressed her displeasure that Northumberland was attempting to claim Durham Place without even consulting her first.[48] In compensation, Northumberland offered her the recently-constructed and very grand Somerset House. Elizabeth did not have enough political clout to refuse Northumberland's request for Durham Place. However, as the full legal owner of Durham Place in 1553, Elizabeth expected and was compensated for giving up Durham Place.

The significance of all these complicated political and legal maneuvers for this study is what it reveals about Elizabeth's political status and how this was expressed in terms of land. Although the broad outlines of her lands had been determined by mid-1547 and she was drawing on their revenues, she did not have legal title to the estates that formed her "assignment." This exposed her to depredations by those in power like Somerset and Northumberland. There was no attempt to requisition Mary's London place or poach her principal residence of Newhall either by Somerset or Northumberland. As an adult, Mary had been able to take full legal possession of her property as early as 1547. She had obtained her patent letters in April 1547 and, since this date, held legal title to her estates. To reassign any of Mary's lands would have required her official permission and the bureaucratic hassle of drawing up of new patent letters. As a legal minor, with no legal title to her estates, Elizabeth could not prevent attempts to purloin Durham Place or Hatfield. Once she obtained her patents in 1550, she held formal legal title to Hatfield and Durham Place among others. Elizabeth might have to bow to political pressure as she did regarding Durham Place but once she obtained legal title to her manors and estates, she was able, at least, to demand compensation for the loss of her property.

The rather involved history of Elizabeth's patents highlights her vulnerability as a minor who could not take legal title to her estates. It was not until she turned sixteen that she began to feature regularly in diplomatic correspondence and, not coincidentally, obtained legal possession of her estates. She could now formally in her own right take oaths of service from her tenants/clients. She could begin to officially "govern" her estates and thereby establish herself as an experienced, landholding, authority figure. Elizabeth could now bring suit in court should anyone damage or infringe on her holdings. She could solicit support from important politicians by championing their applications for reversionary grants of some of her property. She could engage in much of the political activities that was incumbent on landownership in this period.

There was one notable difference between Elizabeth (Mary also) and male landowners. As women, neither princess could hold regional political office, as their landed male counterparts did. Yet even this limited mandate, as a female property owner, had been denied Elizabeth while she was a legal minor. Her age, the political struggle between Somerset and Northumberland, and Northumberland's attempt to steal Hatfield had prevented Elizabeth from obtaining legal title to her estates until March 1550. When Elizabeth's patent letters were sealed, the letters proclaimed more than just the settlement of her lands: they also indicated that she was now an adult "governor" of considerable estate(s).

As this discussion of the complexities surrounding Elizabeth's patent letters highlights, the possession of landed estates was a weighty matter in this period. For the elite landholder, property automatically endowed him/her with regional powers of overlordship, office distribution, and patronage. The decision to confer a substantive endowment of estates on Mary and Elizabeth after Henry VIII's death was a fateful one (see Appendix A). The distribution of estates to each princess allowed them to bestow patronage and build up regional affinities that would enable them, in Mary's case, to resist an attempt to deprive her of the throne and, in Elizabeth's case, to recruit politically important Protestant to her standard before her accession.

MARY'S ESTATES AND REGIONAL AFFINITIES

By May 1547, Lady Mary had received her landed assignment. Her new "estate" was considerable. Her lands generated revenues of £3819 18s. 6d p.a. This was a considerable sum. In terms of her own household history, her revenues in 1547 could fund the costs of what the combined household she had shared with Elizabeth in the 1530s (c. £4,000 p.a.). She could now come close to funding a household on a scale reminiscent of her Welsh household in 1525, which had cost around £4,500 p.a.[49] In fact, throughout the period, Mary presided over a household staff of roughly one hundred. It was not the viceregal household of 1525, which would have been too politically aggressive during the reign of an underage king, but her household/patrimony did constitute a serious political power base. Mary Tudor now had at her disposal revenues that were exceeded only by six other peers in the realm and, of course, the young king.[50]

The lands and affinities of her endowment were centered primarily in Norfolk, Suffolk and Essex and included the significant royal residences of Hunsdon and Newhall (see Map 1). Hunsdon was an impressive country manor, north of London in Hertfordshire. Purchased by Henry VIII in 1525 from Philip Paries, esquire, he later conferred it on Anne Boleyn. After Anne's death, it reverted to the crown and Mary herself lived there off and on through the 1530s as a guest of the crown.[51] When Prince Edward's household was reconstituted to reflect his maturity and certain succession, Hunsdon became his primary country residence. In preparation for his investiture as Prince of Wales in 1546, the king commissioned a portrait of the Prince with Hunsdon in the background.[52]

As evidently important as Hunsdon was, another of Mary's new manors, Newhall in Essex (also known as Beaulieu), was even more so. Oddly enough, Newhall, also had strong associations with the Boleyn family. Anne's father, Sir Thomas Boleyn, inherited it from his mother in 1515. Boleyn entertained Henry there in the same year. The king so enjoyed his stay there that he purchased from his host for £1,000.[53] Henry had refurbished Newhall (as it was now renamed though the name of Beaulieu persisted) in the early 1520s. He commissioned an extensive remodel with an addition of a new gallery, new chimneys for the entry facade, new gatehouse, and new royal lodgings. The king also ordered the addition a new chapel, tennis courts, and a new water conduit.[54] By the time Henry had finished with Newhall's remodeling, it was one of only six royal houses that could accommodate the entire Court—some six hundred people—with ease throughout the 1520s.[55] It cost the king at least £17,000 to complete the remodeling.

After the political disgrace of Cardinal Wolsey, Henry acquired Whitehall and Hampton Court. These residences along with Greenwich and Woodstock became the king's principal residences and eclipsed Newhall. Instead, Mary herself lived there, again at the pleasure of the crown, throughout the late 1520s and early 1530s.[56] From the mid-1530s until the end of Henry VIII's reign, it became the posh residence of its keepers—appointed by the king—such as George Boleyn (Queen Anne's brother), Robert, earl of Sussex and the Marquess of Northampton.[57] One of the more interesting decorations Henry added to Newhall in the 1530s was a stained glass window originally gifted by the king to Waltham Abbey but removed to Newhall after the Abbey was dissolved.[58] It depicted the crucifixion in the central panels with the king and his consort of the moment—Catherine of Aragon—kneeling in the side panels. It is little wonder that Mary would make Newhall into one of her principal residences. It's scale and modernity would certainly have been an impressive setting for all the furniture she selected from Henry VIII's storehouses, which like the stained glass window in Newhall's chapel, reminded onlookers of her royal lineage.

Yet these country manors—Hunsdon and Newhall—which would become Mary's principal residences until her accession, were not even the most impressive of her houses and estates. She took possession not only of important royal manors and estates but also was heir to the patrimonies of friends and enemies alike. In the patent letters, the first manor listed in order of importance was Kenninghall in Norfolk.[59] This had until very recently been the principal seat of the duke of Norfolk before his imprisonment in 1546. It would be Mary's first choice of refuge during the succession crisis of 1553. Her inheritance of this castle and its surrounding estates, lordships, parks, lesser manors, and rectorships meant that she now assumed Norfolk's role as the leading magnate in the northeast of England.

In May 1553, Mary gained further Howard properties when she exchanged her some of her east Essex manors for Framlingham, Eye, and Bungay. Framlingham had also been a residence of Mary's late succession rival and half-brother, Henry Fitzroy, duke of Richmond. It was a strongly fortified castle that served as a costal defense. It was from Framlingham that Mary would later issue her first proclamations as queen.

Mary inherited other impressive holdings formerly belonging to disgraced or defunct titled nobility. From the Duke of Suffolk, the late Charles Brandon, she received the lordship and manor of Melford along with its surrounding estates. An estate—Ware in Buckinhamshire—belonging to her former governess, Margaret Salisbury found its way into Mary's "assignment" from the Privy Council in 1547. The Newhall grant itself derived Thomas Cromwell's patrimony as earl of Essex. The Privy Council (intentionally or otherwise) made Mary Cromwell's de facto heir. As such, she received various manors, lordships, parks, and rectorships that had last belonged to Cromwell (before reverting to the crown); among them were Boreham, Guys Hall, and Cannons Hall.

Surprisingly in view of her later attempts to persuade her nobility to relinquish monastic lands, Mary as princess took possession of vacated church lands.[60] The most significant of these was priory of St. John of Jerusalem, which became Mary's London residence. She received Oldehall in Essex, which had also been a priory. Among Mary's new possessions was Epping manor in Essex, which had recently belonged to the monastery at Waltham. She received the rents and pensions that had formerly belonged to the Thetford monastery in Norfolk. In early 1553, she would accept the lands of Bungay and Norwich abbeys.

In the aforementioned May 1553 grant, Mary received another important residence: Hertford Castle. Although it was by this time, a "lesser house" and not on the scale of Hunsdon or Newhall, it was nevertheless a royal residence. A crown property since the days of Edward IV, it had become a royal nursery manor during Henry VIII's reign.[61] All of his children resided there at one time or another. Mary's receipt of the castle and its surrounding estates was like, Hunsdon and Newhall, a significant manorial expression of her exalted royal status.

Mary received more than just manors. As already mentioned, she also obtained the estates, the parks, forests, and lesser houses associated with major

residences. Her patent letters note that her grant of Kenninghall included its title or "lordship" so technically, she was "lord of Kenninghall." Within this lordship was a rectory whose living was within her gift. Along with the two parks
of Kenninghall, she acquired ten subsidiary manors and two parks. The patent
letters also grant Mary the lordships and manors of Wyveton, Wareham, Barn-
ingham Stafford, Sherringham, Acle, Welles, West Walton, Walpole, Walsoken,
and Hitcham, all in Norfolk. She acquired much the same arrangement with
her Essex holdings near Cannon Hall. She controlled the religious livings associated with her principal manors of Kenninghall, Hunsdon, Newhall, and so
on, to the total of over forty livings now in her gift. She received all profits and
fees that were associated with her new estates including, among others, "the
office of foedary in the county of Norfolk." The parks and woods that Mary now
owned enabled her to feed and victual her household. The offices now in her
gift, while not of national import, did render her as one of the major patrons
throughout Norfolk, Suffolk, and Essex.

Mary also inherited people. She was landlord to her tenants on her lands,
those who leased her lesser houses, farms, and woods. She collected the proceeds from her workers at her mills and presented her clients to the various
rectories and advowsons under her control. She began to recruit household retainers both resident and nonresident. The most important of these was Robert
Rochester, an Essex gentlemen from a distinguished but nonaristocratic family
and now comptroller of her household. Another senior officer, Edward Waldegrave, came from Suffolk—a shire in which Mary held an estate. Other household officers recruited from among the shires where Mary acquired estates were
Henry Jerningham and William Cordell. East Anglian—the epicenter of Mary's
patrimony—gentry families who placed their daughters in Mary's household
and whose menfolk formed Mary's household knights were Coke, Cornwallis
and Dormer.[62] Those who responded so quickly to Mary's standard in 1553 as to
make them likely candidates to be Mary's non-resident affinity are members of
the Bedingfield, Southwell, Shelton, Huddlestone, Drury, and Mordaunt families. These families all hailed from areas where Mary owned significant properties, Norfolk and Suffolk.[63] As I will discuss later, Mary and her household
officers would recruit supporters from other areas in 1553, but it was those who
responded immediately, which became the core of her successful campaign to
gain the throne, and they all came from regions where she was the major landholder.

Part of the reason that her regional affinity responded so quickly to her summons in 1553 may be attributed to her making sure that they knew who she was
and what she stood for. Although, Hunsdon, Newhall, and Copped Hall were to
be her primary residences, there is evidence to suggest that Mary visited almost
all of her manors and stayed in a great many of them. The Imperial ambassador

reported in April 1547, before she had even officially taken legal possession of her estates, that she was planning to visit her Norfolk estates. In the event, she probably did not leave until July.[64] Certainly, she stayed at St. John's Priory whenever she visited the court though the king would also lend her St. James' Palace for her use during these visits. In August of 1551, her major confrontation with Privy Council took place at Copped Hall.[65] Late in 1552, she asked the king and the Privy Council to reimburse her for money she spent effect repairs in her costal properties in Essex suggesting that she had pretty good knowledge of their condition, possibly at first hand.[66] Unfortunately, there are no documents that provide a detailed itinerary of her movements during these years. The variation of her residences and her evident concern for her properties argue that she did not make Hunsdon and Newhall her exclusive residences. Rather, it would appear that she made regular tours of her estates throughout Essex and modern East Anglia.

The Privy Council's decision to award Mary a patrimony resulted in the princess assuming the traditionally masculine role of regional magnate and patron. Evidence suggests that Mary consolidated her position by traveling throughout her properties and putting a face to the name of the national figure and local landlord she had become. Not since 1525 had Mary possessed such an important and concrete political present. She was not just the heir to the throne but a landowner with substantial revenues and considerable patronage obligations.

ELIZABETH'S LANDS

In March 1550 Elizabeth finally received her patent letters and took legal possession of her estates. The most noteworthy aspect of Elizabeth's new patrimony was how unfavorably it compared to Mary's. Mary's lands were worth nearly £4,000, whereas Elizabeth's only just exceeded £3,000. Not only was Elizabeth's estate worth less overall, but her manors were far less impressive than Mary's. Elizabeth's age made her less of a political personage than her sister. This certainly played a role in the delay of her patent letters. As the following shows, Elizabeth's junior status also manifested itself in a less impressive landed patrimony.

The most obvious difference between the two settlements was the overall number of manors; Mary received nearly ninety manors whereas Elizabeth obtained only seventy-five. Much of Elizabeth's settlement was in meadows, parks, woods, and forests. Although these were necessary to ensure that she could feed

her household from fishponds, pasture her herds and have a steady supply of
firewood, the greater preponderance of scattered lands in Elizabeth's allotment
presented no clear advantage to Mary's manor-laden settlement. Quite the re-
verse. Whereas Mary obtained large, capacious residences and their surrounding estates, Elizabeth had to make do with lesser houses and small, dispersed
parcels, which ranged from Northamptonshire to Lincolnshire and Dorset.
The nature of this unequal ratio of lands to manors as compared to Mary's suggest that Elizabeth's settlement resulted from a conscientious effort to ensure
that her assignment provided no more than the stipulated £3,000 in revenue
that Henry's VIII's will had specified as due to her in an annual allowance.
Elizabeth's underage status, both biologically and politically, meant that the
executor-councilors did not need to award her manors on the scale of Newhall
or Hundson. Mary was the adult heir to the throne, a politician with international connections, and therefore she obtained manors and lands far in excess
of the allowance Henry had bequeathed to her. Elizabeth, by contrast, was not
of sufficient political stature to intimidate the Privy Council into treating her
with any special consideration when it came to assigning her estates.

The lands, however, were important to Elizabeth's ability to maintain a
princely household. The revenues were real enough even if they did not, in and
of themselves, directly enhance her political prestige nor, according to her own
statements, cover her household expenses.[67] Nevertheless, Elizabeth took a keen
interest in maintaining her authority over her lands. Her correspondence provides evidence of this interest. An early indication of the importance Elizabeth
placed on her even the smallest parcel of her lands as well as a demonstration of
how her minor status undermined her ability to establish control over her estates comes from two letters.

On January 28, 1549, William Gyffard wrote to Laurence Lee, the steward of
Apethorpe manor that he, Gyffard, had a royal commission to sell certain park-
land abounding Collyweston and Apethorpe.[68] The problem was that both of
these manors and their parks were part of Elizabeth's assignment. The year was
1549, however, nearly a year and an half before Elizabeth obtained legal title to
her lands. In fact, Elizabeth's ability to protect her estate was further complicated by the government investigation currently underway regarding her role in
Thomas Seymour's treasonous activities. While Gyffard was writing to Lee,
Elizabeth was under house arrest. Gyffard and Lee completed the sale of the
specified lands. Despite the distraction of the Seymour investigation, Elizabeth
authorized her surveyor general, William Cecil, to write to Gyffard on February 18, informing him that he must turn over the proceeds of the sale to Elizabeth's officers. According to Gyffard's April reply (Cecil's letter has not survived), Cecil then warned the unfortunate Gyffard that he was not involve

himself in the future with selling royal lands.[69] Despite her difficulties of the moment, Elizabeth had felt is necessary to ensure that swift action was taken to prevent the complete alienation of her revenues from two parks.

An indication that Elizabeth's lands, while generating the necessary revenue, were too scattered to adequately serve her needs exists in a letter she wrote to the Privy Council in May 1553. Due to her "great nede of pastures for my provicions, the lack wherof hath bene to my great chardges," Elizabeth had contracted with a certain "Smyth" to purchase his pastures near Woburn in Buckinghamshire.[70] As far as she was concerned she now "by just ordre of the Lawes justlie possessed" the said pastures. John Russell, earl of Bedford, claimed that the pastures belonged to him and Smyth had no right to sell them. Judging from Elizabeth's letter (the council's has not survived), Bedford had convinced the council to ask Elizabeth to surrender her legal title to the pastures while the courts settled the disputes between Bedford and Smyth. According to the princess, the council had apparently claimed that "it were myne honor and a poynt of commen justice not to imtromit therwith, the matier being litigiouse." Elizabeth protested. Indeed, she flatly refused to surrender her claim to the pastures. She practically threatened the council to award her better lands if it was to have any hope of her giving up the Woburn field: "for I will not god willing forgoo it untill I may be better provided."[71]

Thus far in the letter, Elizabeth had been implicitly, albeit not too subtly, criticizing the disposition of her lands in her settlement. In the closing sentence, she pulled no punches: "And again because it is not unknowne to my Lord [Bedford] nor to any of you all but that it is most requisite for me to seeke some pastures for myself, which had never none out of Lease appointed me by others."[72] In other words, Elizabeth was outraged that the councilors who given her such a haphazard assignment were now trying to prevent her attempts to rectify the situation.

It was not only the quality and location of her lands that Elizabeth found objectionable but also in the quality and location of her manors. Elizabeth's principal manors were Hatfield, Ashridge, Enfield, Collyweston, and her London residence of Durham Place. If Mary was the *de facto* heir to the Howard estates in East Anglia then Elizabeth was heir, in the same manner, to the estates of her paternal great-grandmother, Margaret Beaufort. Beaufort had resided both in Collyweston and Hatfield.[73]

The "best of the rest" was Durham Place, which, as mentioned earlier, Elizabeth was unable to retain being pinched first by Somerset and then by Northumberland. Of the three remaining, two had been used exclusively as nursery households and never used as principal royal residences like Newhall. Collyweston in Northamptonshire had been the principal seat of Elizabeth's grandmother, Margaret Beaufort and then had passed down to Henry Fitzroy, duke of Richmond and, briefly, to Anne Boleyn as part of her jointure.[74] It was very likely in disrepair by the time Elizabeth received it since there was no socially or politically significant person living in it since Richmond's death in 1536. There is no evidence that Elizabeth herself ever stayed there. The two remaining, Ashridge and Enfield, were serviceable but certainly not particularly impressive. There is not much information on them but what little there is suggests that they were adequate to house small-scale royal establishments, such as royal nurseries, but Henry VIII had not modernized them or enlarged them to an extent to render them suitable for the magnate and secondary heir to the throne that Elizabeth had become.

Ashridge was certainly in disrepair to the point of being uninhabitable. In September 1549 Thomas Parry wrote to William Cecil that Elizabeth was not able to go to Ashridge for ten or twelve days because it was not yet ready for habitation.[75] For the period of 1547 until 1553, only four letters survive indicating that Elizabeth was residing at Ashridge. Ashridge was not a royal residence of the caliber of either Hunsdon or Newhall.[76] It was a former monastery acquired by Henry VIII in wake of the monastic dissolutions. Like many monasteries within striking distance of London, it had royal lodgings for when the king paused there during his progresses and hunting trips. Its proximity to London and size meant that it was an ideal manor to accommodate all three of Henry's children while they resided away from court and so there had been chambers permanently assigned for all three of Henry's children. Something of its antiquated condition was evidenced in its outdated method of water supply. Although most royal residences—like Newhall—had newly installed conduit systems, Ashridge drew its water supply from wells with dog-powered pumps.[77] It is likely that Elizabeth was updating the water supply in 1549 in order to make it hygienic. As late as 1551 through 1552, Elizabeth's accounts show that Ashridge was still undergoing repairs.

Less information survives for Enfield. Hardly any of Elizabeth's correspondence for this period places her at Enfield although her accounts for 1551–1552 does indicate that she was carrying out repairs there and that Enfield was a working farm supplying hay to Elizabeth's principal residence, Hatfield.[78]

Given the underwhelming state of both Ashridge and Enfield, it is little wonder that Elizabeth campaigned so vigorously to (re)gain Hatfield, as discussed earlier. Judging by Elizabeth's surviving correspondence—which is admittedly patchy—she preferred far and away to reside at Hatfield.[79] Starkey is doubtless correct to suggest that, contrary to the claims of Elizabeth's modern biographers, she did not request Hatfield, after Northumberland poached it, out of sentimental reasons because it was her beloved childhood home.[80] The simplest reason for her determination to acquire Hatfield was that it was, unlike Ashridge or Enfield, the most palatial of her manors and also convenient to

London. Even so, Hatfield had never been a residence capable of lodging the entire court as Newhall had been. Originally, it had been part of the endowment of the bishopric of Ely and was therefore still popularly known as "Bishop's Hatfield." [81] By 1538, it had attracted Henry VIII's notice and he made it a condition of investing the new bishop that he resign Hatfield to the crown. Thereafter, it became one of the nursery manors, along with Ashridge and Enfield, for the king's children. Henry had probably sought to acquire it because of its parks, ponds, proximity to London and that it was large and comfortable. Nevertheless, what was cutting-edge in 1496 had fallen into disrepair in 1550. Elizabeth's accounts indicate that she needed to employ a small army to effect largely unspecified repairs. One notation in the accounts about tile suggests that the roof probably needed some work. [82] Hatfield possessed the important necessities of deer-filled parks and fish ponds with which to feed a large household. Unlike, Ashridge, Hatfield was at least ready to inhabit and Elizabeth resided there almost exclusively from late 1548 until her accession in 1558.

The distribution of Elizabeth's lands also indicated that her settlement, while generous, was not undertaken with the same careful consideration as Mary's. Mary's lands formed two dense clusters: the Norfolk/Suffolk border and the Essex/Hertfordshire area (see Map 1). Elizabeth's lands were more scattered (see Map 2). The strongest concentrations of Elizabeth's lands formed two arcs sweeping up through eastern Bedfordshire up through south-west Northamptonshire. A small concentration of just over half a dozen manors in Rutland was the focus of the cluster. The second half of the arc swung down along the western border of Cambridgeshire (formerly Huntingdonshire). These estates ringed an area in the three counties, especially in Bedfordshire, in which Elizabeth had no manors. Her major land holding, Missenden in Buckinghamshire, was far from the cluster, although it anchored another much thinner cluster in eastern Buckinghamshire and western Hertfordshire. Her Oxfordshire estates in the western end of the county were a fair distance from her manors in the bordering county of Buckhinghamshire. Many of Elizabeth's Northamptonshire estates ranged far away from her main cluster. Similarly, a few of her Bedforshire estates were relatively isolated in relation to her other holdings. They were, at least, closer to her other properties than her manors in far away Dorset and Gloucestershire.

This relatively thin distribution of her estates was exacerbated in 1551 when Elizabeth had to surrender the entirety of her original patent letters. As I discuss the next chapter, Mary's property exchanges were highly advantageous to her, whereas Elizabeth's new patent of 1551 letters left her worse off than before. Early in 1551 probably around the end of January, Elizabeth surrendered her patent letters for cancellation. The Imperial ambassador reported that she was in London for Christmas 1550 and had stayed on through January 1551. During that time, Stephen Gardiner was arrested and the ambassador reported that Elizabeth immediately asked for one of his manors now that his entire estate had been forfeited to the crown.[83] Either the ambassador was misinformed or Elizabeth was tricked for the new patent letters stripped her of many useful manors in Northamptonshire—considerably weakening her position as the major landholder in that shire—while awarding her small outlying manors that she probably never visited and were not part of the Gardiner estate.

In the reissued patent letters of April 1551, Elizabeth lost her Northamptonshire holdings of Apethorpe, Wadehowe, Woodnewton, Tansor, and Yarwell, which formed the Northamptonshire section of her landed circle. In exchange, she acquired the nearly inaccessible manors of Norton Bawson in Devon and Bysleigh in Gloucestershire along with some small manors in Berkshire, Buckinghamshire, and Essex. She did not receive any of Gardiner's manors.

After this re-issue of her patents in 1551, the most dense concentration of her estates was now scattered. Instead of two close arcs, there was now only the one along south Rutland and western Cambridgeshire. Her other Northamptonshire lands were dotted throughout the county. It is highly unlikely that Elizabeth visited her new manors in Devon and Gloucestershire. A trip to Devon would have been a serious undertaking on a scale with Mary's traveling to Ludlow in 1525 or Elizabeth's later progresses as queen. Given the distribution of her estates, it is little wonder that Elizabeth rarely traveled beyond Hatfield. Mary could shuttle amongst her numerous estates in southwest Essex with ease whereas Elizabeth's nearest manor to Hatfield in Hertfordshire was Redborn, which was getting well toward the other side of the county. Redborn was not even a major holding. The only other plausibly suitable property in the county was Ashridge, which was much farther away than Redborn. Elizabeth later admitted that she had never visited at least one of her major holdings, Donnington Castle: she claimed as late as 1554 that "I neuer laye in it in all my lyfe."[84] The new settlement of her lands in 1551 left her at a distinct disadvantage. Her already scattered estates were now even more thinly distributed.

The immediate beneficiary of the 1551 resettlement was not Elizabeth but Sir Walter Mildmay. He received Elizabeth's surrendered manors at exactly the same day that her new patent letters were issued, April 24, and it was his manors and lands in Devon that the princess received as an exchange. The exchange with Mildmay within the context of Elizabeth surrendering her original patent letters revealed two seemingly opposing aspects of Elizabeth's emerging political status in 1551: her disenfranchisement and her proactive alignment with leading evangelical educators.

Elizabeth did not possess enough political leverage to stabilize her estate or to improve it. Rather, her patrimony was being parceled up so that a rising politician, Walter Mildmay, could obtain lands commensurate with his increasing political status. In a manner of speaking, Elizabeth's political status was less important than that of a government official. But things were not quite so simple. Elizabeth may have surrendered her estates but, by so doing, she was gaining an important political ally. Mildmay now had reason to be grateful to her. The political climate and relative status between Elizabeth and Mildmay was too complicated to assign to either the role of "patron" with the other understood as the "client." It would be more accurate to discuss their relationship as part of a broader political network cemented by shared ideologies and landed properties.

A few months after the Mildmay grants, Elizabeth sponsored a reversionary grant to William Cecil of her manor of Baroughdon in southeast Rutland.[85] In March 1552, Elizabeth granted to Admiral Clinton reversionary interests in her lands near St. Neots in western Cambridgeshire.[86] The Mildmay exchange, the Clinton and Cecil grants all suggest that Elizabeth was publicly aligning herself with some of the more prominent Protestants in her brother's government.

These grants also highlight a point that I need to emphasize here, particularly in view of the earlier discussion on how unfavorably Elizabeth's settlement compares to Mary's. Despite the unequal allotments the princesses received, they both obtained a considerable patrimony. Elizabeth may have objected to a lack of conveniently located pastures and a truly princely residence near London, but she was still one of the wealthiest peers in the realm. Her "lesser houses," like Apethorpe, were good enough to become the principal seats of such rich politicians as Walter Mildmay. She possessed enough lands of good quality that she was able to acquire highly placed allies like Admiral Clinton and reinforce her ties to William Cecil. Elizabeth's settlement was "inferior" only when compared to Mary's. By the standards of the day, she drew on revenues exceeded only by handful of the most exalted peers.

Nevertheless, her estate was indeed substantially inferior to Mary's. This arguably reveals more about Mary's importance than it, necessarily, does about Elizabeth's uncertain political status during her minority. Yet the disposition of Elizabeth's assignment does acquire more significance when considered against the backdrop of her inability to establish her legal title and to retain possession of her estates. That these two issues—her problems establishing her legal rights and retaining possession of her estates—directly impacted Elizabeth's political persona is demonstrated in the letter quoted earlier concerning her pastures in Woburn.[87] As noted earlier, the letter shows her acute sensitivity to the issue of legal title to property. As she was "by just ordre of the Lawes justlie possessed" of the property, she refused to relinquish her legal rights to the pasture.

In light of her difficulties in obtaining her legal title to her estate, it not surprising that she would have been rather touchy on the subject of lawful possession. Elizabeth's objections were not just legal but also political. Throughout the letter, she insisted that it not just "my necessitie" but also, crucially, "myne honor," which was affected by her (in)ability to retain possession of the Woburn field. The princess focused on the correlation between property and public image: she could not risk meekly surrendering the property after having acquired firm legal possession of it "from which to be now rejected were to my great dishonor, syns all the contrey knoweth it." Although "contrey" was more analogous to the modern "county," Elizabeth was convinced that the "controversie" surrounding the Woburn pasture was "not unknowne" in a general sense. In other words, as far as Elizabeth was concerned, her political and social reputation were at risk if she surrendered the Woburn field without favorable and public compensation.

Elizabeth's fears on these grounds were no doubt aggravated by her inability to easily secure a farm for one of her clients. Elizabeth commissioned her steward, Walter Buckler to write to Cecil regarding her suit to have "an honest man," presumably a servant or client, to receive to reversion of a small farm currently part of the endowment of dean of Worcester.[88] Elizabeth held the neighboring manor of Worcester and therefore assumed she was in a position to pressure the dean. To her evident consternation, some of the cannons in the chapter expressed unspecified concerns over the grant. Buckler, writing on Elizabeth's behalf, urged Cecil to advise the king to sign the necessary papers approving the grant that Buckler had thoughtfully enclosed for his convenience.

Elizabeth's letter regarding the Woburn pasture highlights her perception that "honor" or status was linked to property and lordship. Because she did not possess "lordship" rights in Worcester (Mary had obtained lordship rights for nearly all her manors and estates), Elizabeth could not automatically extend the kind of patronage that most regional magnates (including Mary) could to their clients. The initial resistance of the canons of Worcester to Elizabeth's request that her clients be granted a reversionary interest in one of the Worcester farms reflected negatively on her "honor" and status. On the pasture mix-up in Woburn, Elizabeth indicated that she considered it necessary to draw a line in the sand or sacrifice prestige with her clients, neighbors, and tenants. The Privy Council might claim that was a disgrace for someone of her rank (and gender?) to meddle in such an unpleasant legal matter but Elizabeth's letter indicates that she considered their argument to be disingenuous. "Honor" and property were inextricably linked. In her letter, Elizabeth found it incredible that the council would urge her to drop her claims to the Woburn pasture on grounds of "honor" when her "honor" in fact depended on her retaining possession of it.

Elizabeth's pointed reminder that it was the privy councilors who had awarded her an estate without a conveniently located pasture also reveals her recognition that the quality of her settlement—rather than just the total amount of revenues generated—reflected on her political status. Although Henry's will had stipulated that both princesses be treated equally, Elizabeth's underage status meant that council awarded her lands in line with their estimation of her secondary importance compared to Mary. The delay in the issuance of patent letters and the instability of her estate were products of the same assessment of her political significance. Elizabeth's junior status to Mary was directly expressed in the inferior quality of her manors and dispersal of her lands. Despite this, Elizabeth's considerable estates gave her the opportunity to attract important political allies like Admiral Clinton, Walter Mildmay, and William Cecil.

Holding property meant that Mary and Elizabeth were now individuals of considerable consequence. Their tenants and leaseholders were now under their direct authority. The clerical livings attached to their estates were now within their gifts making them the leading patrons in areas where their estates were densely clustered. As Elizabeth's reversionary grants demonstrate, holding property was an excellent method of cementing political/religious alliances. As the next chapter details, the military dimension to landownership was potentially explosive.

NOTES

1. Harris, *English Aristocratic Women* . . . , p. 6
2. S. D. Church, *The Household Knights of King John* [Cambridge UP, 1999], p. 7
3. R. Britnell, *The Closing of the Middle Ages? England, 1471–1529* [Oxford, 1997], p. 19
4. C. Brooks, "A Law-abiding and Litigious Society," from *The Oxford History of Tudor Stuart Britain*, ed. J. Morrill [Oxford UP, 1996], pp. 139–155
5. Mertes, *English Noble Households*, pp. 75–91
6. For typical list and prominence of nobility on these lists, see *CSP Mary Domestic*, 160
7. Harris, *English Aristocratic Women*, p. 38
8. S. Ellis, "A Crisis of the Aristocracy? Frontiers and Noble Power in the early Tudor State," from *The Tudor Monarchy*, ed. J. Guy [London, 1997], pp. 330–339
9. Loades, *Mary Tudor*, p. 176, 180
10. Harris, *English Aristocratic Women* . . . , p. 147
11. In this way, the patrimonies granted to Mary and Elizabeth differed from those granted to younger royal sons or uncles which were entailed on their legitimate heirs and were meant to be permanent alienations of royal estates, Wolffe, *Crown Lands* . . . , p. 31
12. See, e.g., Loades, p. 80

13. BL Cotton Vitellius, C.i, f. 7v.; hereafter cited as "Instructions"

14. *Ibid.*

15. "Instructions", f. 17r

16. See, e.g., Privy Council discussions regarding lands and Henry VIII's will, *APC*, II, p. 43

17. F. Jones, *The Princes and Principality of Wales* [Wales UP, 1969], pp. 87, 93–7. T. P. Ellis, *The First Extent of Bromfield and Yale, Lordships A.D. 1315* [London, 1924], p. 4

18. Gunn, "The Regime of Charles, Duke of Suffolk, in North Wales . . . ," p. 486

19. *LP*, IV, 1500 and *LP*, 4/1, 1690

20. For discussions of decentralized state systems in England, Western Europe, and in the Americas in this period, see S. Ellis, *Tudor Frontiers and Noble Power* [Oxford UP, 1995], A. Cañeque, *The King's Living Image: The Culture and Politics of Viceregal Power in Colonial Mexico* [New York, 2004]

21. A common practice in early modern Europe, see, e.g., S. Kettering, *Patrons, Brokers, and Clients in Seventeenth-Century France* [Oxford UP, 1986]

22. The complete jurisdictional "commissions" Henry granted to Mary's Privy Council are laid out in great detail in the "Instructions," ff. 8r–v, 11r–17r

23. A. N. Palmer and E. Owen, *The History of Ancient Tenures of Land in North Wales and the Marches*, 2nd ed. [London, 1910], pp. 203–204

24. *CPR*, III, 238

25. Starkey, p. 95; P. Johnson, *Elizabeth I: A Study in Power and Intellect* [London, 1988], p. 33

26. *CSP, Spanish*, X, pp. 186, 203, 361; Catholic Imperial ambassadors were not taken into the confidence of Edward VI's Protestant ministers

27. Houlbrooke, *The English Family*, p. 219

28. A. W. Simpson, *An Introduction to the History of Land Law* [London, 1961], ch. 8. For how this all related to wardship, see Elton, *Reform*, p. 147

29. Kantorowicz, *King's Two Bodies*, pp. 9–11

30. She was in residence in the manors later granted to her 1547 through 1550; *CW*, pp. 14–24, 31–36; *APC*, II, p. 120 and Starkey, p. 94

31. *CSP Edward*, 362

32. *CSP Edward*, 362, 363

33. Haynes, *A Collection of State Papers*, p. 96

34. She wrote from Ashridge, Hatfield, and Enfield regularly from 1547 through 1550; *CW*, pp. 14–24, 31–36.

35. *CSP, Edward VI*, 180, 207

36. *APC*, II, p. 120 and Starkey, p. 94

37. *CSP, Edward.*, 36

38. Hoak, *The King's Council in the Reign of Edward VI*, pp. 252–255; Northumberland, at this time, had yet to be granted his ducal title and was known by his then title Earl of Warwick

39. *CW*, letters 7, 16, 17, and 18; *CSP Edward*, 362

40. *APC*, III, 52

41. For an alternate explanation, see Starkey, p. 100

42. *CPR*, III, p. 415

43. *APC*, III, 52

44. Jones and Underwood, *The King's Mother . . .* , pp. 156–157

45. *CSP Edward*, 445

46. *CPR*, II, pp. 240–241

47. *CSP, Edward VI*, 195, 286

48. *CSP Edward VI*, 804

49. Loades, p. 41; BL Additional Charter 67534

50. *CPR*, II, 20. Loades, p. 137 lists the peers whose revenues exceeded Mary's as Somerset, Warwick, Shrewsbury, Pembroke, and Derby

51. In 1537, Mary served as a godmother to a child near Hunsdon; http://www.hunsdon.org.uk/village_history.htm; Thurley, *Royal Palaces* p. 49

52. http://www.tudorplace.com.ar/images/EdwardVIo8.jpg

53. Thurley, *Royal Palaces*, pp. 44–45

54. *Ibid.*, pp. 164, 186, 196, 205

55. The other five being Richmond, Hampton Court, Greenwich, Eltham, and Woodstock; *Ibid.*, p. 73

56. Loades, p. 138

57. Thurley, *Royal Palaces*, p. 83

58. *Ibid.*, p. 203

59. *CPR*, II, pp. 20–23

60. Loades, pp. 245–246

61. Thurley, *Royal Palaces*, pp. 18, 79

62. Loades, pp. 141–142

63. *Ibid.*, p. 176

64. Loades, p. 138

65. *APC*, III, p. 348

66. *CSP Domestic Edward VI*, 776, 777

67. On the eve of her accession, Elizabeth claimed that her landed revenues had never been adequate to her expenses; M. J. Rodgríguez-Salgado and S.Adams, "The Count of Feria's Dispatch to Philip II of 14 November 1558," *Camden Miscellany*, 4th ser., vol. 28 [London, 1984]. Hereafter "FD" for Feria Dispatch

68. *CSP, Edward, Domestic*, 180, 207

69. *Ibid.*

70. *CW*, let.21, pp. 39–40

71. *Ibid.*

72. *Ibid.*

73. M. K. Jones and M. G. Underwood, *The King's Mother: Lady Margaret Beaufort Countess of Richmond and Derby* [Cambridge UP, 1992], pp. 156–157

74. *Stat. Realm.*, III, p. 479

75. *CSP Edward VI*, 362

76. Thurely, pp. 57, 81–82, 163

77. Thurley, p. 163

78. "Accounts," pp. 18, 44

79. BL Harley 6986, art.12., fol.21;Bodleian, Smith 68, fol. 45; BL Landsdowne 1236, fol. 39; BL Harley 39, fol. 14v. All but the last are also printed in *Collected Works*, pp. 13–24, 37–38

80. Starkey, p. 100–101

81. J. J. Antrobus, *Hatfield: Some Memories of Bishop's Hatfield and Its Past*, 4th ed. [Hatfield, UK, 1933], pp. 24–28

82. "Accounts," pp. 43–44

83. *CSP Spanish*, X, p. 214

84. As reported in Foxe, 1563, sig. 1712r–v

85. *CPR*, IV, p. 198

86. *CPR*, IV, p. 373

87. BL Cotton Vespasian, F. XIII, f. 173

88. *CSP Edward VI*, 727

4. ACCOMPLISHING THE FEMALE SUCCESSION

The Succession Crisis of July 1553 and Its Aftermath

Or else the lady's mad. Yet if 'twere so
She could not sway her house,
command her followers,
Take and give back affairs and their dispatch
With such a smooth, discreet, and stable bearing
As I perceive she does.

— William Shakespeare, *Twelfth Night*, 4.3

In this chapter, I continue to pursue the connection between property and status by suggesting that a grant to Mary in May of 1553 was directly linked to the Edwardian succession plan that aimed at disinheriting her in favor of Jane Grey. I conclude the chapter by reviewing the role played by Mary's household and affinity in her defeat of the Grey regime and how Elizabeth prepared to follow her example should anyone challenge her accession. In both cases, the princesses drew on all three of the household's primary resources—display, corporate identity, and property—to help accomplish the female succession.

The chaotic political context that resulted in the breaking of Henry VIII's will was a political paddling pool compared to the last two months of Edward VI's life when he devised a plan for diverting the succession away from Mary and Elizabeth. It has been assumed that neither princess had knowledge or were involved in the discussions to divert the succession away from Mary to Jane Grey. Historians have found no evidence indicating that either princess became involved until directly approached by the Edwardian/Grey government to resign their claims to the crown. No correspondence on the issue survives from the princesses and government officials, no state documents and no official chronicles from the period indicate that there was any negotiation between either princess and the Edwardian government regarding the succession before Edward's death in July 1553. Not surprisingly, therefore, it is now widely accepted that Mary in particular was deliberately kept in the dark about the details of Edward's scheme for depriving her of the right to the English throne.[1]

Property transactions between the princesses and the crown suggest that the political situation may have been considerably more complicated. Two grants, discussed in more detail below, provide hints that both Mary and Elizabeth were better informed about the new succession plan than scholars have previously acknowledged. Applying the Sherlock Holmes principle that once the impossible has been eliminated, then whatever remains, no matter how improbable, must be the truth, this study will explore the question of whether or not these grants provide indirect evidence that the princesses not only knew of the new succession plan, but, initially, consented to it.

MARY'S FRAMLINGHAM/HERTFORD GRANT, NOV.–DEC. 1552, AND THE SUCCESSION CRISIS OF 1553

In May 1553, Mary obtained the ducal seat of the Howard family, Framlingham Castle, along with several other important royal holdings like Hertford Castle.[2] The context for this grant from the crown tracked the swiftly moving political currents generated by the execution of Somerset and intensified by Edward's sudden illness and death in the spring and summer of 1553. As this grant to Mary forms the basis for the argument that she initially consented to her disinheritance in the spring of 1553, it is necessary to discuss its origins and context in some detail. The significance of this grant becomes apparent only when interpreted within highly unusual political context of throughout the year of 1552 and through to the spring of 1553.

In January 1552, the duke of Somerset was executed. Among the charges against him was that he had embezzled royal revenues and had generally mismanaged crown finances. In the wake of these charges, Warwick, now Duke of Northumberland, spearheaded a movement to increase royal revenues.[3] In the

spring of 1552, a royal commission was appointed to investigate how to stream-
line the process of collecting revenues from crown lands. By December, the
council decided to appoint a commission to study how best to generate revenues.[4] The commission recommended a judicious combination of selling off
and exchanging crown lands to raise more revenue. Accordingly, the king requested that Mary, who had received a number of desirable properties in her
"assignment" of 1547, return some of her holdings to the crown. Apparently,
Edward promised to grant her lands in exchange that generated the same revenue as those she would give up.[5] On December 3, 1552, Mary wrote to the king
in reply to his letter (which does not survive) giving her reluctant consent to
exchange her Essex properties of St. Osyth, Clacton, and Weeley. To sweeten
the deal, the king offered to reimburse her for the repairs she had recently undertaken on these manors now that they were to become crown properties.[6]

David Loades, the only one of Mary's biographers to discuss Mary's properties in any detail, acknowledged that Mary's letter indicated, at best, a grudging
acquiescence. According to Loades the proposed exchange "seems to have been
forced upon her."[7] He then suggests that the motivation for the exchange was to
restrict Mary's access to the sea in case she attempted another flight as she had
done in the summer of 1550. This is a reasonable suggestion. Traditionally, the
seat of the Darcy family, Malden, where Mary had attempted to flee the country
from the manor of one of her Malden tenants (at Woodham Water) would pass
out of her hands, as a result of the proposed exchange, and back into that of the
Darcy family.[8] This may well have played a part in why the crown wanted Mary
to surrender these particular manors, which were indeed on the Essex coast.

There may have been additional motives for asking Mary to surrender these
properties. As noted earlier, the crown was interested in reclaiming alienated
properties (such as those now in the possession of Mary and Elizabeth) and re-
selling them at a profit. As true then as it is today, selling real estate was often
dictated by the location of the property. Then as now, coastal properties near a
major urban center were highly desirable. In general when the crown sold an
estate, the asking price was calculated on the basis of twenty times the annual
revenue. So a parcel which brought in £500 p.a. in revenue would be sold on
the open market by the king for £10,000.[9]

Mary's Essex properties were close to the coast while also being near London. Moreover, the crown already had an eager buyer for these properties: Sir
Thomas Darcy. Darcy's eagerness to possess these properties was demonstrated
when he obtained a reversionary interest in them as far back as 1551.[10] As Loades
has already noted, these lands, along with others in Essex which formed part of
Mary's "assignment," were part of the traditional endowment of the Darcy lordship of Chiche, which Sir Thomas received in April 1551.[11] Within the context
of the royal commission's recommendation, the probable plan was to force

Mary to surrender these Essex lands so that the king could sell them to Darcy for a quick, short-term profit. The context also suggests that Mary would receive in return other crown lands which generated approximately the same revenue but were not as desirable on the resale market.

In the end, however, Mary received estates worth far more than those she surrendered and which ran counter the crown's stated objective of selling off its more prize possessions to raise cash. In May 1553, Darcy received his grant of Mary's manors in Chiche, Essex, for an undisclosed sum.[12] In return, Mary obtained the lordships of Eye, Bungay, the manor castle of Framlingham, and the royal residence of Hertford Castle.[13] Far from diminishing Mary's estate, these lands and manors actually increased it to the detriment of the crown. In return for fourteen of her remotest and smallest Essex manors and five parks, Mary received twelve substantial manors, two of which were castles, and twenty-eight parcels of prime real estate in Suffolk, Norfolk, and Essex.

These lands and manors substantially increased the density of her settlement in these areas making her the greatest magnate in East Anglia (see Map 1). Hertford and Hartingfordbury were near Hunsdon so that Mary could travel to them easily. Her two new Hertfordshire manors endowed her with a substantial landed presence in the western half of the county as it formed a dense cluster with Hunsdon and Stanstead. The manors and lordships of Eye, Framlingham, and Bungay provided her with line of manors stretching from southwest Suffolk to the north of the county. These increased Mary's already dense concentration of lands along the Suffolk and Norfolk border. The grant also included Hethersett, Ellingham, and Dychingham in Norfolk which further filled in tiny gaps in this cluster. She now had a manor in northeast Essex with Clavering. Her near-London manors of Eppying and Coppidhall in Essex were now augmented by the addition of Lucton and Chingford (Waltham Forest in modern London). Furthermore, she received all the advowsons with explicit authority to present her clients to all the livings now vacant. The revenue from these estates totaled over £600. This grant greatly increased Mary's revenues and standing within East Anglia.

This was extraordinarily generous especially considering that Mary had recently been in conflict with king and council over her religious nonconformity. Increasing her status and control over a significant portion of East Anglia would appear to be counter-productive to any hopes the crown may have entertained of limiting her political and religious leadership opportunities. Granting Mary these manors also deprived the crown of highly desirable properties that would have fetched a pretty penny on the open market. Even assuming that Mary received lands which generated exactly the same revenue as the ones she surrendered, her surrendered Chiche manors and lands in Essex could not compare to the scale and splendor of Framlingham and Hertford castles.

Framlingham had been the principal seat of Thomas Howard, duke of Norfolk, the preeminent peer of the realm until his arrest in 1546. It was an ancient, massive castle which had recently been remodeled "with an eye for introducing comfort without destroying its feudal magnificence."[14] When Thomas Howard, duke of Norfolk was arrested in late 1546 for treason, his estates were forfeit to the crown. The disposition of the Howard estate had been a matter of particular concern to Henry VIII who considered the Howard estates too valuable to alienate from the crown.[15] Henry's intention had been to gift them to Prince Edward. Although some Howard properties had already been awarded to Mary in 1547 (e.g., Kenninghall), the Privy Council had evidently considered the castle fortress of Framlingham too valuable to leave crown hands from 1547 to 1553.

Curiously, the crown granted to Mary properties in exchange for the Essex lands which would have fetched a good price on the open market. Her new estates of Loughton and Chingford, near London, would certainly have attracted a buyer for their convenient access to London. Mary's new lands and manors, especially Framlingham and the Hertford castles, would have brought in some of the funds the crown needed. As Henry VIII had recognized, Framlingham, in particular was a valuable property which the crown should retain. According to the new financial strategy formulated in 1552, Framlingham should have been sold by the crown for a tidy windfall of cash rather than granted freely to Mary. There were other manors that the crown could have granted to Mary to compensate her for the loss of the Chiche properties.

One conclusion could be that the crown wished to obtain Mary's Essex lands because there was an eager buyer for them without sacrificing Mary's goodwill. So Mary surrendered her Essex properties and received in exchange lands and manors of greater status (like Framlinghan and Hertford castles).

To accept this conclusion is to divorce the grant from the current political and economic situation and the recent tensions between the crown and Mary over religion. The crown's recent confrontation with Mary over religious observance practiced in her household provides no motivation for the crown to place itself at a financial disadvantage when dealing with her. If Loades is correct in suggesting that the crown pressured Mary to surrender the Chiche manors, then this would not be surprising. Mary had embarrassed the Edwardian government with her refusal to institute to Protestant service in her household. The refusal of her senior household officers to obey direct orders from the king and his Privy Council, Mary's personal reprimands to both king and council via her letters, and her appeal to her maternal cousin, the Emperor Charles V, for help all humiliated the Edwardian regime.

This political and economic situation suggest that it would have been in the best interest of the crown to obtain the Chiche manors from Mary and take the opportunity to punish the recalcitrant princess by granting her less "prestige" manors that, nevertheless, generated approximately the same annual revenues. There is reason to suspect that this was the original intention. If Mary had understood she was going to receive Framlingham in December 1552, her aforementioned letter of consent would likely have been more enthusiastic.

The timing of this exchange and the death of Edward VI in July in 1553 suggests a ready explanation. Traditionally, scholars have depicted Edward as a chronically unhealthy boy forever on the brink of dying from tuberculosis. In December 1552, when Mary surrendered the Chiche estates, it is plausible within this traditional scenario to argue that Edward was clearly entering the final stages of the illness that would take his life in July 1553. Government ministers, nervous that they would soon be working for Mary, used the property exchange— originally intended to be unfavorable to Mary—as a way of currying favor with the soon-to-be queen, by ensuring that the grant turned out to be clearly in Mary's advantage.

The problem with this explanation is that the traditional view of Edward as perennially unwell has been convincingly overturned. Jennifer Loach has made a compelling case that the king did not die from a long, wasting illness like tuberculosis nor that he was in chronic ill-health. Rather, Edward, a relatively healthy adolescent, died suddenly from a suppurating pulmonary infection that could not be treated with modern antibiotics and so degenerated into general septicemia.[16] He probably developed his pulmonary infection in mid-February 1553. It was a nasty and intense illness that instantly alarmed contemporaries. By the middle of March, the king himself was concerned enough to draft his plan for the altered succession that he completed by the end of the month. On June 12, 1553, Edward VI publicly unveiled his plan to divert the succession away from Mary to Jane Grey. Edward died on July 6, 1553.

Loach's persuasive diagnosis and chronology of Edward's illness and death has particular bearing on the context for Mary's Framlingham grant in May 1553. If Loach is correct, then Edward displayed no signs of illness in December 1552, when he originally requested Mary to surrender her Chiche manors. Edward's ministers had no reason to suspect that the king was dying. The Privy Council, still smarting from their recent confrontations with Mary and her household over religion, had no motivation for currying her favor. Edward's good health in December 1552, Mary's recent defiance (summer of 1551) of the government's religious policy, and the need to increase royal cash reserves combined with Mary's lukewarm agreement to the surrendering of her Chiche manors all suggest that the original intention was for Mary to surrender her Chiche estates in exchange for, at best, equivalent and probably less prestigious lands. Yet in April 1553, Mary received the "name" properties of Framlingham and Hertford in exchange for surrendering relatively minor lands in Chiche, Essex (although important clearly to Thomas Darcy).

If Mary's Framlingham grant is to be contextualized within the contemporary political situation rather than in an analytical vacuum then it becomes important to assess the differences and similarities of the political situation from December 1552 to April 1553. The most significant development for the country and for Mary, in particular, that took place during these months was the king contracting his pulmonary infection. In December 1552 when Mary was first asked to surrender her Chiche estates, the king was well and the political elite had no reason to think other than that Edward had a long life ahead of him. Everyone probably thought the king would soon be old enough to marry, beget children, and secure a Protestant succession to the crown through an heir of his own body. By the time Mary received Framlingham and Hertford in May 1553, the king was seriously ill. He had drafted a "deuise" diverting the succession away from Mary to their Protestant cousin, Jane Grey. Within a couple of months after Mary's Framlingham grant, Edward would publicly reveal his plan to disinherit Mary (and Elizabeth) in favor of Grey.

If the king originally intended to foist an unfavorable land exchange on Mary in December 1552 when he was well and then, on contracting a serious infection, changed his mind in favor of awarding Mary prestigious manors and estates, another conclusion appears seemingly obvious. While the king was busy trying to engineer the barring of Mary from the crown (which necessitated also barring Elizabeth), the royal officials, judges, and privy councilors hedged their bets by publicly supporting Edward's new plan for succession but, at the same time, ensuring that Mary had reason to be grateful to them by awarding her Framlingham and Hertford. Perhaps many among the political elite reasoned that Mary might prevail in the coming succession crisis.

There are several problems with this conclusion, many of them arising from a superficial consideration of how the Edwardian regime functioned and the legal technicalities involved in alienating crown lands. Both may appear abstruse to the modern reader but they were matters of public concern and discussion in sixteenth-century England. The most obvious problem with accepting the notion that government ministers attempted to mollify Mary with the Framlingham grant at the same time that Edward demanded their support for his new succession plan was that this could not be accomplished without Edward's knowledge. Crown lands were inherited as family holdings by the monarch. These estates were the personal holdings of the previous king's heir. This meant that government ministers could not independently award Framlingham and Hertford to Mary without Edward's explicit knowledge and permission.

For Edward to approve awarding Mary these prestigious manors and lands at the very moment when he was implementing plans to deprive her of the crown would have been counter-productive. The king was adamant about disinheriting Mary. Her gender, her illegitimacy, and, most important, her Catholicism offended him. Because he had spent his formative years at the center of power, he had a precocious grasp of political affairs.[17] If his councilors had advised him to bestow ducal estates on the heir he hoped to bypass, the young king would not have been blind to their intentions. He may have been sick at the time but there is no evidence that he had lost his wits. As his imminent death became more of a certainty, it was Edward who put pressure on his councilors to give their consent to the altered succession.[18] The trajectory of events argues against the councilors having the unilateral ability to ensure that Mary received the Framlingham/Hertford grant. Given the prestige of these manors, it seem highly unlikely that the king would consent to awarding Mary properties that would serve to increase her political and economic standing as a regional magnate in East Anglia. As such, she would (and, eventually, did) pose a real threat to Edward's chosen successor, Jane Grey.

Yet clearly Edward did give his consent since Mary did obtain these manors. If the king's consent is presumed—as it must be—then the timing of the Framlingham grant assumes great importance. In February 1553, Edward contracted his fatal infection; in March he drafted his will disinheriting Mary in favor of Jane Grey; in early May, the princess obtained the Framlingham grant; on May 21, Jane Grey married Northumberland's son, Guilford, thereby strengthening the cohesion (and possibly the resolve) of the king's ministers to agree to his new succession plan; in mid-June, Edward publicly canvassed support for the new succession; in late June, patent letters were drawn up vesting the succession in Grey; on July 6, Edward died; Grey was proclaimed sovereign on July 10; on July 19, Mary was proclaimed sovereign and Grey was arrested. Mary's Framlingham grant occupies an interesting moment in the above chronology. The princess was awarded Framlingham and Hertford just before Edward and Northumberland moved forward with public moves to consolidate the putative successor regime around Jane Grey.

The timing of the Framlingham grant suggests that, in late March/early April 1553, the Edwardian regime first informed Mary of their plans to deprive her of the crown. The Framlingham/Hertford grant was in compensation for Mary resigning herself to her disinheritance. Having secured (as they thought) Mary's acquiescence, Edward and Northumberland proceeded publicly to canvass support for and consolidate the new Grey succession. Grey married Northumberland's son in late May soon *after* Mary obtained Framlingham; the king solicits the support of jurists for the Grey succession in mid-June *after* Mary obtained Framlingham; and the patent letters implementing the new succession are drawn and signed in late June *after* Mary obtained Framlingham.

That Mary could be compensated for the crown with a couple of manors—no matter how grand—will strike many as bizarre. Although two of her female royal progenitors, Margaret Beaufort and Elizabeth of York, had resigned their claims to the throne in return for titles and lands, scholars have hesitated to credit Mary with ability to make pragmatic calculations based on a realistic assessment of the current political situation. The traditional picture of Edward wasting away from an illness for most of his young life, of an oily Northumberland exploiting the ailing king and Mary's political ignorance to press for the succession of his daughter-in-law (Grey) while keeping Mary in the dark is a picture that has been place for some time.[19] According to this scenario, Mary was an ill-informed country bumpkin during the last year of Edward's reign "retired and obdurate in her Suffolk and Hertfordshire manors."[20] Neither Edward nor Northumberland need have anticipated much trouble from such a sad figure. Mary's eventual victory is therefore, usually presented as astonishing event totally unforeseen by contemporaries.

The persistence of this depiction is mainly a result of contemporary testimony of the Imperial ambassadors. Although these ambassadors and envoys were in the employ of Mary's ally and cousin, Charles V, their assessment of Mary often lacked subtlety and deep knowledge of the princess or the English political situation. Mary often represented herself to Imperial envoys as a defenseless maiden in desperate need of Charles's protection.[21] It was a representation that Imperial officials usually took at face value. Mary's self-presentation as a politically unsophisticated victim of the Machiavellian Edwardian regime is one that has continued to persuade subsequent generations.

So compelling was Mary's presentation of herself to the Imperial envoys that even when scholars dutifully note evidence that seems to contradict this picture, they shoehorn the evidence into this preexisting construct largely created by Mary herself. Prescott conscientiously highlighted that, in fact, Mary had been kept informed of Edward's illness by no less a person than Northumberland himself, but Prescott assumed that Northumberland must have been lulling "her into a false sense of security."[22]

If we refuse to let this notion of Mary's political ignorance dictate our interpretation of evidence and events, then other conclusions can be entertained that previously were rejected out-of-hand as implausible. The situation facing the Edwardian regime in late February/early March 1553 was that the young king had contracted a serious infection that might possibly prove fatal. He was unmarried and childless. According the Act of Succession of 1544, which was still in force, the heir to the throne, the next monarch, was the Catholic and formidable Princess Mary. Both Edward and his Privy Council had no reason other than to think that Mary would take great pleasure in reversing the pro-Protestant religious policy to which the king was sincerely committed.[23] Moreover, the privy councilors had special reasons to dread Mary's accession as it was entirely probable that she might hold a grudge against them over her recent confrontation with them over religion, during which her senior household officers were arrested and imprisoned in the Tower. Preventing Mary's accession was, doubtless, an idea that received wide support in principle among the leading officials of the Edwardian regime.

The idea that Mary was deliberately kept in the dark by Northumberland is not credible. For some time now, scholars like Prescott, have acknowledged that Northumberland sent her regular bulletins on the state of the king's health in early 1553. In fact, most of London and the political elite had long known that the king was seriously ill since March 1553 when he was too sick to open Parliament at Westminster but had to do so in a scaled-down ceremony in Whitehall.[24] Moreover, the Imperial ambassador, Jehan Scheve, was sending regular and detailed reports to Charles V, of Edward's decline since February 1553. By early May, the ambassador was predicting Edward's imminent death.[25] If the Imperial ambassador knew this much, it is hard to credit that Scheve would have failed to ensure that Mary was fully briefed as to Edward's condition because Mary's eventual accession was an important aspect of the Imperial agenda in England. Between Scheve and Northumberland, Mary certainly had good reason to anticipate Edward's death.

If Mary was kept informed of Edward's condition, then she could hardly have been ignorant of the new succession plan. She would have to have been spectacularly naive not to have understood the significance of the marriages between the Grey family and those of other Protestant nobility in late May. Certainly by the time that the patent letters were issued in late June outlining the new succession plan, Mary could not have avoided knowledge of the new succession plan even if she had wanted to.

Dispensing with the oddly persistent notion that both Mary and Elizabeth were kept in the dark about the seriousness of Edward's illness in early 1553 and the plans to vest the succession in Jane Grey, conjures yet more questions. If Mary knew about Edward's "deuise" by June (at the very latest), then why did she not publicly protest? This question takes its place besides others that have been asked before. The question that has long puzzled scholars is, why did Northumberland not secure Mary's person in June so that she could not possibly mount a challenge to Jane Grey?[26]

The Framlingham/Hertford grant provides a possible answer to both questions. The grant allows us, in Barbara Harris's phrase, "to look behind the official record"[27] and open up the possibility both that Mary knew of the Grey succession plan and gave her consent (sincere or otherwise) to it, obtaining Framlingham as payment for her consent. Although Mary probably knew about the new succession plan soon after Edward began drafting his "deuise" in March and April 1553, she did not publicly protest afterward because she had already given assurances to Edward and Northumberland that she would not challenge the new succession plan. In gratitude (and probably out of sincere relief), the crown awarded her the plum manors of Framlingham and Hertford.

It was safe to allow Mary to obtain these manors and increase her standing as the leading magnate in East Anglia because she had already privately agreed to abide by the new succession plan. Because of Mary's agreement, there was no need for Northumberland to secure her person. Northumberland could proceed with the marriage of his son to Jane Grey, the other Protestant nobility could openly align themselves to Northumberland, the jurists could support Edward's "deuise" and the patent letters confirming the new succession could be issued within the context of Edward's deteriorating condition because it was widely known among the political elite (which did not include the Imperial envoys) that Mary would not challenge the Grey succession. Edward need not worry in his last days that he was leaving a legacy of civil war by naming Jane Grey as his successor. Northumberland and the others who supported the Grey succession did not do so out blind unthinking devotion to Protestantism but with the knowledge that Mary had pledged to offer no challenge the accession of Jane Grey. The Framlingham/Hertford grant opens up the possibility for viewing those who supported the new succession plan as doing so after having taken the obvious precaution of obtaining Mary's compliance.

Interpreting property grants within the context of high-stakes political power-plays does not originate with this study. As historians have long recognized, Northumberland and the king attempted to strengthen the resolve of the supporters of the Grey succession plan by awarding lands to such important peers as the earls of Huntingdon (whose son married Jane Grey's sister, Catherine in May), Bedford, Pembroke (whose son was betrothed to another Grey sister in May), Shrewsbury, and Clinton.[28] All except Clinton were regional magnates whose support was vital to maintaining order across the country during a time when the country would be called on to support a relative unknown, Jane Grey, as the next sovereign. Clinton was the Admiral of the Navy and, as such, might be called on to repel any foreign invasion designed to destabilize the Grey regime. Most of these landed bribes were completed in the spring and summer of 1553 and so were contemporaneous with Mary's May Framlingham grant. There is no reason to exclude Mary's May grant of Framlingham from such discussions. Surely, no one's support was more crucial to the smooth implementation of the new succession order than Mary's.

The timing of the Framlingham grant when placed within the context of shifting political situation of the spring of 1553 leads me to suggest the following chronology. In November 1552, Edward VI wrote to Mary asking her to surrender her Chiche manors on the spurious excuse that they are not large enough for her. In reality, as the activities of the Privy Council reveal, this was part of an overall strategy to increase crown cash reserves through a systematic program of property exchange and resale that were favorable to the crown. In December, Mary replied giving her grudging consent. In late January/early February, Mary visited the court and probably discussed with the king and the council which manors she will receive in exchange.[29] During Mary's visit, the king contracted a cold which mutates into a pulmonary infection. As the infection resisted available treatments, Edward began drafting plans for altering the succession in March. In early March, Mary in common with others understood that Edward was seriously ill as he was unable to attend the opening of Parliament.[30] At some point in March, Edward and Northumberland approached Mary about resigning her succession claims in favor of Jane Grey. Having little room for maneuver, Mary provided the assurances they seek. As a reward, Edward altered the terms of the property exchange proposed in December 1552 so that it is now favorable to Mary. In May, Mary received the Framlingham/Hertford grant. Having obtained Mary's consent, Northumberland, in late May, moved forward with plans to wed his son to Jane Grey along with other marriage plans consolidating the leadership of the proposed Grey regime. In early June, Edward revealed the new succession order to other important political figures and jurists. In late June, patent letters were drawn vesting the succession in Jane Grey. Throughout June and early July, important regional magnates and political figures received land grants that scholars have identified as incentives offered by Edward and Northumberland to garner support for the Grey succession. In early July, the king died. Jane Grey was duly proclaimed Queen. To Northumberland's dismay and the consternation of other signatories of the succession patent letters, Mary then reneged on the deal she made with Edward and Northumberland. She successfully challenged Grey's succession and proclaimed herself Queen. To add insult to injury, Framlingham served as her headquarters during the succession crisis of July 1553.

The Framlingham/Hertford grant also helps to contextualize the obvious shock occasioned by Mary's eventual challenge to the Grey succession.[31] The Edwardian/Grey regime was clearly unprepared for Mary's challenge. Even those who knew her for many years—Frances Brandon Grey and Jane Dudley—were profoundly shocked and burst in angry tears when they heard the news that Mary had proclaimed herself queen.[32] Leading political figures, including those who had long acquaintanceships with the princess, did not anticipate that she would challenge Jane Grey for the throne. If the impossible is assuming that a collective insanity possessed the major figures of the day, then what remains is the plausibility of the suggestion that no one anticipated Mary's challenge in July 1553 because a few months earlier, she had given assurances that she would mount no such challenge. The Framlingham/Hertford grant with its grand manors and increased standing in East Anglia was her consolation prize.

One thing to keep in mind: the goal of the Grey succession plan was for a smooth transition of power. Edward VI reportedly laid great emphasis on the succession order as a means of preserving civil order: "I desire this all the more ardently to prevent my death from our providing our beloved country with an occasion or proffered opportunity for civil war." According to this same report, Edward was certainly aware of the need to neutralize Mary well before his death if the Grey succession plan was to be successfully implemented; Edward reportedly admitted that Mary "would leave no stone unturned, as the proverb says, to gain control of this isle."[33] The obvious possibility of civil war argues that in order for the new succession plan to succeed, Mary either had to be placated or neutralized. Thus far, studies of the crisis have excluded the former as a possibility and have deliberated on the failure of Northumberland to effect the latter. It is reasonable to suppose that this failure to neutralize Mary by capture or house arrest could be the result of only two things: a shared nervous breakdown by all concerned or certain knowledge that Mary would comply. In effect, Mary's decision to resist precipitated the crisis which Edward VI and the Privy Council judged it had avoided with the Framlingham/Hertford grant. The ease of her later victory can thus be ascribed not so much ineptitude on the part of Northumberland and the Privy Council but rather to Mary's double-cross.

That Mary might feel the need to temporize or, at least, keep her options open in early 1553 by agreeing to the Grey succession plan is not terribly surprising. She was not in a strong bargaining position. Although she had mounted a brave defense of her household's freedom of worship in 1551, she had not prevailed. Neither she nor members of her household could publicly attend any Catholic mass in England. Hindsight tends to simplify what was a hideously complex political situation. When the privy councilors approached Mary about the new succession around March/April 1553, she had already lost her household's right of freedom of worship. If she refused to give the required assurances, she could have had little doubt that she would face immediate imprisonment on the excuse of her religious nonconformity. Despite the drama of her recent confrontation with the Privy Council and Edward over her household's freedom of worship, Mary had been able to do nothing more than score a couple of propaganda points. She could not prevent the arrest of her senior household officers and she was not allowed to continue openly celebrating the Latin mass in her manors. Mary had been forced to back down in the summer of 1551. Although the seriousness of Edward's illness in early 1553 might seemingly strengthen her position on the basis of her status as heir to the throne, this was undermined by the king and the major political figures ranged against her with the goal of depriving her of that very strength—her status as the next heir to the throne.

Another important thing to keep in mind is that Mary could not know for certain the duration of the king's illness. If he survived long enough for the projected Parliamentary session in September 1553—called for the specific purpose of ratifying the new succession order—then there would be little that Mary could do to forestall her own disinheritance.[34] In the 1530s Mary had publicly resisted her own disinheritance to little avail. In 1533, the first Henrician Act of Succession had reaffirmed the ruling of the Church of England that she was illegitimate. In that same year, Henry VIII deprived her of her independent household. The 1544 Act of Succession restored Mary to the succession but did not restore her legitimacy nor her independent household. This history combined with her recent defeat over religion at the hands of the Edwardian government meant that Mary was unlikely to fancy her chances of successfully resisting the new succession plan devised by Edward and his ministers. She had every reason to assume that the Edwardian government would be successful in persuading Parliament to repeal the 1544 Act of Succession and pass a new statute vesting the succession in Jane Grey.

There was little point in Mary offering resistance to her own disinheritance in 1553. In the 1530s, her own father, Henry VIII had deprived her of her independent household and imprisoned (sometimes also executed) anyone who publicly supported her succession rights. In 1550s, Mary may have considered herself fortunate that her brother was offering to allow her to maintain her own independent household and even to enhance her regional standing in East Anglia by granting her the highly desirable properties of Framlingham and Hertford. Essentially, Edward and his ministers made Mary an offer she could not refuse. Mary had little more to lose by accepting the proposal whereas her freedom and perhaps her life were at stake if she refused.

Mary would have understood that her refusal might not only endanger her own life but also risk precipitating a civil war. Civil war was the great political bogeyman of the Tudor period and no one, least of all a royal, lightly undertook a course of action which could lead to such an eventuality. Whether Mary deliberately deceived the king and Privy Council or merely waited on events is not something which cannot be decided here. What Mary's Framlingham/Hertford grant demonstrates is that high-stakes politics usually contained a propertied dimension as scholars have long recognized. The foregoing discussion has highlighted that grants to Princess Mary should be placed in the same political context as contemporaneous grants to other major political figures.

NORTHUMBERLAND'S REVERSIONARY INTEREST IN ELIZABETH'S LANDS, JUNE 1553

This conclusion holds true as well for Princess Elizabeth's property transactions. Because the Edwardian regime's new succession plan also removed Elizabeth from the succession, it is not surprising to find evidence of her collusion in the new succession plan by examining the property transactions she was engaged in during the summer of 1553. Shortly after King Edward revealed his new succession plan in mid-June, Northumberland obtained a reversionary interest in a significant portion of Elizabeth's estate on June 26. Northumberland received a reversionary interest in Estlethorpe and Blakesley in Northamptonshire as well as her estates in Missenden, Buckhinghamshire, which was the largest of her landed holdings.[35]

As with Mary's Framlingham/Hertford grant, the timing of this reversionary grant to Northumberland is highly suggestive. Shortly after Jane Grey married into Northumberland's family and, as the king and his ministers publicly revealed the new succession plan to crown jurists and drew up patent letters, Northumberland obtained a reversionary interest in the bulk of Elizabeth's estate. A reversionary interest indicated that the holder of the reversionary interest had first right of refusal should the property in question became available either through the death of the property holder or a proposed change in ownership. In this case, Northumberland anticipated that Elizabeth's lands would shortly revert to the crown, in the wake of Jane Grey's accession, so he ensured that he would be first in line for her estate by obtaining a reversionary interest. Because the granting of a reversionary interest in her patrimony could only be accomplished with Elizabeth's knowledge and consent, the timing of this reversionary grant suggests that Elizabeth, like Mary, gave whatever assurances were required of her about the new succession in return for a proposed exchange (the details of which have not survived) involving Elizabeth's Missenden lands.

As I have already indicated, it was usual for the landowner to sponsor an application for a reversionary grant of their lands. Northumberland was in a position to stake his claim without Elizabeth's knowledge but this would have been a dangerous move. Elizabeth would likely have learned about a grant involving such a significant portion of her lands. Also, about six months earlier in January, Elizabeth had already expressed some annoyance to Northumberland about his acquisition of Durham Place "without first knowing her mind." If nothing else, this demonstrated both the difficulty in keeping such information from her and her likely reaction on learning it. Significantly, in this instance, Northumberland protested that he had never campaigned for Durham Place and also claimed that he would never willingly offend her.[36] If anything, this should have been more true in June 1553 when her acquiescence to the new succession plan would have been very helpful.

It is reasonable to assume that once Mary had given her assurances about the new succession order and obtained Framlingham in May, there was little reason for Elizabeth to withhold her own assurances. She, therefore, sponsored Northumberland's application for a reversionary interest, completed in June, on the probable understanding that she would shortly receive more desirable property. She was, evidently, unhappy with the disposition of her estates and in chronic debt.[37] The Missenden grant, like the Framlingham grant to Mary, suggests Elizabeth's complicity in the attempt to establish Jane Grey on the throne. The timing of it argues for a presumption that it was somehow linked to the fast-moving political situation precipitated by King Edward's deteriorating health.

The notion that Edwardian ministers would approach either princess about resigning her claims to the crown is based on a reading of a near-contemporary source. William Camden, Elizabeth's first biographer claimed, early in the seventeenth century, that Elizabeth had indeed received an offer "a certaine summe of money and great possessions in Land" from Northumberland in return for her assurance that she not oppose the succession of Jane Grey.[38] Camden was close to Elizabeth's chief minister, William Cecil who himself was prominent in the Edwardian government in the early 1550s. Camden dates the offer to Elizabeth to July 1553, after Edward's death, but the important point is that the idea of offering property to the princesses as an inducement for resigning claims to the crown had indeed been implemented by Northumberland.

As with Mary's Framlingham/Hertford grant, it is difficult to make a credible argument for excluding the Missenden reversionary grant from the contemporary political context. As the political (and biological) futures of both Northumberland and Elizabeth rested on who succeeded Edward on the throne, such firm evidence of them having dealings with each other in an area as intertwined with politics as property must be of interest to those studying the political and religious events of these years.

The Framlingham and Missenden grants reveal the inextricable link between politics and property during this period. Power plays found expression largely, but not exclusively, in land grants. When the Edwardian Privy Council consolidated their power immediately after Henry VIII's death, they did so by exploiting the unfulfilled gifts clause to grant crown estates. Edward VI and Northumberland laid the ground for what they hoped would be a smooth transition of power to Jane Grey by awarding property to important magnates like Shrewsbury and Pembroke. Viewed within the mid-Tudor weave of property and politics, it would be astonishing if the Edwardian regime had neglected to secure the support of two people most vitally concerned, Mary and Elizabeth, by failing to offer some compensation in the form of land in return for them resigning their claims to the crown.

This study of their property dealings in the early summer of 1553 reveals the central importance of their roles as landowners in the inception of the succession crisis. By including Mary and Elizabeth as property holders and politicians as among those whose support was consolidated through property grants, a fuller understanding of how the Edwardian government planned to implement the Grey succession becomes possible.

ACCOMPLISHING THE FEMALE SUCCESSION: THE SUCCESSION CRISIS OF 1553

Edward VI died on July 6, 1553. Mary left Hunsdon on July 4 after being informed of that the king was dying and headed for her Norfolk manor of Kenninghall. On July 8, the Privy Council formally announced the news of the king's death. Two days later, July 10, the Privy Council received Mary's instructions from Kenninghall to proclaim her as queen. Mary and her growing household army moved to Framlingham on July 12. From the 12th to the 14th, important magnates such as Henry Ratcliffe, Earl of Sussex and John Bourchier, Earl of Bath joined her at Framlingham along with regional gentry leaders such as Thomas, Lord Wentworth and Sir Thomas Cornwallis. Five royal ships defected to Mary during this time. On the 14th, Northumberland left London at the head of an army sent to engage Mary's forces and arrest her as a traitor to "Queen Jane." By the time he reached Cambridge on July 19, the Privy Council had proclaimed Mary as queen in London. Northumberland was arrested two days later and Jane Grey and her husband were moved from their royal apartments in the Tower of London to accommodations reserved for state prisoners. The crisis was over. Mary was queen.

Mary's ability to enforce her claim derived exclusively from her roles as head of household and landowner. The themes which have formed the foci of this study—display, corporate identity, and property—figured largely in Mary's victory in the summer of 1553. Various sources from eyewitness accounts to ambassadorial dispatches indicate that, as the owner of fine manors, extensive lands, and material wealth, Mary was able to impress those who rallied to her cause with her status and resources. Because she ruled a large household of loyal servants, she was able to exploit the household's military potential and turn the household into an administrative center and military headquarters. This, in turn, allowed her to organize her tenants, neighbors, and retainers into a military force credible enough to intimidate the Privy Council, who themselves controlled all the military resources of the crown.

There are indications that hospitality and material display played a central role in Mary's strategy for consolidating support among her affinity and those who joined her forces from outside her estates during the two weeks she fought for the throne. On July 12, Mary decided to relocate her headquarters from Kenninghall in Norfolk to her newly acquired manor in Suffolk, Framlingham. An eyewitness, Robert Wingfield claimed that Mary made this move on the advice of her household officers for strategic reasons because Kenninghall was too small and not as defensible as Framlingham.[39] Scholars have had little reason to doubt Wingfield's assertion.[40] There may be yet another reason for Mary's relocation. Mary moved her headquarters to Framlingham because it was a materially more impressive setting in which to stake her claim to the throne. Wingfield's explanation is worth quoting in full to comprehend all the factors which he lists:

> Now that men from all ranks of life were joining her every day, the queen's forces were wonderfully strengthened and augmented, and on their sovereign's instructions her personal council discussed how they could best move their headquarters; for with consummate judgment the queen recognized that her house was utterly inadequate to withstand an enemy attack or fitly to accommodate her much increased forces and household. Therefore after suitable consideration they very wisely chose Framlingham, the strongest castle in suffolk, and the ancient capital seat of the famous dukes of Norfolk, where they might await further reinforcements and, if necessity demanded, fight a determined enemy.[41]

Framlingham was indeed larger than Kenninghall. It was, in fact, a castle-stronghold, although it had not been used for defense purposes since well before the end of the fifteenth century. Framlingham's position in east-central Suffolk placed allowed Mary to establish her headquarters in a location from which she could easily call to arms her tenants and neighbors of her northeast estates in the county.

However, in some ways the move to Framlingham was, strategically, counterproductive. Framlingham was much nearer to London than Kenninghall meaning that Northumberland's forces could reach the princess much sooner. Framlingham was at the outskirts of Mary's patrimony. While Mary resided at Framlingham, Northumberland could reach her without having to circumvent or neutralize any of her other estates; he could simply proceed directly to Framlingham from London. If Mary had remained at Kenninghall, then the duke would have had to take her many estates from London to Norfolk into account—it was a longer and more difficult journey for Northumberland to make with his army. Relocating to Framlingham meant that Mary risked facing a battle with Northumberland's experienced troops (the 1549 rebellions) before her *ad hoc* army was fully organized. At Framlingham, the princess had no buffer zone of estates, as she would have had at Kenninghall, between her

and Northumberland's approaching forces. Indeed, Kenninghall's remote location in the midst of her densest estate cluster was probably the reason she
had initially retreated there.

According to this quotation, the move from Kenninghall to Framlingham
was not simply to provide a larger camp for Mary's forces but also to "fitly accommodate her much increased . . . household." By the time Mary decided to
relocate, important magnates such as the earls of Sussex and Bath, Lord Wentworth and other significant local gentry had joined her cause. They were given
command of the army and, naturally, lodged within Mary's manor at Kenninghall. Although Kenninghall was a large, very fine, manor house, it was not on
the scale of Framlingham.[42]

Mary was no longer just a royal landlord on an inspection tour for which
times Kenninghall was a suitable residence. In the summer of 1553, she was a
candidate for the throne rallying her subjects. Men like Sussex and Wentworth
came to her with obvious reluctance since the Grey regime appeared to hold all
the cards: the treasury, royal navy, the support of the political elite of the Edwardian regime (including the clergy of the national church), and the authority
to raise troops on a national scale. Being lodged in crowded accommodations at
Kenninghall would have done little to relieve the minds of important figures
such as Sussex and Wentworth as to their decision to join Mary. The move to
Framlingham—which placed her in dangerous proximity to Northumberland's
London forces—makes sense only if Mary was exploiting the scale and recent
remodeling of Framlingham to bolster the confidence of her understandably
nervous supporters. Local gentry, like Wingfield, certainly appreciated Framlingham's scale and history as this quotation evidences. As the principal seat
of the duke of Norfolk, it very likely contained his most expensive and richly
decorated tapestries and furniture. The size and splendor of the castle would
help to reassure Mary's worried supporters that she was not without impressive
resources. It would remind them of her recent role as one of the preeminent
magnates of the realm, her shared political and religious agenda with the
Howard family, and her landed inheritance after Henry VIII's death as one of his
heirs. In short, it was a more "fit" setting for her to stake her claim to the throne.

Offering fit accommodation and hospitality emerges as something of theme
in Wingfield's account. It was not simply Mary whom he presented as a political
hostess but also those who sheltered Mary on her way to Kenninghall and, later,
on her triumphal progress to London after Northumberland conceded defeat
on July 20. Wingfield carefully noted who received Mary on her way to Kenninghall as such an action was itself a declaration of allegiance. Sir John Huddleston welcomed Mary at Sawston Hall although it was "at the dead of night"
on July 4, the night the she fled Hunsdon heading for Kenninghall. The next
day, she found shelter at the house of Lady Burgh at Euston whom Wingfield

praised "for her ready and courteous services to her sovereign."[43] Mary did not undertake these visits because she had no manors of he own in the area. She had many, especially near Euston. Mary was taking the opportunity of her necessary journey to Kenninghall to ascertain the level of support she could expect from her neighbors by "dropping in" unannounced to see how she would be received. The "courteous" reception of her by her neighbors and tenants was a form of political hospitality for the highest stakes and did not go unnoticed by Mary's enemies. On his way to engage Mary's forces at Framlingham, Northumberland paused to burn down Sir John Huddleston's Sawston Hall, the first place Mary had visited on her way to Kenninghall on hearing of Edward's death.[44]

Even after Northumberland admitted defeat on July 19, the politics of hospitality continued to figure in Wingfield's narrative. Although the Privy Council had proclaimed Mary, the situation was still tense since not all of the supporters of the Grey regime had been secured: the duke of Suffolk and Northumberland's sons were still on the loose. The privy councilors could easily change their minds and send another army to intercept Mary. After July 19, receiving Mary still posed some risk (although it now arguably posed as much, if not more, risk to refuse her shelter). When Mary arrived at Colchester a day or so after July 19, she stayed in the house of her mother's former privy chamber lady, Muriel Christmas whom Wingfield praised as "scarcely without equal in birth and modest conditions."[45] Henry, Lord Abergavenny, declared his support for her by hosting her and her household between Colchester and Ipswich.

When Mary came to her old manor of Newhall, she remained there for several days. Its location near London made it a serviceable place from which she could begin to take the reins of power into her hands. Doubtless, she was exhausted from the events of the last two weeks. As with Framlingham, however, there is a hint in Wingfield's narrative that Mary was also displaying another of her impressive residences for the admiration of her relieved supporters. Wingfield, no stranger to domestic magnificence, referred to Newhall as "the lovely house" and praised Henry VIII for building it as another of his "admirable monuments."[46] It was from here that Mary held her first court as queen. Backdropped by her expensive and elaborate tapestries, sitting beneath her sumptuous cloth of estate and on richly appointed chairs, she publicly rebuked and imprisoned Henry Manners, earl of Rutland for supporting Northumberland. Her supporters would have joined their queen at prayer in a chapel decorated with a window proclaiming her lineage with its depiction of her parents.[47]

At Newhall, Mary received her old friend, Frances Brandon, duchess of Suffolk and granted her suit for a pardon for her husband and hinted that her daughter, Jane Grey, might also receive a pardon in due time.[48] The Imperial ambassadors arrived there on the 29th for their first audience with the new queen. The crush of suitors became so great that the nearby towns and villages could no longer bear the strain of supplying food and supplies. Mary broke up the court on July 31 and made her way quickly to London stopping for overnight stays at Sir William Petre's house and at the crown manor of Havering. On August 3, after much deliberation with her Privy Council, she entered London for the first time.[49]

Mary's entry into London (where Jane Grey had been proclaimed queen) as sovereign was a ceremonial event laden with political importance, signified primarily through household display and urban hospitality. It was an opportunity for the Mary to impress on her rebellious capital her royal status. She did this by displaying her household wealth. London residents, familiar with royal splendor, were, nevertheless, struck by the scale of Mary's household display. The London undertaker, Henry Machyn, claimed that Mary's household retinue contained one thousand footmen in velvet coats and three thousand knights mounted on horses.[50] The Tower chronicler, in the *Chronicle of Queen Jane and Queen Mary*, had more conservative estimates but was still impressed.[51]

For its part, London attempted through decoration to erase memories of having accepted the accession of Queen Jane. The gates, roads, storefronts and houses were all festooned with decorations. Crowds pressed Mary on all sides expressing their relief at her accession. Wingfield praised the "magnificent preparations" of the city and the later "magnificent pomp" of her entry to the Tower on August 10.[52] Some of this preparation and pomp had, of course, been orchestrated by the government so it was not a unadulterated expression of urban loyalty to the queen. Yet there is little reason to doubt Wingfield's description about the high level of tension in the capital and London's use of the queen's entry as an opportunity to display its loyalty. London was, evidently, determined to welcome her as its sovereign and indicated this by eagerly participating in the "magnificent preparations" for her entry. In return, Mary was equally determined to overawe her subjects with her household wealth, to declare her undoubted right to the throne by displaying for all to see in her richly attired domestic staff.

In Mary's last days as a princely head of household, before her accession as queen, she continued to exploit her household's potential for material display. At a crucial moment in the succession crisis, Mary was able to reassure and consolidate her supporters by lodging them in Framlingham, a setting lavish enough to add substance to her claim to throne. The move from Kenninghall to Framlingham arguably resulted in material display playing a determinative role in her eventual victory over the Grey regime. At Framlingham, more than at Kenninghall, Mary could display herself amid the architectural and material trappings of power. She continued this strategy when she held her first court at Newhall. Not only was Newhall impressive but it was one of her manors as princess. Mary's residence there, after Northumberland's concession of defeat, established a link between her recent past as a princess and her present as queen; she was the rightful heir to the throne because she had lived in the style of one for the last seven years. Mary persisted in reinforcing this link when she entered London with a household retinue of footmen and knights, admittedly augmented by new recruits among the gentry and aristocracy. This display of her household staff served to underscore that Mary had already assumed a position of authority well before successfully claiming the throne.

PRINCESS MARY'S HOUSEHOLD CAMPAIGN FOR THE THRONE

Mary's success in claiming the throne resulted from her ability to exploit her authority as a householder. According to Wingfield, Mary immediately enlisted the help of her household staff when she decided to claim the throne:

> Having first taken counsel with her [household] advisers, she caused her whole household to be summoned, and told them all of the death of her brother Edward VI; the right to the Crown of England had therefore descended to her by divine and by human law after her brother's death, through God's high providence, and she was most anxious to inaugurate her reign with the aid of her most faithful servants, as partners in her fortunes. Roused by their mistress's words, everyone, both the gently-born and the humbler servants, cheered her to the rafters and hailed and proclaimed their dearest princess Mary as queen of England.[53]

Wingfield stated that Mary asked for more than their aid but also for their ultimate sacrifice. She "passionately" exhorted "her followers at Kenninghall to try the hazard of death if need be." She was not exaggerating the dangers. One of her servants, Thomas Hungate, "eagerly offered" to deliver her letter of defiance to the Privy Council. "Shooting the messenger" was acceptable practice in this period, so Hungate was literally risking his life by undertaking the commission. On delivering Mary's letter, the Privy Council ordered Hungate to be taken to the Tower. According to Wingfield, Northumberland hinted darkly to Hungate that he would not leave it alive: "Hungate, I am truly sorry that it was your lot to be so immature and thus rashly to throw yourself away in this embassy."[54]

While Hungate counted his days in the Tower, Mary sent out "swift messengers in all directions" to rouse her affinity and to proclaim her accession.[55] Like Hungate, these messengers were undertaking dangerous missions. Those dispatched to towns and villages carried with them copies of Mary's proclamation of her accession. One of the messengers fled for his life after he proclaimed Mary in Ipswich in defiance of the local elite's decision to proclaim Jane.[56] Norwich officials refused to allow Mary's messengers entry into the city because they claimed that they had not received confirmation of the king's death. One of Mary's senior officers, Sir Francis Englefield, suffered imprisonment for his efforts on her behalf during this period.[57]

Perhaps even more risky was to fulfill Mary's command to recruit support from outside her affinity. By approaching those who had already declared themselves in support of the Grey regime, Mary's agents revealed themselves to the enemy and declared an allegiance that would jeopardize their fortunes, perhaps their lives, if Mary should lose or withdraw her claim. These risks were not merely conjectural. When one of her servants, Thomas Wharton, tried to persuade the Earl of Sussex to switch his support to her cause, he narrowly avoided an ambush laid for him by Northumberland's son, Robert Dudley who had evidently been tipped off by Sussex.[58] Despite these risks, Mary's servants carried out her orders to a remarkably successful degree. Wingfield's narrative—which contains more than a whiff of the heady atmosphere at Mary's headquarters as news of successes reached Framlingham—dwells at length on how Mary's servants were able to turn such important magnates as the Earls of Sussex and Oxford and to entice seven crown ships to defect to her cause.

The first prize won by Mary's agents was the Earl of Sussex. The circumstances of his switch from Northumberland to Mary reveals the stakes involved and the means that she and her agents were prepared to employ to achieve their ends. According to Wingfield, Sir John Huddleston happened "by a lucky chance" to meet up with Henry Ratcliffe, the second son and namesake of the Earl of Sussex.[59] Young Henry was on his way to London with letters from his father to the Privy Council outlining suggestions for how the government could secure Mary's arrest. Huddleston brought Henry before Mary, whom Wingfield claimed was "delighted with his arrival, just as much at the return of Huddleston, whom she greatly valued." The princess and her advisors promptly inspected the letters which gave them valuable intelligence as to the Privy Council's plans. At first obliquely, Wingfield hints that Henry was detained against his will at Kenninghall in order to secure the allegiance of his father: "she hoped to be able to win over the elder Henry to her cause through his son."

Whether Huddleston had been deliberately sent to intercept young Henry or just to bring in whoever might be useful, Wingfield's narrative suggests that Ratcliffe was forcibly apprehended by Huddleston. He was evidently searched and the letters discovered. Mary then kept him as hostage until his father, the earl, withdrew his support from the Grey regime. Part of the reason that Mary may have had to resort to such tactics was that Sussex had already refused to answer Mary's summons sent via Thomas Wharton. Mary's detention of Sussex's son changed the earl's mind. At this point Wingfield does not bother to disguise the true nature of the hostage situation "When the earl was told of his son's *capture*, he made haste to come to the queen."[60] After the earl swore fealty to Mary, Wingfield noted that only then was the earl himself "finally sent off to return on an appointed day with a large military force." Tellingly, Wingfield does not mention if young Henry left with his father; it is highly probable that he remained with Mary, still a hostage, until his father returned with the promised troops. Fortunately for the young Ratcliffe, his father fulfilled his promise a couple days later.

Mary and her household were clearly prepared to play hardball. It may have been in retaliation for the kidnapping of the son of their prominent supporter, Sussex, that the Privy Council informed three prisoners in the Tower who were either Marian supporters or related to families associated with Mary to prepare for death. These prisoners were: Thomas Howard, duke of Norfolk; Stephen Gardiner, bishop of Winchester; and Edward Courtenay, earl of Devon.[61] Northumberland's decision to burn Sawston Hall may also have been in retaliation not only for Sir John Huddlestone sheltering the princess her on her way to Kenninghall but also for his role in the kidnapping of Henry Ratcliffe.

Another important recruit who was, at least pressured, if not strong-armed, was Sir Thomas Cornwallis. He was a member of a distinguished gentry family in Suffolk and currently serving as sheriff of Norfolk and Suffolk. He, along with other important local men such as Thomas, Lord Wentworth, had complied with the Edwardian edict to proclaim Jane as queen at Ipswich and helped to chase away Mary's messenger. Had the situation remained like this, it would have been a serious setback for the princess as Ipswich was close to Mary's estates. If she could not win Ipswich which was part of her affinity, then how could she hope to sway the country as a whole to her cause. Noting a general lack of enthusiasm for Queen Jane, Cornwallis hastened to London to confer with the Privy Council. On the way he ran into John Colby, a Marian agent, "quite by chance."[62] Colby claimed that he had just returned from London and that the populace did not support the Grey succession. He managed to convince Cornwallis to return to Ipswich and proclaim Mary. As Mary journeyed to Framlingham, Colby brought Cornwallis before her to do homage. Mary's reception of Cornwallis suggests both the importance of securing Ipswich for her cause and perhaps hints that Cornwallis did not switch to her side voluntarily. According to Wingfield, Mary "seemed to berate the man for being somewhat slow and stubborn and less mindful of his duty than he ought to have been despite the repeated requests of her letters."[63] Wingfield claims that only the intervention of one of Mary's most trusted household officers, Sir Henry Jerningham, spared Cornwallis further unspecified embarrassment, possibly imprisonment at Mary's hands.

Wingfield's narrative does not given any overt indication whether Thomas, Lord Wentworth, one of the leading magnates of East Anglia and head of Wingfield's own regional affinity, was brought to Mary's side through fair means or foul.[64] What Wingfield does admit was that Mary dispatched two of her servants, John Tyrrell and Edward Glemham with specific orders "to draw into her party Thomas Wentworth." Later Wingfield admitted that Tyrrell and Glemham had given Wentworth's "the queen's command." Given Wentworth's known Protestant sympathies and his insistence on proclaiming Jane as Queen in Ipswich, it is worth considering what possible means of persuasion Tyrrell and Glemham could have used to induce Wentworth to desert the Grey regime. Wingfield, as one of Wentworth's clients, was at pains to exonerate his patron by claiming that Wentworth was only following orders when he proclaimed Jane at Ipswich but that "his inner conscience constantly proclaimed that Mary had a greater right to the throne."[65] Perhaps.

There was another ready inducement available to Tyrrell and Glemham: the proximity of Mary's forces to Wentworth's Suffolk estates. Mary had waited until she was established in Framlingham, near the very center of the county, before she sent her agents after Wentworth. From Framlingham, Mary could threaten almost any estate in the county. At the time Mary's agents may have been threatening Wentworth on July 13, she posed much more of a threat to him than Northumberland would on learning of Wentworth's allegiance switch. Northumberland had not yet left London (which he did finally the next day). Mary's forces could raid Wentworth's estates long before Northumberland could reach him with reinforcements. If Northumberland did eventually prevail, then Wentworth could legitimately claim that he had little choice but to temporarily surrender to Mary in order to preserve his estates. Wentworth had much more to lose by not heeding Mary's (possible) threats.

The princess had selected Tyrrell and Glemham to deliver her "command" because they were among Wentworth's closest associates.[66] Perhaps she hoped that Wentworth would believe their testimony as to Mary's military strength and her intentions. If Wentworth did not believe Tyrrell and Glemham, then he might believe yet another of her household officers. Mary had dispatched one of her senior household officers, Sir Henry Jerningham to check on Tyrrell's and Glemham's progress with Wentworth.[67] Mary's decision to send Jerningham after Tyrrell and Glemham is an indication of just how complicated and delicate the situation was regarding Wentworth. Tyrrell and Glemham were close to Wentworth and so there was a risk that they themselves would be persuaded by Wentworth to switch allegiances rather than the other way around. Mary evidently sent Jerningham to ascertain the situation and, probably, to issue more dire threats against Wentworth if Tyrrell and Glemham had failed in their commission or gone over the other side. Mary's proximity and the growing number of her forces could certainly help to explain the quick success of Tyrrell and Glemham's commission.

Not only were Mary's agents prepared to resort to thuggish tactics to secure magnate support for their mistress, they were also on the alert for exploitable opportunities. On their way back from their meeting with Wentworth, Tyrrell and Glemham met Sir Henry Jerningham on July 14.[68] Jerningham informed them that he had along the way conferred with another of the princess' agents, Philip Williams, and learned that there were approximately half a dozen ships lying off the nearby harbor of Orwell. According to Williams, the crews of these ships were on the point of mutiny. Wingfield claims that the crews' discontent arose over the Grey succession but scholarship suggests that the crews were more concerned over poor conditions and lack of pay.[69] The end result was that Jerningham persuaded the crews to mutiny and declare for Mary. Jerningham had secured for his mistress royal ships "laden with soldiers and weaponry."[70] This was such a piece of good fortune that Jerningham insisted that the squadron leader accompany him back to Framlingham in order to personally inform Mary "of this happy and unexpected arrival to the queen."[71] Thus, Mary not only received an unlooked for windfall of naval support but more importantly weakened, if mainly on the symbolic level, the Privy Council war effort.

As if these considerable activities were not enough, Mary's agents also engaged in rumor-mongering and they opened up a second military front. I am persuaded by David Loades's speculation that when Mary's messengers proclaimed their mistress Queen, they did not hesitate to exaggerate the size of her forces or the level of support she enjoyed amongst the populace.[72] The rumor mill was particularly active during the crisis and logic suggests that the princess' servants were behind such damaging false reports such as the one that claimed she had already defeated and captured Northumberland's son and lieutenant, Lord Robert Dudley. The Imperial ambassadors, who reported that the Privy Council was shaken by the Robert Dudley rumor, also sent dispatches to Charles V indicating the court was feeding on (Marian?) disinformation exaggerating the size of her army.[73] The ambassadors themselves were duped by these rumors. Initially, Mary had attempted to keep the ambassadors informed but the speed of events and her own movements to Kenninghall and then Framlingham meant that she was unable to send word to them until later and then only to ask for Imperial troops.[74]

Around July 17, two of her servants, Sir Edward Hastings and Sir Edmund Peckham even organized an armed uprising on her behalf in Northamptonshire and Buckinghamshire, hoping to force Northumberland to split his forces as he made his way to Framlingham via Cambridgeshire.[75] Hastings's connection to Mary's household, if any, is unclear; he certainly acted as if he were one of her retainers because his support of Mary placed him at odds with his brother, Francis Hastings, earl of Huntingdon, ardent supporter of the Grey regime who was allied to the Grey family by marriage. Wingfield identified Peckham as one of Mary's servants. Wingfield reported that Northumberland began to despair when he heard of the Peckham/Hastings uprising. Rather than quelling what Northumberland considered a minor household insurrection, he now faced two simultaneous uprisings on either side of his advancing army. Within a couple of days of this new Marian uprising, Northumberland conceded defeat and himself proclaimed Mary as queen at Cambridge.

Mary's exploitation of her elite household and regional standing was in line with a long standing tradition of medieval lordship and regional affinity that remained current in sixteenth-century England. As recently as 1549, the earl of Arundel had suppressed rebellions against royal authority in Sussex, the location of his estates. Arundel performed his commission largely by mobilizing his household and affinity.[76] In Mary's cause, her household culture of reverence foreshadowed this display of deep commitment and unswerving loyalty by her household officers and non-resident affinity. Mary's household—resident staff and nonresident retainers—obeyed her in this as it had done so often before. Her staff risked their lives, their possessions and their freedom to help Mary make good her claim to the throne. If she had lost, then Mary's agents and officers would not have only had to answer to Northumberland and the Privy Council but also to the earl of Sussex, Sir Thomas Cornwallis, and Thomas, Lord Wentworth. Kidnapping an earl's son and threatening a local magnate were not the means to prolong one's life in mid-Tudor England. Unlike the Privy Council, Mary did not have the authority to muster national troops, she did not have a navy or access to the royal treasury. Nor did she have the support of the nobility, judges, and government ministers. What she did have, which Queen Jane apparently did not, were servants and agents prepared to risk everything on her behalf. As Wingfield put it: "they did not hesitate to face an untimely death for their queen."[77] Another important asset that Mary possessed and her rival did not was an affinity.

The most important of the commissions that Mary's household servants fulfilled were her orders to raise her affinity—her neighbors, tenants, leaseholders. Her gentry neighbors, in particular, functioned as informal household retainers, judging from their behavior during the succession crisis. Their support, arguably, was instrumental to Mary's eventual victory in that the commitment of her affinity to her cause bestowed on the princess the appearance of a popular mandate to assume sovereign authority.

Wingfield's narrative placed great emphasis on Mary's support amongst the East Anglian gentry. This is not surprising because Wingfield was himself a member of an established gentry family in Suffolk. To my knowledge, there is no evidence that contradicts Wingfield's assertions; scholars generally accept that the strength of Mary's following came from where her estates were located.[78] As her visits to Huddlestone and Burgh indicate, Mary's first impulse was to raise her affinity. She quickly dispatched messengers "to draw all the gentlemen of the surrounding countryside to do fealty to their sovereign."[79]

The list of those who first joined her at Kenninghall were almost exclusively magnates and gentry whose estates were near hers. Gentry from Norfolk and Suffolk like Sir Henry Bedingfield, Sir Richard Southwell, and Sir John Mordaunt were with Mary by July 12. Other gentry from these counties who responded quickly to Mary's call were Sir William Drury, Sir John Shelton, Clement Heigham, John Sulyard, Sir Edmund Peckham, and Sir John Huddleston. They all possessed estates in the same counties were Mary's lands were most densely clustered—Norfolk, Suffolk, and Essex. In fact, there was a sizable contingent of gentry supporters from nearby Mary's cluster on the east Suffolk/ south Norfolk border. Among them were: Sir Edward Rous; Owen Hopton; the aforementioned John Tyrrell; Thomas Steynings, formerly steward of the Howard estates centered on Framlingham; Francis Jermy; Alexander Newton; the aforementioned Edward Glemham; and Edward Mone.[80]

These local gentlemen did not simply bring themselves to Mary's service. When Mary arrived at Framlingham on the evening of July 12, Wingfield reported that there were "as many as possible of the local gentry and justices, together with a crowd of country folk" who had answered her summons. Edward Mone came to Mary "laden with the money that he had collected" as part of his duties as King Edward's tax collector, which he now offered to the princess. Many brought other family members: Bedingfield brought his brothers, Drury his son, John Brewse brought his brother. More importantly, men like Bedingfield and Southwell came to the princess "amply provided with money, provisions and armed men."[81] They brought their own retainers, tenants, and clients—their own affinities.

Mary was gathering together a gentry power base centered on her estates in east Suffolk and south Norfolk. It is in this context that her determination "to draw" Thomas, Lord Wentworth "into her party" should be seen. Wentworth's influence had been primarily responsible for Cornwallis's decision initially to proclaim Jane in Ipswich despite Mary's repeated orders to the contrary. Wentworth's extensive estates in Suffolk gave him the power to become, indeed he had already become during the crisis, a dangerous counterweight to Mary's sphere of influence in the county. The goal therefore, must be not simply to neutralize Wentworth but to win him over. When Wentworth finally made the decision to support Mary (or merely knuckled under her threats), he brought with him "a not inconsiderable military force."[82] Wentworth brought with him

over a dozen representatives of leading county gentry families in his train all
with their own retainers. Wingfield's narrative lingers over the list of Wentworth's followers: Sir Richard Cavendish, Sir Henry Doyle, Lionel Tollemache,
Edward Withipoll, John Southwell, Francis Nunn, and John Colby. These men
would never sit on the Privy Council nor hold government office of national
import, but they, along with other regional gentry, formed the foundation of
Mary's army. The harsh recruitment of Sussex was undertaken with similar
hopes of a gentry windfall. Holding his son as hostage, Mary was able to force
Sussex to not only refrain from lending his considerable support to the putative
Grey regime but to swell Mary's forces with his "cohort of both horsemen and
foot-soldiers."[83]

Mary's support was, of necessity, drawn mainly from her gentry affinity.
Other regional magnates had all signed Edward VI's "Device." Of the three
leading magnates which she did eventually recruit to her standard—the earls
of Bath and Sussex and Lord Wentworth—only Bath joined her voluntarily.
Significantly, John Bourchier, earl of Bath held estates which were near Mary's
Hunsdon. By right of his wife, Margaret Kitson, Bath held the impressive
manor of Hengrave Hall, which he made into his principal seat after his marriage.[84] Wingfield records that as Mary journeyed from Hunsdon to Kenninghall stopping off at Thetford, the earl of Bath met her and pledged his support. His knowledge of her whereabouts suggests that she summoned him to
her on her way from Hunsdon to Thetford.[85] Bath was the one magnate whose
proximity and behavior suggests that he served in an informal capacity as her
retainer. Like Sussex and Wentworth, Bath brought with him "a large band of
soldiers."

David Loades has persuasively argued that Mary thwarted the Edwardian
succession "because her affinity was strong enough to throw down an initial
challenge."[86] He identified her gentry support among her affinity as the element, which tipped the balance in Mary's favor. Loades also pinpointed the efforts of her household officers as ultimately responsible for the success of the
whole enterprise. My investigations into how Mary's household functioned, its
agenda and culture, the extent of her properties, and the still-important feudal
role of landlord/overlord supports Loades's argument. It also supports his suggestion that the suspiciously swift response of many of Mary's neighbors such as
Sir Henry Bedingfield and Sir Richard Southwell was evidence that they had
previously been alerted—most likely by Mary's servants—to ready their household retinues. Also, Mary was able to equip all of her many messengers with
proclamations suggesting they had been drafted beforehand in preparation. As
Loades observed: "It takes very careful organization to create such effective
spontaneity."[87] The king's illness was well known and the new succession an
open secret. The Framlingham grant suggests that Mary knew of the Edward-

ian succession plan since mid-April and therefore, had plenty of time to galvanize her household to make preparations should she decide to indulge in one of her favorite pastimes—gambling—by reneging on her deal with the Privy Council and challenging the Grey succession. This time, she was participating in high, indeed, the highest-stakes gambling risking her life, her properties, her status and those of her dependents and supporters.

Jennifer Loach has pointed out that those who initially supported Mary's bid were overwhelmingly Catholic. Protestant families within Mary's Norfolk affinity such as the Heydons and the L'Stranges did not answer her summons.[88] Loach emphasized that the propaganda issued by the Grey regime—proclamations, speeches, and letters—all emphasized Mary's traditionalist beliefs. Loach concludes that Mary herself was "not making the fatal error of which historians usually accuse her when she assumed that her triumph had proved that Catholicism was still a political force."[89]

The Protestantism of both Sussex and Wentworth accounted for their reluctance to join Mary's standard and helps to explain why she and her household/affinity felt it necessary to resort to force and threats of violence. As Loades argued, it was the quick response of Mary's affinity, which ensured her victory but, as Loach asserted, it was her Catholic affinity that initially answered her summons, whereas the more important Protestant holdouts, such as Wentworth and Sussex, had to be "persuaded." I would further argue that it was not just the Privy Council who stressed Mary's Catholicism but also her household propaganda machine. As Loach noted, Mary's traditional beliefs were shared by the majority of her subjects. It seems quite likely that along with exaggerating the size of Mary's forces, her "scouts," as Wingfield called her staff, also emphasized her Catholicism to those favorable to it while downplaying it to those who were not.[90]

Wingfield insisted on listing all the senior officers and other members of the household who had been especially active during the crisis because "it is unfitting to relegate to the obscurity of an unthankful silent the names of those to whom their country and their most gentle sovereign owe so much."[91] Wingfield is surely correct in his declaration that Mary owed her household a profound debt. When she asked them to sacrifice all in her cause in Kenninghall, they complied. They drafted proclamations, alerted her affinity, kidnapped nobles, posted her proclamations in hostile towns, spread rumors, encouraged mutiny on royal warships, carried her defiance to the Privy Council itself and through it all risked and endured imprisonment and depredations to their goods. Thus, Mary was elevated to the throne not just because of her blood, parliamentary legislation, or general support among the populace, but through the activities of her household staff on behalf of "their dearest princess."

ELIZABETH'S SHADOW COURT:
JULY 1553–NOVEMBER 1558

It is unfortunate for this study that I cannot devote equal space to the ways in which Elizabeth was able to utilize her household to effect her accession. Historical events contrived to limit Elizabeth's ability to fully exploit her position as head of a princely household. No sooner had Elizabeth left her teens—turning twenty in September 1553—and beyond doubt mature enough to rule her household and stabilize her estates than she found herself deprived of her household. Queen Mary suspected her sister's complicity in the Wyatt rebellion of January-February 1554 and imprisoned the princess throughout 1554 either in the Tower or under strict house arrest. Thereafter, Elizabeth was kept under less strict conditions but was not officially in command of her household until the end of Mary's reign in November 1558. Although Elizabeth's freedom of movement was more constricted than Mary's had been when she was Edward VI's heir, I argue that Elizabeth was still able to exploit the same household assets—display, corporate identity, and affinity—that Mary employed so successfully in the summer of 1553. Like her sister before her and despite her not being in technical command of her household, Elizabeth was able to draw on her household resources to ensure that there was a smooth transition of power from one queen to another—to continue the female succession.

As noted earlier, Elizabeth's actions during the succession crisis are difficult to pinpoint concretely. Her reversionary grants to Northumberland present good evidence that she, like Mary, initially colluded with the Grey succession plan. Mary's victory over the Grey regime was also a win for Elizabeth. With Mary's victory, Elizabeth was now incontestably the heir to the throne. She was now more than ever a figure of national significance. The princess wasted no time in demonstrating her grasp of her new status and her determination to exploit it through a display of household force. As Mary progressed toward London from Newhall in July 1553, Elizabeth entered London in anticipation of greeting Queen Mary at the city gates. She entered London on July 29, a couple of days before the queen's expected arrival. As the princess rode through the city streets on her way to her manor of Somerset Place, her household made quite an impression on the populace—doubtless the whole point of the exercise—as recorded by the diarist, Henry Machyn:

> The sam day cam rydyng thrugh London my lade Elysabeths grace, and thrugh Fletstreet, and so to my [lord of] Somersett('s) place that was, and yt ys my lade grasys [place; attended] with ij M horse, with speres and bowes and gunes, and odur [weapons and the cloth according to their qualities] . . . and spesyall sir John Wyl-

liam, sir John Brygys, master Chamb[urlain] all in gren gardyd with whytt welvett saten taffaty.[92]

Two days later, Machyn reported that "rod thrugh London my lade Elysabeth to Algatt, and so to the qwens grace her sester, with a M1. hors with a C. velvett cotes."[93]

The significance of this household display of military force becomes apparent in Camden's biography of Elizabeth. He cut the number by more than half of Elizabeth's household retainers from the figure quoted by Machyn. Camden also justifies the display and thereby highlights its controversial aspect: "MARY proclaimed Queene through all parts of *England,* who comming toward the Citie of *London* with an Armie, ELIZABETH (not to bee wanting, her Sisters cause and hers being yet disquieted) went accompanied with fiue hundred Horse to meet her vpon the way."[94] In actuality, the "cause" had been decided for almost two weeks. Thus, Camden's declaration that Elizabeth's forces were there to aid Mary's bid for the throne was either the result of his confusion over the progress of the crisis or an attempt to gloss over some of the more aggressive implications of Elizabeth's household retinue.

If Elizabeth's armed household was not strictly necessary from a military viewpoint then the logical conclusion was that she was making an unsubtle and highly public statement about her new status as heir to the throne. Elizabeth was flexing her household muscle to impress on onlookers that she was a person of consequence second only to the Queen. Just as her sister had, Elizabeth was prepared to take the throne by force should anyone challenge her claims.

It is unlikely that Elizabeth intended to upstage or embarrass Mary appears to have been concerned about Elizabeth's household display. Although Queen Mary greeted Elizabeth's senior household officers with overt affection (probably paying special attention to those who had served in combined household she shared with Elizabeth in 1530s), she, nevertheless, issued a spate of proclamations the very next day ordering a general disarmament.[95] She commanded that all soldiers, "other than such as arre by specyall commandemente appoyntede to attende uppon the Quenes Highnes' person," to return home.[96] The Queen ordered that certain noblemen now London to disperse their household forces. Elizabeth was not named in any of these proclamations but nor were her forces exempted under the "specyall commandemente" designation. Under the terms of the proclamations, Elizabeth would have to disband her household retinue. Queen Mary had, in fact, already issued a similar proclamation on July 21.[97] There should have been no need to issue another such proclamation after less than ten days of issuing the first one. It is hard to avoid the conclusion that Mary's decision to reissue the earlier proclamation the very day after she was confronted with her heir's impressive household army was aimed specifically at Elizabeth.

Whatever Elizabeth's intentions, it was a risky undertaking to display her household forces to a monarch who had just successfully taken the throne through her own exhibition of household might. From this time, Queen Mary would demonstrate an acute sensitivity toward Princess Elizabeth's household. Before the year was out, around the end of November, Queen Mary admitted to the Imperial ambassador that she did not like to think of Elizabeth succeeding her because the princess' household was staffed by Protestants.[98] This was an ominous statement that presaged a campaign of government harassment of Elizabeth and her household from February 1554 until, with varying degrees of intensity, the end of the reign in November 1558. Throughout, Elizabeth's role as head of household and landowner was under hostile crown scrutiny.

An instance of Mary's keen interest in the activities of Elizabeth and her household occurred in the wake of the Wyatt rebellion. In January 1554, Sir Thomas Wyatt led a rebellion against Queen Mary in response to her announcement that she would marry Prince Philip of Spain. In February, Wyatt was arrested after nearly taking London. The government suspected Elizabeth not only had prior knowledge of the plot but may have been one of the conspirators since Wyatt confessed that the aim of the rebellion was replace Queen Mary with the princess. Among the charges leveled against Elizabeth was that she had placed her residences on alert on Wyatt's warning. Specifically, the government interrogators focused on reports that Elizabeth had fortified one of her manors, Donnington. During an interrogation in the Tower, the princess had an exchange with Stephen Gardiner, bishop of Winchester (Queen Mary's chief minister) which has become famous through dissemination in popular biographies of Elizabeth. The original source of the story is Foxe who probably derived it from the testimony of one of Elizabeth's servants. Significantly for this study, Gardiner's investigation hinged on the state of Elizabeth's manors and her rights as a property owner:

[Gardiner and the Privy Council] examined her of the talke that was at Ashridge, betwyxte her and Syr James Acroft [one of the rebels], concerning her remouing from thence to Donnington castel, requiring her to declare what shee ment thereby. At the fyrste, she beyng so sodaynlye asked, dyd not well remember any such house but within a whyle, wel aduisiyng her self, she sayd: In dede (quoth she) I do nowe remember that I haue suche a place. But I neuer laye in it in all my lyfe. And as for any that hath moued me therunto I do not remember . . . [Gardiner brings in Croft and Elizabeth says she has nothing to say to him] And as concerning my going vnto Donnington Castel, I do remember that mayster Hoby and mine officers, and you, Syr James Acrofte had such talke: but is that to the purpose, my Lordes, but that I may go to my owne houses at al times.[99]

Elizabeth's biographers have included this episode as a demonstration of the princess' quick-thinking. Having temporarily dropped the ball with the patently unconvincing statement that she did not remember owning a place called Donnington, she then recovered and asserted that as a property owner, there was nothing sinister in and of itself in scheduling a visit to any of her manors. What is especially important for this study is that Elizabeth's position as head of household and landowner both provided her with exploitable opportunities and furnished evidence against her. Although her fortifications of Donnington had provided suspicious indications that she was in league with Wyatt, it was her role as head of household, which helped preserve her status whilst she answered government interrogators in the Tower.

Foxe again is the source of another interesting episode that has rarely found its way into the narratives of the legion of Elizabeth's biographers. Perhaps, its mundane focus on how to properly serve food to a princess has failed to excite much interest in modern readers. For the purposes of this study, it is Foxe's concern with how Elizabeth's servants campaigned to see that their mistress received service due to an heir to the throne that makes it worth quoting at length here:

> . . . that daye or there aboutes, diuers of her own officers . . . [requested the Lord Lieutenant of the Tower] to geue such order that her viands [food] might at al tymes be brought in by them which were appointed therunto. Yea syrs, sayd he, who appointed you this office? They answered, her graces Cou[n]sel. Counsel (quoth he), there is none of the[m] which hath to do, either in that case, or any thing else with in this place: and I assure you, for that shee is a prisoner, she shal be serued with the Lieutenauntes men as other the prisoners are. Wherat the gentlemen [of Elizabeth's household] sayd that they trused for more fauour at hys handes, considering her personage . . . [100]

According to Foxe, Elizabeth's servants successfully maintained her status as heir to the throne at a time when she was, officially, a prisoner of the state on suspicion of treason. By preventing Tower officials from employing their own "common" servants from waiting on Elizabeth, her staff ensured that the princess literally received special treatment. Moreover, her staff insisted that their authority derived from their position as members of her household Privy Council, which the Tower constable properly claimed had little authority within the Tower itself. Foxe, nevertheless, claimed that the crown upheld the authority of Elizabeth's servants to regulate her environment.

In essence, there were two parallel authoritarian structures within the Tower thanks to the efforts of Elizabeth's household staff. There was the traditional establishment of the lieutenant of the Tower and his staff and now also that of the Princess Elizabeth and her staff. This was unusual. Even noble prisoners had to petition the Privy Council to have just one of their household servants attend them in the Tower or to have the Tower officials prepare special meals for health considerations.[101] In contrast, Elizabeth's staff had so established their authority (according to Foxe) that they were able to defy the Lieutenant himself and refuse his order that his cook serve Elizabeth's food. Only "her own sworne men" were worthy enough to serve the heir to the throne.

There is some corroboration of Foxe's depiction in the correspondence of the princess' subsequent jailer, Sir Henry Bedingfield. Bedingfield escorted Elizabeth from the Tower in April 1554 to the manor of Woodstock. Shortly after her arrival, the princess' staff began immediately agitating that the house be outfitted to properly reflect her position as heiress presumptive. On May 27, Bedingfield complained to the Privy Council that: "Cornwallys, the gentleman usher, dydde move me to assente that the cloth off estate sholde by hanged upp for hyr grace, wherunto I directlye sayde naye tyll yor lordeshipps plesures were known therin."[102] Elizabeth's servants considered that she was entitled to the cloth of estate as a material expression of her place in the succession. The crown's response to this request has not survived.

According to Bedingfield, Elizabeth's servants were not just interested in maintaining the princess' status as heir but also as head of household and property owner. As already noted, Elizabeth's household refused to disband during the princess' incarceration. Not only did the household remain intact and menacingly nearby but also it continued to function as the administrative headquarters for managing her properties. On May 28, the Privy Council authorized a Mr. Smith to visit Elizabeth to discuss one of her properties because it "doth moche importe hym to speke wth the ladye Elizabeth."[103] The biggest thorn in Bedingfield's side was Thomas Parry. As Elizabeth's cofferer, Bedingfield despaired that he was unable to "avoyde by enye possible mene, butte that daylye & howerlye the sayde Parye maye have & gyve intelligence" on nefarious "enterprises" both to and from Elizabeth by virtue of his necessary daily contact with his mistress. Parry's anonamalous status as Elizabeth's senior household officer, meant that he enjoyed nearly unrestricted freedom of movement even though the princess was herself under house arrest. This rendered him, according to Bedingfield, "wonderouselye fytte to dooe theys enterp[ri]ses yff he be disposed thereto."[104]

Not only were Elizabeth's servants exploiting the situation to their and the princess' advantage, keeping her informed of events and smuggling in forbidden books, and so on, but Elizabeth herself agitated to gain recognition as mistress of princely household.[105] She claimed, through Thomas Parry, that she needed authority to issue her own warrants in order to see her household adequately supplied with venison. Parry supported her in this by claiming that the keeper of Enfield Park refused to recognize the order that did not come from Elizabeth herself. The Privy Council denied Elizabeth's request to issue warrants in her own name; she was a state prisoner whose legal status was, at best, unclear.[106] Elizabeth campaigned, again unsuccessfully, to chose her own servants to replace the queen's agents who staffed Woodstock.[107] When Bedingfield pointed out that, officially, he was the governor of her household and thus "appointed there to be one of her officers," the princess snapped: "From such officers good lord deliuer me."[108]

Foxe related an episode involving one of Elizabeth's many attempts to assert her household authority and Bedingfield's stiff resistance. Again, it is worth quoting at some length, as it illustrates the convergence of status and household authority and how Elizabeth considered herself humiliated by her inability to deploy her own servants on even mundane errands:

> . . . and standinge by her while she wrote (whiche he [Bedingfield] straightly obserued) all wayes she being wery, would carry away her letters, and bring them agayn when shee called for them. In the finishing therof, he wold haue bene messenger to the quene of the same whose request her grace denied saying, one of her owne men should cary them, and that she would neither truste him, nor none of his therabouts. Then he answering againe said: none of them durst be so bolde he trowed to cary her letters being in that case. Yes quod she, I am assured, I haue none so dishonest, that would deny my request in that behalfe, but willbe as willing to serue me now as before. Well, sayd he, my commission is to the contrary, and may not so suffer it . . . [109]

This quote contains an interesting instance of the correlation between household authority and political standing. When Bedingfield claims that none of Elizabeth's servants will dare to carry her letters to the queen, he is declaring that the princess' political disgrace is so complete that her servants are reluctant to be identified, especially in London, as members of her household. This prompted a hot denial from Elizabeth that her servants are not distancing themselves from their positions as her staff, they are not "dishonest." Bedingfield's accusation also elicited another angry rejection of his services as her officer.

Given the ceaseless efforts of her household and of the princess herself to have her status as heir to the throne and householder recognized and maintained, Bedingfield found his assignment nearly impossible to fulfill. Within a few months, in August, he wrote the council begging to be relieved of duty.[110] It was extremely difficult to keep Elizabeth under strict house arrest while also allowing her to remain a property owner with an attendant household so that she could pay the costs of her household and that of her jailer as well. The princess and her officers clearly exploited the situation whenever they could.

Although the queen was unhappy over the prospect of Elizabeth succeeding her, she does not appear to have had any interest in reducing the princess' status as a landowner and householder. Queen Mary could have certainly deprived Elizabeth of some of her lands or proposed unequal exchanges such as Edward VI had initially done with Princess Mary in late 1552. In fact, the queen seems to have colluded with Elizabeth's servants in maintaining her status. Among her initial instructions to Bedingfield was the warning that he was to carry out his duties as jailer "in suche goode & honorable sorte as maye be agreable to or honor and hir [Elizabeth's] estate & degree."[111] Evidently, the queen's policy was to deprive Elizabeth of the opportunity to fully exploit the resources of her princely household—no more household armies, fortified castles, or resident devoted servants—but not of her administrative headquarters to collect revenues and supply the household.

The motivations for this policy were mostly economical and, to a lesser degree, political and personal. Elizabeth was paying for her imprisonment not just in political currency but also in literal currency. Because Bedingfield and his brothers and their personal servants were technically now members of her household, Elizabeth must pay for their room and board, much to Thomas Parry's disgust.[112] Of course, Elizabeth was still responsible for her own servants who had set up headquarters at the nearby inn. Allowing Elizabeth to keep her lands meant that she had the means to bankroll her own imprisonment.

The political situation provided further incentive to refrain from depriving Elizabeth entirely of her household and property. Mary's continued childlessness and the 1544 Act of Succession meant that Elizabeth was heir to the throne. Having fought herself to uphold the Act, Mary was unwilling to publicly sponsor any serious moves to repeal it.[113] She was even willing to allow Elizabeth something of her princely estate through her household but, ostensibly, shorn of much of its military and political power.

Finally, it is important not to lose sight that Mary and Elizabeth had enjoyed cordial relations until Mary's accession. Mary's reluctance to condone extreme action against her sister, her concern that Elizabeth be well treated, and her unwillingness to deprive the princess of her estates is not too surprising considering their blood ties and formerly good relationship. The evidence suggests that Mary wished to contain and neutralize the destabilizing potential which Elizabeth, as the legal heir, represented rather than to permanently remove her from the succession other than by means of Mary producing an heir of her own body.

Whatever the motivation, the crown's decision not to deprive Elizabeth of her estates and the actions of both the princess and her servants to exploit this meant that she was virtually unimprisonable. As a landowner, Elizabeth had to maintain some kind of household to serve as an administrative center even while she herself was under house arrest. This, in turn, necessitated that she consult regularly with her treasurer. It also provided an excuse for her household to remain constituted even if separated from her physically. This allowed her servants to agitate on her behalf, to bring her contraband books and correspondence, to ensure simply by wearing her livery on errands that the public did not forget her status as heir. Those few servants allowed to reside with Elizabeth took full advantage of the situation to insist that the princess receive preferential treatment and the material trappings of royalty. Like her sister, Elizabeth benefitted from the corporate household which, in part, derived its identity from her. This corporate identity motivated her servants to take such actions as they could to maintain her public image as heir apparent and head of a princely household. Without her household and estates, Elizabeth would likely have faced a stricter imprisonment and a much more complete political eclipse. Elizabeth's household ensured that Mary's policy of containment would enjoy, at best, only limited success.

Bedingfield's warning that Thomas Parry could convey "intelligence" to the princess is an indication that Elizabeth's servants were performing yet another important function for their mistress: maintaining her political network. As detailed later, Elizabeth continued to reach out to leading politicians during Mary's reign as she had done in Edward's. Again, her household provided the safe context in which to do this. The difference now was that Elizabeth was doing more than acquiring useful political contacts; she was recruiting for her future administration. As Queen Mary's childlessness continued and her health deteriorated, it became increasingly clear that a new succession was imminent. The succession crisis of 1553, however, meant that it was unwise for the princess or her servants to assume that her accession would receive no challenge. Accordingly, Elizabeth's princely household performed one last but vital service for her: they alerted her affinity to be ready to defend the princess' accession by military force.

As Mary lay dying in November 1558, her husband, Philip II of Spain, dispatched Gómez Suárez de Figueroa, Count de Feria as a special envoy to protect Spanish interests during the upcoming transfer of power and to remain as a resident ambassador. He arrived on November 9 and quickly concluded that, as far as Mary was concerned, there was no hope of her recovery.[114] On his initial arrival, Feria noted that the privy councilors were extremely nervous regarding the way that Elizabeth would treat them once she became queen. Nevertheless, Feria already understood that at least one, Sir John Mason was a "gran fauorido de Madama Ysabel" who was known to keep the princess informed on Privy Council deliberations.[115] The next day, November 10, Feria visited Elizabeth and quickly learned that the princess had suborned more than just Sir John Mason, she had a transition team in place preparing for her imminent accession.

Feria found Elizabeth staying at Brockett's Hall, the home of her tenant, Sir John Brockett. Feria immediately noted the presence in the house of Elizabeth Fitzgerald Fiennes, Lady Clinton, the wife of Admiral Clinton. She was apparently visiting and was invited, along with Feria, to dine with the princess. The political hospitality on offer was successful as Feria confessed that he thoroughly enjoyed himself.[116] During what Feria considered to be an unsettling interview afterward, Elizabeth readily admitted that she had been in contact with most of the important noble and political figures of the day and they had all sent assurances of their loyalty. Feria evidently could see for himself that all the Protestant nobility and gentry had already flocked to Elizabeth.[117] Among them, according to Feria, were: Francis Russell, Earl of Bedford; Lord Robert Dudley; Sir Nicholas Throckmorton; Sir Peter Carew; and John Harrington (who had married one of Elizabeth's privy chamber women, Isabella Markham). As far as Feria was concerned, they were all either heretics or traitors. They were certainly all Protestant and had all been involved in either the Grey succession or in the Wyatt and Dudley rebellions in Mary's reign.

It was clear to Feria that Elizabeth's support was not merely drawn from those who opposed the Marian regime. According to Feria, the princess knew everyone of importance in the kingdom.[118] Feria then named specific ministers in Elizabeth's pocket and it was an impressive list. The chancellor, Nicholas Heath, bishop of Worcester; William Paget, Lord Privy Seal; Sir William Petre, Secretary; Dr. Nicholas Wotton, former ambassador to France and now one of the commissioners at Cercamp negotiating for a peace with France; Edward Fiennes, Lord Admiral Clinton who was keeping Elizabeth informed of events in Germany; William Lord Howard of Effingham former Lord Admiral and currently a privy councilor; William, Lord Grey de Wilton captain of Guisnes and [although at the time of the Feria visit, he was currently a prisoner of war]; Thomas Ratcliffe, Earl of Sussex (older brother of the lord whom Mary had kidnapped), lord deputy of Ireland.[119] In fact, she had more allies than Feria realized. Two the earls of Arundel and Pembroke—whom Feria specifically claimed were not part of Elizabeth's circle would, in fact, receive appointments to her Privy Council within weeks of her accession suggesting that, unbeknown to Feria, they had been in contact with the princess before Queen Mary's death. These two earls were well worth cultivating. Henry FitzAlan, Earl of Arundel, was, at the time of the Feria interview, Lord Steward, privy councilor, and commissioner at Cercamp. William Herbert, Earl of Pembroke, was currently serving as a privy councilor, captain-general of English contingent at St. Quentin, and lord president of the council in Marches of Wales.[120]

Those whom Feria named as hostile to Elizabeth, in fact, indicate just how far the princess had spread her net. These men were Thomas Thirlby, Edward

Hastings, Sir Thomas Cornwallis and Cardinal Pole. There is a hint in the Feria dispatch that their exclusion from Elizabeth's network was more by their own choice rather than the princess'. When Feria questioned her about Pole, Elizabeth claimed that her hostility toward Pole resulted from his refusal to enter into negotiations with her by sending an envoy to her: "Díxome que nunca el cardenal la auía embiado a visitar ni a dezir ninguna cosa hast aora."[121] It was not Elizabeth who shut the door initially but Pole and possibly it was also the same story with Thirlby, Hastings, and Cornwallis. These men—Cardinal Pole especially—were particularly devoted to Mary, and two, Hastings and Cornwallis, had escorted Elizabeth to London in February 1554 to face years of imprisonment. Despite this, Elizabeth's comment about Pole being the one who was unwilling to come to terms suggests that she was reaching out to anyone, no matter her past relations with them, in order to ensure her smooth accession.

The "point man" for this remarkable network was one of Elizabeth's nonresident household officers, Sir William Cecil, her surveyor. He was also currently a government secretary if no longer principal secretary as he had been under Edward VI. Cecil was in a position to contact the aforementioned privy councilors on Elizabeth's behalf just as he had done for her during Edward's reign. He was also connected to the Protestant nobility, serving as the earl of Bedford's steward in 1557 while the earl fought in France. In the days leading up to Elizabeth's accession, he was in negotiations with Chancellor Heath over what role the latter would play in the new regime.[122] Feria already understood by November 10, well before Queen Mary's death, that Cecil would assume the post of principal secretary on Elizabeth's accession.[123] It would have been easy for Cecil to discreetly solicit support for Elizabeth's accession in early November at the muted court of the dying queen. Envoys, such as the one that the princess had expected from Pole, would have been directed by Cecil to Elizabeth's current residence to deliver the verbal allegiance of their masters and mistresses.

If Cecil was in charge, primarily, for securing political support for Elizabeth's accession, her cofferer, Thomas Parry ensured that the princess would receive military support should her accession be challenged. The setting of Feria's interview, Brockett's Hall, was the clue. J. E. Neale uncovered evidence that Thomas Parry was coordinating projected military operations from Brockett Hall.[124] Because confirmation of military support often came in writing, Elizabeth's residency at Brockett's Hall would ensure that whatever incriminating documents arrived would remain at Brockett's Hall rather than one of Elizabeth's own residences in the increasingly unlikely event that Mary recovered. From late October through early November, Parry solicited support from regional gentry like Sir John Thynne. Neale argued that Thynne's correspondence during these weeks, while not specifically mentioning military forces, were indications that Thynne was alerting his Wiltshire retainers to be on stand-by in case military action was necessary. This is supported by a 1592 letter from Thomas Markham to Cecil referring back those weeks in late 1558 when Markham led a band of three hundred footmen at Berwick. Markham claimed that he had been instructed by Parry to "leave his own band with such other captains as he could trust to be in readiness with their bands likewise to serve the maintenance of her [Elizabeth's] royal estate and dignity."[125] Markham claimed that he arrived at Brockett Hall in late 1558 with signed undertakings promising the aid of ten thousand men. It is likely that Parry had secured, for Princess Elizabeth, a much more broad-based support than Princess Mary had enjoyed in 1553. It was not simply Elizabeth's household affinity that Parry was utilizing but rather he was preparing to muster troops throughout the land, even as far away as Berwick on the Scottish border, to support the princess' accession. In the event, Parry did not need to call out these troops. Cecil's groundwork was enough to guarantee Elizabeth's easy accession. Within hours of Mary's death on November 17, Chancellor Heath announced Elizabeth's accession to Parliament.[126]

The actions of Princess Elizabeth's household during Queen Mary's reign were perhaps less dramatic than Princess Mary's during the succession crisis but they were just as crucial in accomplishing the second half of the female succession. Elizabeth's household was instrumental in maintaining her political profile during her imprisonment. Her servants insisted that government officials acknowledge her status as heir to the throne through such seemingly prosaic things as food service and household decor. As a landowner, Elizabeth was allowed to retain her household in order to administer her lands.

The result was that the Marian policy of isolating and containing Elizabeth could not be successfully carried out. Bedingfield was powerless to prevent Parry from conveying information to Princess Elizabeth or from her during their daily consultations. Because he could not forbid contact between the princess and her senior officers without jeopardizing the efficient management of a household on which he himself was dependent, Bedingfield could not completely isolate Elizabeth from her friends and allies who could contact her through Parry and her other household staff. It was also Parry who prepared for military action in the days before her accession. Cecil, associated with Elizabeth's household since 1548, practically guaranteed her smooth succession by preemptively soliciting the allegiance of the leading magnates and politicians of the realm.

Although Mary and Elizabeth used their preaccession households in very different ways, the result—the female succession—was the same. Princess Mary probably initially deceived the Privy Council over her acquiescence to the Grey succession and then relied on her household and affinity to actively oppose its efforts to crown Jane Grey as queen. Princess Elizabeth's strategy was quite different. During Queen Mary's reign, Elizabeth continued her previous policy of securing allies on the Privy Council she had begun during Edward's reign. She used her household contacts not to oppose the Privy Council but bring them around to supporting her accession. Elizabeth's household prepared for the possibility of military action but it had already obtained the necessary political support to guarantee her accession. The princess was able, through her household, to recruit many of the leading figures of her future regime. Thanks to her household, when Elizabeth assumed sovereign authority, she could count on ready-made friends and allies to help her govern. In the final days of Mary's reign, Elizabeth's household had functioned as a shadow court which easily translated into a royal court on her accession.

These different strategies were successful in accomplishing the female succession because of their reliance on the three main assets of an elite household: display, corporate identity, and property. Princess Mary's decision to remove to Framlingham, which placed her and her army within closer proximity to enemy troops and Princess Elizabeth's armed household retinue that greeted Queen Mary outside London gates were architectural and military expressions of household display. This display, in both cases, was intended to make manifest the princesses' royal status and sovereign potential. The devotion of their household servants was instrumental, in Mary's case, in completing the often risky and sometimes unpleasant tasks necessary to win a throne from a regime in command of all the crown resources. Elizabeth's staff so strongly identified with their mistress and with the household that they had created that they remained constituted, well beyond what was strictly necessary, as Bedingfield pointed out, during her incarceration. Elizabeth's role as a landowner helped to provide some justification for her household to remain constituted. Princess Mary's role as overlord and neighbor enabled her to call out an affinity sufficiently large enough to turn the tide in her favor during the succession crisis of 1553.

Both princesses needed different resources to accomplish their accessions: Mary required a military power base to challenge the Grey succession and a reverential following willing to risk their lives and possessions in her cause. Elizabeth needed a household independent enough to agitate on her behalf even without the benefit of her leadership and thus, prevent her complete political eclipse during Queen Mary's reign. Moreover, Elizabeth was able to exploit the household's reputation for Protestantism to solicit the allegiance of leading politicians and nobles who were also her co-religionists. This helped to helped to ensure a smooth transfer of power from the Marian regime to hers. Both found the necessary resources to accomplish the female succession in their preaccession households.

NOTES

1. Loades, *Tragicall History*, p. 97

2. *CPR*, V, pp. 176–177

3. *CSP Edward VI*, 590; Elton, *Reform and Reformation*, p. 356

4. Elton, *Reform and Reformation*, p. 357

5. *CSP, Edward VI, Domestic*, 778

6. *CSP Edward VI*, 777. See also, APC, IV, 188

7. Loades, p. 139

8. Harris, *English Aristocratic Women . . .* , p. 203

9. Palliser, *The Age of Elizabeth*, p. 89

10. *CPR*, IV, p. 134

11. Loades, *Mary Tudor*, p. 139

12. *CPR*, V, 1553, pp. 97–99

13. *CPR*, V, pp. 176–177

14. D. MacCulloch, " 'Vain, Proud, Foolish Boy': The Earl of Surrey and the Fall of the Howards," from *Rivals in Power*, ed. D. Starkey [London, 1990], p. 111

15. APC, II, p. 17 as quoted and cited in E. W. Ives, "Henry VIII's Will: The Protectorate Provisions of 1546–7," *The Historical Journal*, 37/4 (1994), p. 903

16. The following chronology and reaction to Edward's illness is from Loach, *Edward VI*, pp. 162–169

17. Jordan, *Edward VI: The Threshold of Power*, pp. 200–256

18. Loach, *Edward VI*, p. 164

19. Elton, *Reform and Reformation*, p. 374; Prescott, *Mary Tudor*, pp. 163,165; Starkey, *Elizabeth*, p. 116.

20. Prescott, p. 160

21. *CSP, Spanish*, X, pp. 124–135

22. Prescott, pp. 163, 165

23. D. MacCulloch, *Thomas Cranmer* [Yale UP, 1996], p. 538

24. As noted in the diary of a London undertaker, Henry Machyn. *The Diary of Henry Machyn, Citizen and Merchant-Taylor of London, From A.D. 1550 to A.D. 1563*, ed. J. G. Nichols [London, 1847] , p. 32; hereafter cited as "Machyn"

25. As noted by Loach, *Edward VI*, p. 161

26. Bindoff, "A Kingdom at Stake 1553," p. 648; Elton, *Reform*, p. 375; Loach, *Edward VI*, p. 170

27. Harris, *English Aristocratic Women . . .* , p. 141

28. Loach, *Edward VI*, p. 165

29. For Mary's visit (though not the reason for visit or possible topics for discussions), see Machyn, p. xlii, as noted in Loach, *Edward VI*, p. 159, fn. 1

30. Machyn, p. 32

31. R.Wingfield, *Vita Mariae Reginae* ed. D. MacCulloch, from Camden Miscellany, XXVIII, 4th ser. [London, 1984], p. 261

32. Prescott, p. 168

33. *Vita*, p. 247

34. *Vita*, p. 249

35. *CPR*, V, p. 171

36. *CSP, Edward VI, Domestic*, 804

37. On the eve of her accession, Elizabeth claimed that her landed revenues had never been adequate to her expenses; M. J. Rodgríguez-Salgado and S. Adams, "The Count of Feria's Dispatch to Philip II of 14 November 1558," *Camden Miscellany*, 4th ser., vol. 28 [London, 1984]. Hereafter "FD" for Feria Dispatch

38. W. Camden, *Annales the true and royall history of the famous empresse Elizabeth, Queene of England* . . . [London, 1625], p. 28; accessible at http://gateway.proquest .com/openurl?ctx_ver=Z39.88-2003&res_id=xri:eebo&rft_id=xri:eebo:citation: 99843074

39. Pictures of Framlingham can be accessed at http://www.framlingham.com/ visit/framlinghamcastle/framlinghamcastle.html

40. Loades, p. 177; Loach, p. 171

41. *Vita*, p. 255

42. Kenninghall, like Framlingham, had recently been remodeled by the Duke of Norfolk before his imprisonment in 1546. Macculloch, "Vain," p. 111

43. *Vita*, p. 251

44. *Vita*, p. 262

45. *Vita*, p. 270

46. *Ibid.*

47. See discussion in ch.3

48. *Vita*, p. 271

49. Loades, pp. 184–188

50. Machyn, p. 38

51. *Chronicle*, p. 14. The chronicler estimated that Mary's household retinue of footmen numbered no more than 740

52. *Vita*, p. 271

53. *Vita*, p. 252

54. *Vita*, p. 253

55. *Ibid.*

56. *Vita*, pp. 255–256

57. *Vita*, p. 269

58. *Vita*, p. 254

59. *Vita*, p. 254

60. *Vita*, p. 254. My italics

61. *CSP Spanish* XI, p. 80

62. *Vita*, p. 256. Colby does not appear on any household lists or accounts. He probably was not a resident member of Mary's household. His efforts on Mary's behalf as detailed in this incident suggest that he was, like Bedingfield and Southwell for example, an informal household retainer

63. *Vita*, p. 256

64. For Wingfield's status as one of Wentworth's followers, see the Introduction to *Vita*, p. 186

65. *Vita*, pp. 257–259

66. *Vita*, p. 297, fn.37

67. *Vita*, p. 258

68. *Ibid.*

69. J. D. Alsop, "A Regime at Sea: the Navy and the 1553 Succession Crisis," *Albion*, XXIV (1992): 577–590

70. *Vita*, pp. 258–259

71. *Vita*, pp. 258–259

72. Loades, p. 180, fn. 1

73. *CSP Spanish, XI*, 86

74. Prescott, p. 165, 170

75. *Vita*, pp. 252, 260

76. Lawrence Stone, "Patriarchy and Paternalism in Tudor England: The Earl of Arundel and the Peasants Revolt of 1549," *Journal of British Studies* 13/2 (May, 1974), pp. 19–23

77. *Vita*, p. 253

78. Loades, pp. 176–179; Loach, *Edward VI*, pp. 172–178; A. Whitelock and D. Mac-Culloch, "Princess Mary's Household and the Succession Crisis, July 1553," *The Historical Journal*, 50/2 (2007), pp. 265–287

79. *Vita*, p. 253

80. *Vita*, p. 257 and p. 296, fns. 33, 34

81. *Vita*, p. 254

82. *Vita*, p. 259

83. *Vita*, p. 257

84. J. Gage, *The History and Antiquities of Hengrave in Suffolk* [London, 1822], p. 124.

85. *Vita*, p. 257 and p .296, fn. 35

86. Loades, p. 183

87. Loades, pp. 176–177

88. Loach, *Edward VI*, p. 176

89. Loach, *Edward VI*, p. 179

90. *Vita*, p. 260

91. *Vita*, p. 252

92. Machyn, p. 37

93. Machyn, p. 38

94. Italics original; Camden, *Annales*, [1625], p. 28; accessed at http://eebo.chadwyck.com.proxy.lib.utk.edu:90/search/fulltext?ACTION=ByID&ID=D000009984307 40000&WARN=N&FILE=../session/1186609084_28701&DISPLAY=ALPHA

95. Machyn, p. 38

96. *APC*, vol. IV, p. 306; July 30, 1553;"other that" in the original

97. *APC*, IV, pp. 300–301

98. *CSP, Spanish, XI*, 395

99. Foxe, 1563, sig.1712r–v

100. Foxe, [1563], sig.1712v

101. *E.g. APC*, IV, pp. 331, .332, 344, 346; *CSP, Mary*, 756

102. BP, p. 163

103. BP, p. 167

104. BP, p. 176

105. BP, 161

106. BP, pp. 184, 188

107. BP, pp. 169, 184, 189, 205

108. Foxe, [1563], sig.1714r, 1729; available at .

109. Foxe, [1563], sig.1714r; p. 1729; available at http://www.hrionline.ac.uk/johnfoxe/main/12_1563_1729.jsp

110. BP, p. 206

111. BP, p. 158, dated May 31, 1554

112. BP, pp. 176, 180

113. The Spanish ambassador reported that Gardiner tendered a bill to the effect of excluding Elizabeth from the succession but there is no corroborating evidence to support this, no indication in the parliamentary registers or minutes; *CSP, Spanish*, XIII, 131

114. FD

115. FD, pp. 319, 329

116. FD, p. 330

117. FD, pp. 320–321

118. FD, p. 322

119. FD, pp. 331–332

120. FD, p. 340

121. FD, p. 322; "She told me that the Cardinal had never sent an envoy to visit her."

122. BL Cotton Vespasian F. XIII, f. 287 as cited in FD, p. 339, fn. 12

123. FD, p. 323

124. J. E. Neale, "The Accession of Queen Elizabeth I," first published in *History Today* (Coronation Issue), May 1953 and subsequently reprinted in *The Age of Catherine de Medici and Essays in Elizabethan History* [London, 1958; 1963], pp. 131–144. Citations from this article refer to the reprinted version in *The Age* . . .

125. As quoted in Neale, "Accession," p. 135

126. Neale, "Accession," pp. 138–142

CONCLUSION

The Female Succession, Elite Households, and Further Research

Although the 1544 Act of Succession mandated that should Edward VI die childless his half-sisters, Mary and Elizabeth, should succeed him, there was no enforcement mechanism. After the passage of this act, after its reluctant acknowledgment in Henry's will, there was no guarantee that the female succession would take place should Edward die without issue. Indeed, Edward himself attempted to bar the princesses from the throne. Interestingly, Edward nominated another woman, Jane Grey, to succeed him. Jane Grey had the nomination of the king, the support of most of ruling elite including her father-in-law, John Dudley, Duke of Northumberland, and the resources of the capital city and of the crown. Yet she was not able to reign for longer than nine days. Jane Grey lacked the one thing that her rival, Mary Tudor, had possessed intermittently since childhood and consistently for the previous six years: an independent household.

Exploiting her role as head of household and property-owner, Mary Tudor was in a position to insist on her succession rights. Without her household, it is almost certain that Mary would have not been able to quell so easily Jane Grey's putative regime. It was Mary who had already established herself as authority figure by presiding over her own independent household since 1547 and who had established herself as a patron, landlord, neighbor, and magnate in East Anglia. Although her attempt to preserve the religious autonomy of her household during her brother's reign ultimately failed, she nevertheless established herself (via her defense of her household) as the undisputed leader of his Majesties loyal Catholic opposition. Unlike Jane, Mary had once enjoyed viceregal status as the *de facto* Prince of Wales. Mary was the independent authority figure in 1553 whereas Jane (rightly or wrongly) was widely regarded as Northumberland's puppet.

With an independent household of her own, even one that she merely managed it as Guildford Dudley's wife rather than headed it in her own right, Jane Grey would have been able to acquire clients, tenants, servants, and neighbors whose loyalty would have been as much to her as to her husband and his family. A few years as a household manager would have endowed Jane with some individual political status rather than merely the dependent status she had in 1553 through her natal and marital ties. As David Loades noted in 1989, of the two women, "It was Mary who represented self-determination, not Jane."[1]

Elizabeth was not directly challenged for the throne, as Mary was, but she was prepared to fight for her succession rights when it was her turn to accede in 1558. Like Mary, she was able to draw on support from her servants, clients, neighbors, and tenants. Both Tudor princesses recognized and exploited the opportunities provided to them by virtue of their roles as heads of household. Without their households, there is reason to doubt that either princess could have acceded to the throne.

The main reason to doubt the ability of the Tudor princesses to successfully attain the throne is that Tudor England was a patriarchal political system. Women were excluded, not simply subordinated within, major social, educational, legal, and political systems. Yet two women consecutively assumed the highest position of authority as reigning monarchs.

The traditional explanation for this curious happenstance, as mentioned in the Introduction, is that Mary and Elizabeth were the last eligible members of the royal family. In France, when the male royal line died out then males from collateral branches of the royal family would accede to the French throne through marriage to the most senior female representative of the previous royal line. Thus, François I became the first Valois king of France when he married Claude, daughter of Louis XII. Marrying Mary or Elizabeth off to collateral royal males was a viable option in Tudor England and would have spared the patriarchal state the embarrassment of a female succession.

Until Henry took steps to disinherit Mary in 1527, England's foreign and domestic policy centered on ensuring that Mary wedded a man who could either credibly claim the throne himself or possessed enough political stature to rule England as Mary's husband. James V of Scotland was Mary's first cousin, the son of her paternal aunt, Margaret Tudor. The close blood relationship would have needed a papal dispensation but it also indicates how credible a candidate for the English throne James was. In 1536, James indicated that his marital and diplomatic ambitions lay in France when he married first a French princess and, after her death, a French noblewoman. By this time, Mary's value on the marriage market had been considerably undermined by her parent's "divorce," the birth of her half-sister Elizabeth in September 1533, and the Acts of Succession in 1533 and 1536, which declared her illegitimate and ineligible to inherit the throne.

Other domestic candidates for the throne or for marrying either Mary or Elizabeth are Edward Courtenay, earl of Devon, Henry Darnley, and Henry Hastings earl of Huntingdon. None were ideal: Courtenay was Catholic and prisoner in the Tower until 1558, Darnely was not born until 1545 and Huntingdon was descended from a rival royal house, the Plantagenets, whom the Tudors had supplanted. It was possible—indeed, desirable from a patriarchal standpoint—to marry off either Mary or Elizabeth into a foreign royal house. Negotiations for Mary to wed Charles V, the Habsburg emperor, were a feature of Anglo-Habsburg diplomacy in the 1520s. Before Henry took steps to disinherit Elizabeth in 1536, he entered into negotiations to wed Elizabeth into the French royal house.

If Tudor England had clamored for a male monarch, there were options available either in the form of collateral royal males or through the marriages of Mary and Elizabeth to foreign royalty. For various political and religious reasons, these options were not exercised. The existence of these male candidates along with the statutory illegitimacy of Mary and Elizabeth meant that neither princess could simply passively wait for the throne to come to them should Edward VI die childless.

Their anomalous roles as heads of elite households and property owners empowered Mary and Elizabeth to adopt a proactive approach toward their political goals, agendas, and futures. As heads of their own independent establishments, the Tudor princesses had more control over their own destinies than previous English princesses had possessed. In theory, the monarch could contract a marriage for them outside of the realm without their consent. In practice, however, Mary found it impossible to force her half-sister Elizabeth to marry outside the realm since Elizabeth's refusal would be supported by her clients, such as William Cecil and Edward Fiennes (Lord Clinton) with whom she had cemented a relationship by granting them either household appointments or reversionary interests in her lands.[2]

Elite households could provide this level of protection and power because such households were only partially domestic establishments. As seen in this study of the Tudor princesses, elite households were the means by which Tudor England was governed. As scholars have been documenting for the last twenty years, Tudor England was not a centralized state.[3] The monarch governed by means of the nobility and the gentry who, in turn, presided over establishments that employed local people as servants. Households of regional magnates or gentry JPs were centers of patronage, culture, religious instruction, production, and politics. National policy may have been determined by the crown but the policy was implemented (or not) at the level of the elite household. England was governed by households—from the royal one in London to the vertical and horizontal network of households spread across the land like fine mesh.

By heading their own households, Mary and Elizabeth were able to exploit perhaps the single most important element of social organization in late medieval Western Europe. All but the very poor were members of a household. The household was a marker of identity as socially important as name, gender, family, and profession. As mentioned in the Introduction, a grocer to Princess Elizabeth's household, considered a slur on her to be an insult to him because he identified her interests with his own as a member (although nonresident) of her household. In the Introduction, I stated that the household was greater than the sum of its parts. It was not simply a collection of individuals but a Geertzian meeting ground where individual identities were articulated within a larger social hierarchy. The poor and the rich understood their roles in relation to each other within a Tudor household. The elite household in sixteenth-century England was predicated on the smooth interaction between the head/manager of household and the servants up and down the ranks.

This description of Tudor England as a decentralized state governed loosely by inclusive households applies not just to England.[4] Across Western Europe, late medieval/early modern elite households functioned as regional political and cultural centers accessible to people of nearly all economic backgrounds. As David Herlihy pointed out, for fifteenth-century Florentine households "a large proportion of the population—more than could otherwise be expected—[gained] some exposure to elite society and its way of life" via membership in the elite household.[5]

None of this is to claim that the elite household was a force for social or gender egalitarianism. Those of divergent economic status interacted in the elite household but not on terms of equality. Mary and Elizabeth might know the names of their kitchen servants, but they did nothing to equalize relations between themselves and their servants or even between the ranks of the servants. The household was very strictly hierarchical.

It is possible to argue that one form of social inequality—economic—helped to mitigate (without entirely eliminating) prevailing gender inequality for *some* women. Women of high social status, wealth, and property such as Mary and Elizabeth could (and certainly did) exercise authority over their male servants, tenants, and neighbors. Later they would reign in similar manner over their male subjects. Women of lower socioeconomic status suffered the double penalty of gender and social subordination in keeping with widely articulated pejorative attitudes toward gender and economic deprivation. Women and men endowed with natural gifts could, with luck, negotiate, even overcome such attitudes—but this was extremely rare.

This study of the preaccession households of Mary and Elizabeth Tudor indicates that the elite household provided a forum in which elite women did not need to negotiate with or circumvent patriarchal attitudes. The household, as both a public and private space, occupied a conceptual space in which formal and informal power overlapped. As the wife of an elite male householder, a widow, or (like Mary and Elizabeth) an heiress, elite women were expected to exercise authority over all servants, to dispense patronage (even if this meant little more than influencing their husbands), and catechize the children of the household "family."

This study of the preaccession careers of Mary and Elizabeth Tudor has revealed the similarities between how they functioned and how other elite women of the time lived. Like other noblewomen, the Tudor princesses ruled over their servants, tenants, and neighbors. They were responsible for religious and secular education of their dependents as were other elite female household managers/heads. The princesses exploited, as did other high-born women, the patronage opportunities attendant on elite household in order to secure clients and to implement their political and religious agendas.

To put it in unfashionable terminology: the elite household endowed these noblewomen with agency. It was an agency not purchased as a result of sly manipulation of loopholes within patriarchal legal and social norms. Elite women exercising authority within the household was not only expected but encouraged. Writers of most prescriptive literature, even those who accepted without question a wife's subjection to her husband's authority, assumed that the elite housewife would undertake serious responsibilities within the "domestic sphere" that could have political and religious ramifications.

More research is needed to more fully flesh out the *informal* articulation of political and religious power. The informal, the private, the domestic was neither hidden nor subordinate. Building on all the many fine studies of families of sixteenth-century England, future researchers would make a useful contribution to our understanding of this period by focusing on the household as public center of political and religious patronage. For a period so well studied as Tudor England, the practical application of power and patronage, usually emanating from households, is poorly understood.

This study of Mary and Elizabeth as property holders has underscored the importance of conveyancing documents as sources of political-patronage relationships and how women participated in these relationships. This discussion necessarily focused on Mary and Elizabeth Tudor but future studies would add greatly to the overall picture of Tudor England by examining how women of property (as owners and/or managers), both real and moveable, participated in significant social, economic, cultural, and political trends of the period.

Whereas this study has focused on how Mary and Elizabeth Tudor transitioned from *informal* to *formal* power, from heads of household to heads of state, an important caveat must be kept in mind. Most sixteenth-century noblewomen were not able to make this transition. This was an important distinction between men and women of this period. A man could head his own household and serve in public office. Often a woman could do neither. Elite women usually managed their households but in their husbands' name (even if their husbands were dead) or their sons'. It was rare for a woman to hold public office.

Studying the preaccession careers of Mary and Elizabeth can provide insight into the opportunities available to other elite women. Like Mary and Elizabeth, noblewomen dispensed patronage and ruled over their servants. The experiences of the Tudor princesses, however, can also highlight the unmovable obstacles women faced in this period. A noblewoman might exercise authority over her servants but she rarely did so in her own name—usually it was an authority she exercised in the name of her husband, son, brother, or father. In some ways, Mary and Elizabeth had this also in common with other women of their time. They would consecutively claim the throne as the last representatives of their patriline.

The centerpiece of this study is the transition that Mary and Elizabeth made from heads of household to heads of state. The mechanism for this transition was made up of many factors: patrilineal descent, parliamentary statute, and the elite household. The last was a platform available to other noblewomen, but only the Tudor princesses could exploit its full potential. By itself, the elite household was not enough to propel Mary and Elizabeth to sovereign power but without it neither princess could have acceded to the English throne as established authority figures.

NOTES

1. Loades, *Mary Tudor*, p. 182
2. For details of the proposed marriage for Elizabeth and Mary's ambivalent attitude toward it, see S. Doran, *Monarchy and Matrimony* [London, 1996], pp. 19–20; for grants to Fiennes, Cecil, and an early one to Northumberland, see *CPR*, III, pp. 88, 112, 198; V, p. 171
3. See essays on the court as household in *The English Court from the Wars of the Roses to the Civil War*, ed. D. Starkey [London, 1987]; S. G. Ellis, *Tudor Frontiers and*

Noble Power: The Making of the British State [Oxford UP, 1995]; M. K. McIntosh, *Controlling Misbehavior in England 1370–1600* [Cambridge UP, 2002]

4. See, in particular, the problem of discussing the "state" or "state-building" within a sixteenth-century Western European and colonial context in A. Cañeque, *The King's Living Image: The Culture and Politics of Viceregal Power in Colonial Mexico* [New York, 2004], pp. 4–11

5. D. Herlihy, *Medieval Households* [Harvard UP, 1985], p. 156

APPENDIX A

Henry VIII's Will and The Bequests to Mary and Elizabeth, 1547

In mid-1547, Mary and Elizabeth began funding their household expenses from the revenues of crown lands assigned to them for their use. They were the first English royal spinsters to live as landed magnates in establishments free from crown oversight. Unlike their own combined household during Henry's reign, their post-1546 separate households were not funded directly from the king's Privy Purse or chamber accounts. Traditionally, unmarried English princesses lived at court or, as Mary and Elizabeth had done during Henry's lifetime, at the king's expense. The novel nature of Mary's and Elizabeth's financial independence during Edward VI's reign has not been emphasized by previous scholars. However, as this study is positing a relationship between Mary's and Elizabeth's preaccession political status and their abilities to assume sovereign power in a patriarchal state, a detailed exploration of how and why the Tudor princesses acquired their innovative landed endowments is of great importance. At times, the following discussion of the legal mechanisms that resulted in Mary and Elizabeth acquiring land becomes quite technical.

The headache-inducing complexities of conveying land in Tudor England confers substantial appeal on the current explanation for how the Tudor princesses obtained their landed patrimonies. The traditional explanation for why Mary and Elizabeth received such generous landed allocations in 1547 was that it was in accordance with Henry VIII's last will and testament.[1] This explanation derives, not unreasonably, from the wording of the contemporary conveyancing documents—the patent letters—by which the princesses received their lands. These patents claim that the princesses received their lands "in fulfilment [*sic*] of Henry VIII's will."[2] Elizabeth's most recent biographer has interpreted this apparent bequest as a reflection to Henry's concern for the welfare of the princesses because he "had realized that the world would be a difficult place for his daughters" after his death.[3]

There are three reasons to revisit the claims in the patent letters that Mary and Elizabeth obtained their patrimonies courtesy of bequests in Henry VIII's will. The most obvious is that the will contains no bequest of land to either of his daughters. Second, such a bequest would have violated the purpose of the will which was to conserve the royal demesne. Finally, Henry was unlikely to bequeath land to his unmarried daughters as it would have represented an unnecessary innovation in the living arrangements traditionally made for royal spinsters.

The actual provision made for Mary and Elizabeth in Henry's will bequeathed cash not lands:

> Further our Will is that, from the furst Howre of our Death until such Tyme as the sayde Counsaillours canne provide either of them or bothe of sum honorable Mariages, they shall have eche of them *Thre Thousande Poundes, ultra reprisas* ["final discharge" or net], to lyve on, willing and charging the forsayde Counsaillours to limite and appoinct to either of them such sage Officers and Ministers for ordering thereof, as it may be employed both to our Honour and theirs.[4]

Although the phrase "ultra reprisas" often appeared in grants of property, it was not, in and of itself, a term that referred to property. Its appearance in property documents is explained by the need to specify that the recipient of a parcel land was due a certain amount of net revenue. The sum of landed revenue, qualified by the term "ultra reprisas," meant that the exact sum thus qualified was due to the recipient and no further charges (for collection, conveyancing, etc.) could be deducted from that amount. "Ultra reprisas" here means that Mary and Elizabeth were to net £3,000 and that nothing further could be deducted from this sum. As the will itself translated the phrase, in another bequest (discussed later) the princesses were to receive this sum "over all charges."[5]

Certainly, the will's executors did not comprehend the phrase "ultra reprisas" to mean that the £3,000 in the bequest to the princesses should be raised in landed revenues. In their initial performance of Henry's bequest to his daughters, the will's executors (who were also King Edward's privy councilors) assumed that the bequest referred to a yearly allowance, a "pencion" for each princess to "lyve on." Consequently, the executor-councilors ordered that allowances ("pencions") be paid to the princesses. On April 11, 1547, the Privy Council deputed Sir Edward Peckham, cofferer (treasurer) of King Edward's household, to distribute to each princess "the summe of oone cii, to be accompted as parcell of her Graces pencion to her allotted by the testament of our late Souveraine Lord."[6] As the executor-councilors initially interpreted and performed it, Henry's will granted allowances to Mary and Elizabeth, not lands.

The executor-councilors were, initially, on solid ground in their original interpretation of Henry's will because there are almost no landed bequests in the will. There is only one landed bequest in Henry's will and it reads quite differently from the cash bequest to Mary and Elizabeth. The will clearly and *explicitly* bequeaths land to the clerics of St. George's chapel Windsor:

> Also We wool that with as convenient Spede as may be doon after our Departure out of this World, if it be not doon in our Liefe, that the Deane and Channons of our Free Chaple of Sainct George within our Castle of Winesor, shall have Manoures Landes Tenementes and spiritual Promotions, to the yerely Value of Six Hundred Poundes over all Charges, made sure to them and their Successours for ever . . .[7]

This type of precise language stands in marked contrast to the bequest to the princesses. There is no reference to "manoures landes tenementes" in the bequest to Mary and Elizabeth. If Henry wished his daughters to have lands, there was no reason for him to be coy about it. He could simply have employed the explicit wording in the princesses' bequest that he did for the clerics of St. George's.

In fact, the near absence of landed bequests in the will posed a problem for the executor-councilors. In his will, Henry had designated the will's executors to serve also on King Edward's first Privy Council. To compensate them for their service, the will bequeathed each executor-councilor specific cash sums. This, however, was not the type of compensation that the executor-councilors coveted. As the terms of these testamentary clauses were common knowledge even before Henry contracted his last illness, his secretary William Paget was in consultation with Henry on how to augment these cash bequests during the last few months of Henry's life. According to Paget's later deposition, Henry had agreed to bestow titles and lands for the executor-councilors. The intention had been for Henry to bestow these lands and titles on the named executor-councilors during his lifetime but he died before could do so.[8]

The wording of the will's bequests meant that the executor-councilors could not obtain the lands and titles they sought because the will bequeathed only cash to the named executor-councilors. As with the bequest to Mary and Elizabeth, Henry's will bequeathed cash not lands to the executor-councilors. The executor-councilors overcame this restriction by invoking the will's "unfulfilled gifts clause." This clause directed the executors to pay Henry's debts, complete any ongoing transactions involving crown lands and accomplish any outstanding "promises" made by the king. This clause, intended to authorize the executors to complete any conveyancing transactions still in process at the king's death, was seized on by the executor-councilors. They argued that this clause allowed them to perform not Henry's will but rather his last known intentions; his "unwritten will."[9] Not surprisingly, the executor-councilors determined that Henry's last known intentions were to freely bestow lands from the royal demesne on all of the executor-councilors and other important political figures.

Paget and others deposed that Henry had promised to grant land to his executors but died before he could initiate the legal process (drawing up patent letters or revising the will). The result of these depositions was that all the property grants to the executor-councilors, which were theoretically in fulfillment of Henry's intentions, contained lengthy preambles citing the unfulfilled gifts clause and the details of the depositions.

A further complication that likely impeded Henry from bequeathing land to anyone in his will (except to the clerics of St. George's) was the legal difficulties involved when an underaged monarch (Edward VI) attempted to alienate crown lands. As a legal minor, Edward VI did not come into full possession of the lands he inherited from his father. Therefore, he could not alienate them away from the royal demesne. He could not initiate any transactions involving crown lands until he came of age when he turned eighteen (which would have been in 1555 had he survived). Edward's legal deficiency in this regard was, in the late sixteenth century, legally recognized by Elizabethan judges to be compensated for by his royal status as a monarch (the doctrine of the king's "two bodies"). In 1547, however, the boy-king's abilities to convey crown lands solely on his own authority was not firmly established under the law.[10]

An indication of the problems involved in Edward initiating an alienation of crown lands can be seen in the legal difficulties surrounding the lone landed bequest in Henry's will. Although Henry had specified that the bequest to the clerics of St. George's should be funded from lands, he had not initiated the process by which crown lands could be granted to the clerics. Henry's heir, Edward VI, at only nine years of age, was not in full legal possession of these lands. Therefore, according to the legal advice obtained by the will's executors, Edward could not solely on his own authority, alienate crown lands to fund his father's testamentary bequest to the clerics of St. George.

In 1547, crown jurists recommended that the only unassailable method by which Edward could initiate a grant crown lands to the clerics of St. Georges was to employ a tripartite indenture.[11] This was a legal agreement between three parties comprising on the one hand the recipients (e.g., clerics of St. George's), King Edward as the second party and, as the third, the executor-councilors.

The executor-councilors were acting, essentially, as cosignatories for the under-aged monarch. Furthermore, the Privy Council ruled that anyone who had been engaged in property conveyances (and could produce the documents) involving crown lands at the time of Henry's death could henceforth complete their transactions only in the form of a tripartite indenture.[12] Thus, when the dean and cannons of St. George's eventually received their lands, their patent letters contained a preamble stating that they held their lands per a tripartite indenture.[13]

In fact, the invocation of the gifts clause in Henry's will allowed the executor-councilors to circumvent the legal problem posed by King Edward's legal minority. The executor-councilors were, essentially, arguing that their later grants of crown lands were in completion of those that Henry VIII meant to initiate but died before he could begin the legal process. When the executor-councilors obtained their lands in 1547, they did so on the adult (although dead) Henry's authority rather than upon Edward's contested authority as a legal minor. Because there were no actual conveyancing documents in process regarding the lands the executor-councilors claimed that Henry had "promised" them, a tripartite indenture was not relevant to complete their (nonexistent Henrician) grants.

There was yet another problem that Henry would have had to consider had he genuinely wished to bequeath land to his daughters. Bequeathing land to females, even elite females, was a dicey business that often ended in conflict with women having to bring suits in the court of Chancery in order to obtain the lands bequeathed to them.[14]

Henry's will contains no landed bequest to Mary and Elizabeth in the *explicit* wording of the text. In fact, there is only one landed bequest in the will at all. As the bequest to clerics of St. George's Chapel, Windsor, illustrates, if Henry had intended to bequeath land to his daughters, he could have done so overtly and specifically. Yet as the bequest to the clerics at St. George's also testifies, bequeathing land from the royal demesne was fraught with legal difficulties when the succeeding monarch was a minor. Finally, Henry would have been well aware that bequeathing land to his daughters was an inefficient method of bestowing land on females in Tudor England.

This near absence of landed bequests in the actual text of the will accords with the overall goal of Henry's will: to ensure the financial and political safety of Prince Edward should he accede to the throne as an underaged monarch.[15] The best way to ensure young Edward's safety as an underaged monarch was to ensure that royal finances were stable and self-sustaining. This financial stability was, in Henry's will, combined with new organization of the crown government designed to prevent the political dominance of a relative (like a Richard III–like uncle) who could Edward's sovereignty and/or life.

To ensure Edward's financial stability, Henry's will contains bequests of cash rather than of lands (with one exception already noted). This made sound fiscal sense. Crown lands not only generated revenues for the monarch but royal estates could be sold to land-hungry elite for a quick profit. Henry's desire to preserve the royal demesne intact for his son helps to explain the near absence of landed bequests in his last will and testament.

That Henry would seek to preserve crown lands for his successor may surprise historians who have documented Henry's lavish grants of land from the royal patrimony throughout his reign, which deprived the crown of much-needed revenues.[16] Nevertheless, at the end of his life, Henry attempted to preserve the royal demesne intact for his successor. Furthermore, he expressed unwillingness to deprive his heir of even the crown's most recently acquired lands.

In February 1547, William Paget deposed that in the weeks immediately preceding Henry's death that he and Henry discussed plans for the late king to distribute to the executor-councilors the forfeited estates of the recently arrested, Thomas Howard, duke of Norfolk. Paget, however, admitted that Henry, while initially receptive to the idea of distributing the Norfolk estates to the executor-councilors had, in the end, changed his mind. Paget confessed that Henry "altered his determinacion for geving any of the said Dukes londes . . . but sayd he wold kepe them to him self," reserving much of the Norfolk estate for the crown.[17]

If Henry rejected the proposal for distributing the Norfolk estates before his death, it is unlikely he intended that the cash bequests in his will should be funded from the sale of any crown lands even those recently acquired like the Norfolk properties. Given Henry's attitude regarding the Norfolk lands, it is likely that his last will and testament, with its overwhelming preference for cash rather than landed bequests, accurately reflected Henry's hopes for the fiscal strategy that would be employed by those governing the realm after his death (in reality if not in name) until his son came of age.

That Henry would prefer to fund his testamentary bequests from cash rather than lands is more comprehensible when considering his entire financial "portfolio." Henry, the Citizen Kane of his day, had accrued a vast amount of "stuff." It has recently been estimated that Henry's collection of tapestries and goods amounted to £1,200,000.[18] This was a staggering resource, roughly equivalent to £300,000,000 today.[19]

Henry acquired the royal goods not only to decorate his many palaces but to function as liquid assets. These goods could be sold to raise the cash necessary for funding the royal Privy Purse. From his Privy Purse, the king could bankroll the incidental expenses of his own household, the households of his dependents, and even, on occasion, foreign embassies.[20] As royal goods were the personal property of the monarch, they could be sold at will without jeopardizing the main source of crown revenues: rents from royal lands and various fees, customs, and excises. The royal goods were petty cash, whereas crown lands were the revenue-generating capital to be preserved and, if possible, increased. It was, therefore, much more sensible for Henry to bequest a portion of royal goods (or cash from the sale of them) to all his beneficiaries, including Mary and Elizabeth, instead of crown lands.

As already noted, the near-absence of landed bequests in Henry's will was a matter of consternation to those charged with performing the will, the executor-councilors. As they initially understood the will, nearly all the testamentary bequests were in cash. There was no question that the text of the will referred to cash bequests to all beneficiaries (except the clerics of St. George's chapel). The problem for the executor-councilors was that the wording of nearly all the will's bequests was entirely too specific, too obviously meant to be funded from cash (like the bequest to Mary and Elizabeth), which served as too great a constraint upon the executor-councilors.

The executor-councilors claimed that there was a problem "if we perfourme the legacies and promises of our late Souvergiane Lorde with such money as was remayneng at the tyme of his deathe." According to their argument, the problem was that the government might run short of funds necessary for national defense "if we shulde have solde such juelles, plate or other riche hanginges for the said perfourmaunce of the will." In a complete dismantling of Henry's strategy of funding the testamentary bequests from cash, rather than lands, the executor-councilors argued that it was better "to perfourme the promesses of lande made by our late Souveraigne Lorde" rather than liquidate any of the royal moveable property to fund the will's bequests.

As the will's executors initially understood Henry's will, there were no landed bequests except to the clerics of St. George's. All other bequests, including that to themselves as well as to Mary and Elizabeth, were to be funded from cash raised from the sale of "juelles, plate or other riche hanginges" from the royal coffers. Like nearly all the other bequests in the will, the executors assumed that Henry's bequest to his daughters was of cash. As far as contemporaries were concerned Henry bequeathed cash allowances ("pencions") to Mary and Elizabeth. As noted earlier, this understanding guided the initial performance of Henry's will by the executor-councilors, who initially distributed to each princess the "pencion to her allotted by the testament of our late Souveraine Lord."

In 1547, both Mary and Elizabeth received landed patrimonies. However, they did not receive them because their father, Henry VIII, had left them estates in his last will and testament. There is no bequest of lands to the princesses in his will. There was no widely understood but unspoken assumption that the bequest to Mary and Elizabeth each of £3,000 *p.a.* should be raised by endowing them with land that generated revenues that equaled the specified amount.

Rather, the executor-councilors performed the bequest as it was written and distributed to each princess the cash allowance that their father had bequeathed them in his will. As the executor-councilor originally understood Henry's will, almost none of the bequests were to be funded from landed revenues. The executor-councilors assumed that the will directed them to perform all bequests from cash that should be raised, as the executors themselves understood it, from the sale of royal jewels, plate, and tapestries.

One final point regarding the improbability of Henry bestowing lands on his daughters in his will. Had Henry truly intended for Mary and Elizabeth to preside over independent establishments and to possess substantial landed revenues, this would have represented a dangerous innovation the living arrangements of English spinster princesses.

Endowing Mary and Elizabeth with landed patrimonies would have created "overmighty subjects" who could challenge the authority of the underaged king and his government. Princess Mary did indeed question the young king's right and that of his government to her household to conform to the nationally mandated religion. From her own manors and amid her regional affinity, Mary successfully overturned Edward's provisions for the succession to the throne. Princess Elizabeth was able to acquire important political allies from among the privy councilors serving during her brother's and sister's reigns by sponsoring reversionary interests in her lands. None of this would have been possible had the princesses lived as previous English princesses had done, that is, at court or at the financial discretion of the crown.

Allocating estates to each princess required far more bureaucratic energy than simply continuing the usual policy of funding the household expenses of the princesses from the crown privy or chamber accounts. Lacking the benefit of hindsight, contemporaries would have had no reason to regard Mary and Elizabeth as eligible for anything other than the usual fate of English princesses: marriages abroad negotiated for the realm's advantage. Indeed, this is the future that Henry's will explicitly addressed.

The patent letters by which the princesses received their estates made fraudulent claims. Mary and Elizabeth did not obtain landed patrimonies because their father bequeathed them estates in his will. There was no bequest to them of lands in the will. None of the executor-councilors deposed (as Paget did regarding lands and titles for the executor-councilors) that Henry had contemplated bestowing lands on his daughters but died before he could initiate the conveyancing process. There was no long preamble in the princesses' patents citing the unfulfilled gifts clause in the will as there was in the patents by which the executor-councilors received their own lands. Nor did Mary and Elizabeth obtain their lands via a tripartite indenture as did the only beneficiaries of a landed bequest from Henry's will: the clerics of St. George's.

Henry bequeathed cash allowances to his daughters, not land. This was the initial understanding of those charged to perform the will, the executor-councilors, who ordered that each princess receive the cash allowance "allotted by the testament of our late Souveraine Lord." Yet by April 1547 Mary (and probably Elizabeth, too, but not officially) began drawing their income from the revenues generated by their landed assignments. This was a clear violation of Henry's last will and testament. Appendix B examines the political context that generated the erroneous claims in the princesses' patents, which claim a fraudulent relationship between the estates awarded to Mary and Elizabeth in 1547 and the testament of their father, Henry VIII.

Although Henry had provided Somerset and his ally, Paget, with an opportunity to suggest that another, much more of important provision in the will be set aside. Henry's will proposed a scheme for a collective regency during Edward's minority vested in the will's executors whom Henry nominated to sit on Edward's privy council. This council of executor-councilors was to rule the kingdom until Edward came of age. Somerset and Paget proposed their own alternative a few days after Henry died on January 28. They suggested that one man, Somerset (at the time earl of Hertford only), should rule as regent rather than maintaining collective sovereignty in the Privy Council as a whole. Somerset and Paget could anticipate that many of their colleagues would readily accept the practical utility of having one ruling regent rather than a collective body.

It was far more logical for Henry to bequeath cash allowances to Mary and Elizabeth. Granting lands to Mary and Elizabeth would have undermined Henry's financial and political strategy in the will, the goal of which was to ensure Prince Edward's safety as an underaged ruler. Henry's provisions for the ruling Privy Council indicates that he was desperately worried that a Richard III–like figure could emerge to threaten Edward's sovereignty.[21] So Henry's stipulations regarding the Privy Council were a series of regulations designed to prevent any one councilor from assuming personal sovereignty at Edward's expense.[22] Bequeathing a large estate to the adult Mary, in particular, would have placed considerable material and political resources at the disposal of one of Edward's potential rivals. Essentially, Henry would have staked any bid that Mary might make to become a Richard III–like figure herself.

Yet, in April 1547, Mary did obtain a vast landed estate that, according to her patent letters, was in performance of Henry's will. The question is why the patent letters make this claim when there is no such bequest in the will. The claim also contradicts the initial performance of the bequest by the executors as bestowing *allowances* on each princess rather than *revenues* from estates. The registers of the Privy Council preserve the contemporary distinction between "pencion" (allowance) to be paid out from the sale of royal goods or the Privy Purse and "revenues" derived from property.[23] The question now becomes:

what made the executor-councilors alter their initial understanding of the Henrician bequests to Mary and Elizabeth?

Hindsight makes it easy to forget that political situation taking shape after Henry's death in late January 1547 initially appeared unstable. The new king was nine years old and his right of legitimate succession was not instantly accepted by the international community.[24] The paradoxical result of Henry's matrimonial adventures and his break with the Roman Catholic Church was that, Mary, of all his children, was the only one widely accepted as legitimate—at least, by the politically powerful outside of England. Domestically, Mary had served as the *de facto* princess of Wales in 1525, she was instrumental in brokering an Anglo-Habsburg alliance in 1545, and was part of powerful female network that included Katherine Parr and Anne Seymour (wife of Somerset).

Because Mary did not make a bid for the regency, it is easier still to forget that she was a very credible rival to Somerset for the regency. She was well connected via her Habsburg cousins, highly educated, and possessed legitimate blood claims to the throne herself. As the king's half-sister, she was more closely related to him than was Somerset, the king's maternal uncle. It was usual practice on the Continent for royal women with Mary's qualifications to assume the regency for an underaged male king. Although this was not the practice in England, Mary's suitability for the regency was not lost on the English political elite. Two years later, in 1549, the some Edwardian privy councilors would offer Mary the regency.[25]

Mary was close to the center of power and in a position to know the contents of Henry VIII's will.[26] This is significant because the executor-councilors had quickly decided to violate the will's gifts clauses almost immediately after Henry VIII died. To violate the will in any degree jeopardized the already shaky legitimacy of the sovereign Privy Council because their powers and offices derived solely from the will. The will should have been a sacrosanct document but the executor-councilors had personal reasons to creatively interpret some of the will's stipulations even at the risk of undermining their own authority. The princess was in a position to object. If Mary publicly voiced her objections then she could call into questions the legitimacy of the new regime.

But Somerset wished to be more than merely a "first among equals." He persuaded the executor-councilors to allow him to personally assume regal authority so that he ruled alone consulting the Privy Council only at his discretion. To induce the executor-councilors and other important politicians to accept this diminution of their collective power and the significant violation it represented of Henry's will, Somerset and Paget determined that it would be necessary to bribe the political elite, primarily but not exclusively the other executor-councilors. As discussed by numerous scholars, these bribes took the form of property grants.[27] This is the context that, as detailed later, helps to make sense of how and why Mary and Elizabeth were the first princesses in English history to obtain landed patrimonies before marriage.[28] Historians generally cite Paget's May 30 grant as the first of these landed bribes.[29] Significantly, Mary obtained her estates two weeks before Paget did.

Mary's grant was dated May 12, 1547. The lack of a landed bequest to the princesses in Henry's will means that the will need no longer serve as a distraction when interpreting Mary's grant. It now becomes possible to appreciate properly the significance of the date on which her grant was completed. Mary obtained her properties at the same time that other politically important people were receiving the lands that Somerset had promised them. The timing of Mary's grant alone argues that the princess was one of the recipients of Somerset's landed bribe. Indeed, it is now hard to explain the timing of Mary's grant without reference to these other grants and to Somerset's wholesale landed bribe of the political elite.

To excerpt Mary's grant involves arguing that the timing of her grant alone is somehow unrelated to the establishment of Somerset's regency while the other grants were connected. It would be quite a coincidence if Mary's grant was completed at this time and yet had nothing to do with the political situation that generated the contemporaneous grants to Paget, John Dudley, Thomas Seymour, and William Herbert. There is a telling phrase preserved only in Mary's patent letters. It is significant that this phrase appears in her patents rather than in Elizabeth's, dated three years later. Mary's patents stated that she obtained her estates "by the advice of the Protector [Somerset] and the executors."[30] As Mary's patents admitted, she received her lands through the efforts of Somerset and the executor-councilors. Following the reasoning of previous scholars in linking the contemporaneous grants to Paget, Seymour, Dudley, et al. to Somerset's bid for the regency, this study proposes a connection between Mary's patrimony granted in May 1547 to Somerset's consolidation of power.

The political significance of Mary's grant lies not only in its timing but also in its scale. Indeed, the scale of her estate combined with its rapid settlement suggests that Somerset and the councilors delayed the completion of their own property grants until after Mary's lands had been assigned. Mary's grant was completed before Paget's (May 30), Dudley's (June 23), and Thomas Seymour's (August 19). Somerset himself did not obtain the patent to his own lands until July 9.[31]

Moreover, Princess Mary received far more lands than any of the privy councilors or executors—a lot more. Although £1,000 in landed revenues was the minimum enjoyed by most noblemen, Mary's lands generated revenues that totaled just over £3,800 *p.a.*[32] This is significant for two reasons: it is far in excess of what Henry VIII specified in his will (thus further eroding the relationship between her estate and Henry's will) and the scale indicates the importance Somerset assigned to neutralizing the threat Mary posed to his bid for the regency.

Mary's patrimony provided her with annual revenues that not only placed her on a par with dukes and earls, but it was in far in excess of the total amount Somerset used to bribe the executor-councilors. In fact, the combined total of revenues from the land grants to all of the executor-councilors in 1547 has been estimated at an aggregate total of only £3,200—about £600 less than the landed revenues granted to Mary alone![33] The comparison serves to illustrate the extraordinary scale of Mary's land grant. Somerset himself initially obtained lands generating an annual revenue of £1,100 to support him in his new dignity as Protector of the Realm and Duke of Somerset.[34]

This grant to Mary resulted in her becoming a regional magnate with many livings and offices in her gift. After receiving her patent letters in 1547, Mary formally obtained "lordship" rights the offices and livings associated with her estates. This made her a political patron of considerable local influence in East Anglia. Eventually, Mary would exploit this local influence to raise an army to successfully challenge Jane Grey and enforce her own succession to the throne in 1553. Arguably, Mary took possession of the throne as an overmighty subject as much as a prince of the blood.

In response, the potentially volatile political situation in the wake of Henry VIII's death, Protector Somerset "freely adapted" Henry's testamentary bequest to his daughters in order to remove Mary as a possible threat to the stability of the young king's regime by bribing her with a landed estate. This (temporary) alienation of crown lands was then justified (as preserved in the phrasing of the patent letters) by claiming it originated as a bequest from Henry's will. The illusion was reinforced by converting Elizabeth's Henrician cash bequest into property as well (though worth considerably less than the estate awarded to Mary). The conveyancing documents for these estates—the princess's patent letters—therefore reveal a legal fraud in falsely claiming a relationship to Henry's will. Mary and Elizabeth obtained heir landed estate not through Henry's will but due to the obvious political dangers inherit in the situation of a underaged monarch, a ruling Privy Council, and an adult, politically ambitious royal sibling.

Somerset and the executor-councilors were encroaching upon the royal demesne in direct contravention of Henry VIII's will when they awarded themselves lands. The estates that Somerset used for bribing the executor-councilors derived from the royal demesne. If Mary had publicly objected, if she had warned her brother, informed the Imperial ambassadors, written to Continental Catholic powers, and conferred with leading courtiers, she certainly could have caused trouble on the basis that she was the king's closest relation. A person of Mary's status publicly calling attention to the actions of Somerset and the executor-councilors could potentially have served to undermine an already tenuous regime.

Somerset and the executor-councilors could not see into the future and be assured of Mary's compliance. They could, however, enjoy a measure of security on this issue if Mary accepted the bribe of a landed estate. Moreover, this bribe could be cloaked by claiming a false relationship to Henry VIII's will. The will's bequest of a respectable (though not excessively generous) allowance to Mary enabled Somerset and the executor-councilors to bribe the princess on a massive scale under the cover of performing Henry's will.

That Mary was, essentially, bought off is further evidenced by the unequal treatment of the princesses. Because both Mary and Elizabeth were treated equally in the will (save for the order of succession), especially regarding annual income and marriage portions, they should have received roughly the same amount in household goods. Instead, Elizabeth's estates totaled to just over the required £3,000, nearly a thousand less than Mary's. Clearly, Mary's settlement was more generous than Elizabeth's. The will provided no justification for treating Mary any differently in this regard than Elizabeth. Rather, Henry's will leaves little room for doubt that both sisters were to receive exactly the same income. The lopsided allocation to Mary argues that the Edwardian government was at pains to buy her goodwill.

Endowing the princesses with substantial estates that would be reflected in their households was the last thing Henry VIII would have wished. The king's overriding concern throughout the will is Edward's safety as an underage monarch. Henry had deliberately refrained from granting Mary her own independent household after 1533. Indeed, he demonstrated nervousness about even allowing her to assume dominance in the conflated household of the princesses in 1536. Around May 1537, Mary personally wrote to Cromwell assuring him that the reports of her entertaining politically important guests behind the king's back were greatly exaggerated: the "strangers that you wryte . . . hath been reported to the wurst." If Henry at the height of his power in the 1530s had felt threatened by the idea of Mary, in particular, having her own fully independent household, how much more would he have worried about her having an household which approached (although did not equal) her welsh viceregal household of 1525? Henry had "Money Plate Jewlez and Householde Stuffe" literally bursting his palatial storehouses. The crown could easily afford to sell the fraction of it to provide the necessary income for Mary and Elizabeth.

As the will reads, and contrary to what scholars have asserted, Henry's intentions appear rather to undermine the princess' status as heirs. The linkage of the marriage portion of £10,000—if they married abroad—with the £3,000 *p.a.*

provides motivation for both the princesses and the privy councilors to marry them off quickly. The longer their marriages were delayed, the more the Privy Council would have to sell to pay their pensions. From Mary's and Elizabeth's viewpoint, the real money would come to them only upon marriage. Henry most likely intended for them to continue living in the combined household that would be richly furnished with some of his goods, whereas some were sold to pay their pensions until they were soon married abroad. On paper, it was an excellent method for neutralizing the political threat they could pose during Edward's minority. Undermining the status of female heirs was very much in keeping with Henry VIII's policy since he began divorce proceedings against Catherine of Aragon in 1527.

That Henry's primary concern regarding his daughters would be their marriage portions is not surprising. It was quite common for men of any means at all to leave instructions in their wills regarding the marriages of their single daughters.[35] Henry's provision for his daughters was clearly designed to motivate the Privy Council to do what he himself had failed to do: secure husbands worthy of the princesses. Henry bequeathed allowances to his daughters that the Privy Council would need to pay through the sale of royal goods or the siphoning off of royal revenues much as had been done in Henry's lifetime. Payment of this allowance would require considerable energy and planning by the Privy Council, which Henry clearly hoped would soon prompt the executor-councilors to arrange suitable marriages for Mary and Elizabeth and, thus, spare themselves the trouble of having to arrange for the payment of the annuities to the princesses.

If Henry's primary concern had been the economic and political security of his daughters, then he could have named them as coexecutors of the will. Unmarried women were recognized as legal persons in their own right in all jurisdictions in England so they were eligible to be named.[36] Being executors would have allowed Mary and Elizabeth to exercise some control of the dispersal of the assets specified in the will and the fulfillment of their own bequests.

Henry was relentlessly conventional in his provision for his daughters. The concern over their marriages was reflected in the wills of other elite men and, more particularly, the strictures Henry placed on Mary's and Elizabeth's freedom of choice was another instance of Henry following testamentary convention amongst elite fathers. Like other contemporary elite fathers, Henry specified that his daughters marry with the consent of the will's executors so as to prevent the princesses from marrying beneath them or "dishonorably."[37]

The Privy Council's decision to convert these bequests into lands undid Henry's attempts to contain and marry off his daughters. Their considerable estates robbed the princesses of any motivation towards marriage. They now wielded authority as two of the country's wealthiest magnates. As events were to play out, the Privy Council would have done better, in terms of their long-term political careers, to adhere to the original stipulations of Henry VIII's will. The conversion of princesses' bequests from "stuff" to property elevated them from the status of barely-acknowledged heirs to overmighty subjects.[38] This was very probably the outcome which the late king had tried to avert. The 1544 Act of Succession had created the opportunity for the female succession but it was the Privy Council's decision to confer princely estates on Mary and Elizabeth, which gave them the financial and military resources to accomplish it.

NOTES

1. Loades, p. 137; see also MacCaffrey, p. 11

2. *CPR*, II, p. 20

3. Starkey, p. 65

4. T. Rymer, ed. *Fœdera*, 3rd ed. (1741) (facsimile, Hants., 1967), vol. VI, pt. 3, p. 145. The italics are original and indicate places in the manuscript that were left blank and later filled in by Henry's clerk, William Honnynges (*LP*, XXI, pt. 1, 634). The official sealed, witnessed, and registered copy of the will, dated December 30, 1546, is in the PRO E23/4/1. It is the PRO copy that is transcribed in *Fœdera*, VI, pp. 142–145. For a lucid discussion of copies, drafts, and the official PRO version, see E. W. Ives, "Henry VIII's Will—A Forensic Conundrum," *The Historical Journal*, 35/4 (1992): 779–804 [hereafter Ives, "Forensic"]

5. *Fœdera*, VI, p. 143

6. *APC*, II, pp. 83, 84, 86. 92, 100, 110, 120, 122, 141, *passim*

7. *Fœdera*, VI, p.143

8. *APC*, II, pp. 14–19 for Paget's deposition

9. Miller "Henry VIII's Unwritten Will," pp. 87–105

10. Kantorowicz, *The King's Two Bodies* . . . , pp. 7–9

11. *APC*, II, p. 38

12. *Ibid.*

13. *CPR*, 1547, p. 148 (Oct. 7th); for other grants that employed the tripartite indenture regarding property in conveyance when Henry VIII died, see *CPR*, 1547, pp. 4; 13; 23; 39; 116; 151; 157; 161; 178; 179; 239; 241

14. Harris, *English Aristocratic Women*, p. 134

15. Houlbrooke, "Henry VIII's Wills', p. 893; E. W. Ives, "Henry VIII's Will: The Protectorate Provisions of 1546–7," *The Historical Journal*, 37/4 (1994), p. 913 [hereafter: Ives, "Protectorate"]

16. R. Lockyer, *Tudor and Stuart Britain*, 3rd edition [Harlow, UK, 2005], p. 82; R. W. Hoyle, "War and Public Finance" in *The Reign of Henry VIII*, ed. D. MacCulloch [London, 1995]; Elton, *Reform and Reformation*, p. 244

17. APC, II, p.17 as quoted and cited in Ives, "Protectorate," p. 903

18. *The Inventory of King Henry VIII*, (Society of Antiquaries of London, 1998), vol. 1, p. x

19. J. J. McCusker, "Comparing the Purchasing Power of Money in Great Britain from 1264 to Any Other Year Including the Present," *Economic History Services* (2001), available at http://www.eh.net./hmt/ppowerbp

20. D. Starkey, "Intimacy and Innovation: The Rise of the Privy Chamber, 1485–1547" from *The English Court from the Wars of the Roses to the Civil War*, ed. D. Starkey (London, 1987), p. 95

21. H. Miller, "Henry VIII's Unwritten Will: Grants of Lands and Honours in 1547," in *Wealth and Power in Tudor England: Essays Presented to S. T. Bindoff*, eds. E. W. Ives, R. J. Knecht, and J. J. Scarisbrick [London, 1978], pp. 87–105

22. Ives, "Forensic," pp. 779–804; R. A. Houlbrooke, "Henry VIII's Wills: A Comment," *The Historical Journal*, 37/4 (1994), pp. 891–899; Ives, "Protectorate," pp. 901–914

23. See change in terminology from "pencions" to "revenues" in registers referring to the performance of princesses' Henrician bequest

24. Loades, p. 135

25. Hoak, *The King's Council*, pp. 254–262

26. She later told the Imperial ambassador, Van der Delft, that she had no idea of the will's contents, *CSP*, Spanish, IX, 123. Queen Mary's later efforts to suppress the will because of the marriage clause suggest that she had a pretty good idea of the will's stipulations (the clause stipulated that she must obtain the executors' consent before marrying or forfeit the throne); *CSP Mary*, p. 207, fn. 6. Queen Elizabeth, too, sought to suppress the will; Levine, *Tudor Dynastic Problems*, p. 113

27. Miller, "Henry VIII's Unwritten Will," p. 87; D. Starkey, *The Reign of Henry VIII: Personalities and Politics* (London, 1985), p. 163; G. R. Elton, *Reform and Reformation* (London, 1977), p. 333; Houlbrook, "Henry's Will," p. 898; P. Williams, *The Later Tudors: England 1547–1603* (Oxford UP, 1998) pp. 34–35; J. Loach, *Edward VI* (Yale UP, 1999), pp. 26–27

28. The records of these land grants are transcribed in the *CPR 1547–8*, (London 1924), pp. 6–7, 17, 23, 25, 42, 45, 124, 190, 193, 240, 243–245, 252. Mary's grant is erroneously dated in *CPR 1548–1549*, p. 20

29. Miller, "Henry's VIII's Unwritten Will," p. 97

30. *CPR*, II, p. 20

31. *CPR*, 1547–1548, pp. 25, 45, 190, 252

32. Harris, *English Aristocratic Women*, p. viii; according to Mary's patent letters, her annual landed revenues were £3,819, see *CPR*, II, p. 22

33. The total for all the estates of the privy councilors in landed revenues is given in Miller, "Henry VIII's Unwritten Will," p. 87; Starkey, *The Reign of Henry VIII*, p. 164 suggests that this may be a conservative estimate

34. Houlbrooke, "wills," p. 896. Somerset would substantially increase his lands and revenues of the course of the next two years

35. Harris, *English Aristocratic Women*, p. 46

36. See Harris, *English Aristocratic Women*, p. 55, fn. 91 for three instances in which fathers nominated their daughters as executors

37. Harris, *English Aristocratic Women*, p. 57 for instances of other elite fathers placing similar strictures on their daughters

38. Using Crown lands to create overmighty subjects had been a concern of political commentators since the mid-fifteenth century, Wolffe, *Crown Lands* . . . , pp. 36, 91

APPENDIX B

The Fraudulent Claims in Mary's and Elizabeth's Patent Letters, 1547

In Appendix A, the supposition that Mary and Elizabeth had received their landed patrimonies courtesy of bequest from Henry VIII's will was challenged because, most obviously, the will itself contains no such bequest. The confusion on this point was not the result of later "inventions" or a lack of rigor by scholars. Rather, historians have cited historical sources contemporary with Mary and Elizabeth to document the claim that Henry VIII bequeathed landed estates to his daughters. These documents are the patent letters by which the princesses obtained their properties. These patents claim that the properties conveyed to Mary and Elizabeth from the royal demesne were in performance of Henry's will. Historians had little reason to suspect that these patents made fraudulent claims.

This appendix will focus on the political context that generated the fraudulent claim in the princesses' patent letters concerning the origin of their patrimonies. After highlighting the lack of supporting evidence for the claims in the princesses' patents, the appendix will concentrate on exploring reasons why the patents would falsely claim a relationship to Henry's will. Mary's estate is crucial here. The timing of her patrimony (when she first began drawing revenues from it) and its scope further erodes the supposed connection between her patrimony and Henry's will. These factors also indicate that the proper context for her (and Elizabeth's) patrimonies was not Henry's will but, rather, the unusual political situation taking shape after Henry's death. Mary (and Elizabeth) received their estates not as bequest from their father but as part of a widely dispersed landed bribe of the political elite in return for accepting the political hegemony of Edward Seymour, duke of Somerset.

The claims in the princesses' patents were deliberately fraudulent. The statement in the patents that Mary and Elizabeth received the lands in performance of Henry's will was not a result of a simple misreading of the will by a negligent clerk. Rather, the patents were suspiciously imprecise regarding Henry's will because there was no supporting documentation for the claim that the princesses obtained their estates as beneficiaries of the will. As the following discussion illustrates, because the will itself contained no *explicit* bequest of lands to the princesses, there were only two legal options available for claiming that Mary and Elizabeth obtained their estates as beneficiaries of their father's will: citation of the will's unfulfilled gifts clause or a tripartite indenture. The lack of either meant that there was no documentation supporting the claimed relationship between the princesses' estates and Henry's will. The reference to Henry's will in the princesses' patents was unusually imprecise because those responsible for issuing the patents had no specific evidence that Henry had bequeathed land to his daughters.

The general lack of landed bequests in Henry's will meant that those who coveted properties from the royal demesne, as the executor-councilors did, had to invent documentation entitling them to obtain grants of crown lands ostensibly on Henry's authority. Henry failed to bequeath land in his last will and testament not only to Mary and Elizabeth; he also refrained from bestowing properties on his executors. Under the terms of the will, only the clerics of St. George's Chapel, Windsor, were entitled to estates from the royal patrimony. In order to obtain lands for themselves, the executor-councilors argued that the crown lands they petitioned to obtain were in fulfillment of Henry's unrealized intentions and promises that the will's unfulfilled gifts clause, authorized them complete. This interpretation allowed the executor-councilors to claim that the will and the depositions of Paget and others regarding Henry's intentions served as supporting documentation. Hence, the patents conveying royal land to the executor-councilors in 1547 and 1548 contained lengthy preambles citing this clause in the will and the interpretation or "spin" of the executor-councilors put on it.[1] There is no such preamble in the patents issued to Mary and Elizabeth.

The absence of a similar preamble in the princesses' patents is significant. The patents of the executor-councilors contain these preambles and reference the depositions of Paget and others, detailing the grants Henry had intended to initiate to the executor-councilors before his death. The depositions with their details of titles and the value of the lands Henry discussed awarding to the executors provided necessary supporting evidence concerning Henry's "intentions" and supposedly justified the land grants. Hence, the citation of the will's gift clause and the depositions in the patents of the executor-councilors. The absence of such references in the patents of the princesses suggests that neither Paget nor anyone else could recall Henry discussing plans for bestowing land on his daughters. Because there was no evidence indicating Henry's uncompleted intentions to grant estates to the princesses, the will's unfulfilled gifts clause was not applicable in their case.

The other method whereby Mary and Elizabeth could have obtained lands as a bequest from Henry's will was to employ a tripartite indenture. As discussed elsewhere, the executor-councilors mandated that all those who were engaged in property transactions with the crown when Henry died could only complete their transactions in the form of a tripartite indenture. This legal mechanism required the executor-councilors to act as cosigners for the underaged Edward VI. Because the one isolated bequest of land in the will (to the clerics of St. George's) involved the alienation of crown lands, the executor-councilors—acting on advice of crown jurists—ruled that this bequest could only be performed via a tripartite indenture.

Given the concern of the executor-councilors regarding the will's lone *explicit* landed bequest and the legal problems involved in an underage monarch completing property transactions begun in the reign of his predecessor, the lack of a tripartite indenture in the conveyancing process by which the princesses obtained their lands is revealing. Employing a tripartite indenture required supporting documents. In conveying royal land under the authority of Henry VIII, one of two types of supporting material was necessary: either citation of a passage in Henry's will or material documenting that the recipient of land was involved in a transaction when Henry died. Neither was available to Mary and Elizabeth. There was no passage in Henry's will bequeathing land to them. Furthermore, neither princess was in the midst in a property transaction involving crown lands when their father died. Lacking any supporting documentation, Mary and Elizabeth were unable to obtain their lands via a tripartite indenture.

The princesses' patent letters contain the bald and carefully unspecific notation that Mary and Elizabeth obtained their estates in performance of Henry's will. There was no citation of a specific bequest. The patents contain no reference to the unfulfilled gifts clause or to the depositions of Paget and others. A tripartite indenture could not be used to convey crown lands to the princesses because there was no specific passage in Henry's will bequeathing land to them. Nor was either princess midway through a property transaction with their father that would generate documentation to support completing the transaction through a tripartite indenture.

Unlike other similar grants from the royal demesne ostensibly completed under Henry VIII's authority, the princesses' patents make no reference to supporting documents. This, combined with the text of the will itself, indicates not only did Henry fail to bequeath land to his daughters, but also he expressed no intentions of ever doing so. At least, no one in 1547 or later was prepared to go on record as recalling that Henry had expressed such intentions.

Another detail in Mary's patents that serves to further erode the claimed relationship to Henry's will is that Mary's patrimony generated revenues far in excess of the cash allowance that Henry bequeathed to her in his will. Mary's lands generated revenues that totaled just over £3,800 *p.a.*[2] Elizabeth, by contrast, received a patrimony which generated almost exactly the sum of £3,000 *p.a.* that Henry had bequeathed as her cash allowance. Henry's will provides no justification for this unequal treatment. Both princesses should have received roughly the same amount in cash allowances. If the idea was simply to convert the cash allowances to landed revenues in order to perform Henry's will, then both princesses should have received roughly equivalent patrimonies. There was no justification in Henry's will for awarding Mary so much more than Elizabeth. Rather, Henry's will leaves little room for doubt that both sisters were to receive exactly the same income.

The lopsided allocation in favor of Mary provides the key to understanding the fraudulent claims in the patent letters. Unlike Elizabeth, Mary was the heir to the throne should Edward die childless. Henry's will not recognize this distinction between the princesses, but the executor-councilors clearly did.

There is another phrase that appears only in Mary's patent letters and it reveals the political context that generated her grant. Mary's patent letters claim that her estate was not only (if erroneously) awarded in performance of Henry's will but also the estates were granted to her "by the advice of the Protector [Somerset] and the executors."[3] Because this phrase appears only in Mary's patents, it is her patrimony on which this appendix will focus. The circumstances surrounding the issuance of Elizabeth's patents are discussed. The wording of Mary's patent letters indicates that the proper context for assessing the origin and significance of her patrimony is in the unique political situation taking shape in the days immediately following Henry VIII's death.

Henry died on January 28, 1547. He was succeeded by his nine-year-old son Edward. In his will, Henry had laid out a scheme for a collective regency vested in a sovereign privy council. This council of executor-councilors was to rule the kingdom until Edward came of age. Henry's obvious intent in suggesting this collective regency was to prevent the emergence of a Richard III–like figure who could threaten Edward's sovereignty perhaps even his life. The last minor to inherit the throne was Edward V who, along with his younger brother, entered the Tower of London and was never seen alive again, while his uncle assumed the crown as Richard III.

However laudable Henry's scheme was, it was also immediately deemed impractical. Within days, Henry's brother-in-law, Edward Seymour, Earl of Hertford (soon elevated to the dukedom of Somerset) proposed that he should assume the title of "Protector of the Realm" and rule as regent for his nephew in all but name. Somerset enlisted the aid of Henry's secretary William Paget. Somerset and Paget suggested that one man, Somerset, should rule as regent rather than maintaining collective sovereignty in the Privy Council as a whole. Somerset and Paget could anticipate that many of their colleagues would readily accept the practical utility of having one ruling regent rather than placing sole sovereignty in a collective and contentious body.

There were two separate but related problems with implementing the new scheme of a Somerset regency: it represented a deviation from Henry's will by which the privy councilors had received their own appointments and the second was the political stature of Princess Mary.

To induce the executor-councilors and other important politicians to accept the diminution of their collective power that a Somerset regency would entail and the significant violation it represented of Henry's will, Somerset and Paget determined that it would be necessary to bribe the other executor-councilors. As discussed by numerous scholars, these bribes took the form of property grants.[4] Historians generally cite Paget's May 30 grant as the first of these landed bribes.[5] Significantly, Mary began drawing revenues from her estates six weeks before the date of Paget's grant.

Mary's began drawing revenues from her lands on April 12, 1547.[6] At the risk of stating the obvious, Mary could not draw revenues from lands that had not already been assigned to her. Therefore, her estate had been settled by April 12. Mary obtained her properties at the same time that other politically important people were receiving the lands that Somerset had promised them. The timing of Mary's revenues alone argues that the princess was one of the recipients of Somerset's landed bribe. Indeed, it is now hard to explain the timing of Mary's revenues without reference to these other grants and to Somerset's wholesale landed bribe of the political elite.

To isolate Mary's grant involves arguing that the timing of her revenues alone is somehow unrelated to the establishment of Somerset's regency while the other land grants were connected. It would be quite a coincidence if Mary's estate was completed at this time and yet had nothing to do with the political situation that generated the contemporaneous grants to Paget, John Dudley, Thomas Seymour, and William Herbert. Following the reasoning of previous scholars in linking the contemporaneous grants to Paget, Seymour, Dudley, et al. to Somerset's bid for the regency, this study proposes a connection between Mary's estate settled in April 1547 and Somerset's consolidation of power.

The political significance of Mary's estate lies not only in its timing but also in its scale. Indeed, the scale of her estate combined with its rapid settlement suggests that Somerset and the councilors delayed the completion of their own property grants until after Mary's lands had been assigned. Mary's estate was completed before Paget's (May 30), Dudley's (June 23), and Thomas Seymour's (August 19). Somerset himself did not obtain the patents to his own lands until July 9.[7]

Moreover, Princess Mary received far more lands than any of the privy councilors or executors—a lot more. Although £1,000 in landed revenues was the minimum enjoyed by most noblemen, Mary obtained over £3,800 in landed revenues.[8] Mary's patrimony provided her with annual revenues that not only placed her on a par with dukes and earls, but it was in far in excess of the total amount Somerset used to bribe the executor-councilors. The combined total of revenues from the land grants to all of the executor-councilors in 1547 has been estimated at an aggregate total of only £3,200—about £600 less than the landed revenues settled on Mary alone.[9] The comparison serves to illustrate the extraordinary scale of Mary's land grant. Somerset himself initially obtained lands generating an annual revenue of £1,100 to support him in his new dignity as Protector of the Realm and Duke of Somerset.[10]

The timing of Mary's settlement is suggestive but the implications of it diverge from the widely accepted narrative of this historical "moment" and Mary's part in it. In general, historians tend to portray Somerset's rise to power as logically inevitable and to cast Mary as a marginalized from the jockeying for political position that took place amongst the executor-councilors during the first two months of Edward VI's reign.[11] Hindsight makes it easy to forget that the political situation taking shape after Henry's death in late January 1547 initially appeared unstable. The new king was nine years old and his right of legitimate succession was not instantly accepted by the international community.[12] The paradoxical result of Henry's matrimonial adventures and his break with the Roman Catholic Church was that, Mary, of all his children, was the only one widely accepted as legitimate—at least by the politically powerful outside of England. Domestically, Mary had served as the *de facto* Princess of Wales in 1525, she was instrumental in brokering an Anglo-Habsburg alliance in 1545, and was part of powerful female network that included Katherine Parr and Anne Seymour (wife of Somerset).

Because Mary did not make a bid for the regency, it is easier still to forget that she was a very credible rival to Somerset for the regency. She was well connected via her Habsburg cousins, highly educated, and possessed legitimate blood claims to the throne herself. As the king's half-sister, she was more closely related to him than was Somerset, the king's maternal uncle. It was usual practice on the Continent for royal women with Mary's qualifications to assume the regency for an underaged male king. Although this was not the practice in England, Mary's suitability for the regency was not lost upon the English political elite. Two years later, in 1549, some of the Edwardian privy councilors would offer Mary the regency.[13]

Mary was close to the center of power and in a position to know the contents of Henry VIII's will.[14] This is significant because the executor-councilors had quickly decided to violate the will's cash bequest clauses almost immediately after Henry VIII died. To violate the will in any degree jeopardized the already shaky legitimacy of the sovereign Privy Council because their powers and offices derived solely from the will. The will should have been a sacrosanct document but the executor-councilors had personal reasons to creatively interpret some of the will's stipulations even at the risk of undermining their own authority. The princess was in a position to object. If Mary publicly voiced her objections to this violation of Henry's will, then she could call into question the legitimacy of the new regime.

In response to the potentially volatile political situation in the wake of Henry VIII's death, Protector Somerset "freely adapted" Henry's testamentary bequest to his daughters in order to remove Mary as a possible threat to the stability of the young king's regime by bribing her with a landed estate. This (temporary) alienation of crown lands was then justified (as preserved in the phrasing of the patent letters) by claiming it originated as a bequest from Henry's will. The illusion was reinforced by converting Elizabeth's Henrician cash bequest into property as well (though worth considerably less than the estate awarded to Mary). The conveyancing documents for these estates—the princesses' patent letters— therefore reveal a legal fraud in falsely claiming a relationship to Henry's will. Mary and Elizabeth obtained their landed estate not through Henry's will but due to the obvious political dangers inherent in the situation of a underaged monarch, a ruling Privy Council and an adult, politically ambitious, royal sibling.

Somerset and the executor-councilors were encroaching on the royal demesne in direct contravention of Henry VIII's will when they awarded themselves lands. The estates that Somerset used for bribing the executor-councilors derived from the royal demesne. If Mary had publicly objected, if she had warned her brother, informed the Imperial ambassadors, written to Continental Catholic powers, and conferred with leading courtiers, she certainly could have caused trouble on the basis that she was the king's closest relation. A person of Mary's status publicly calling attention to the actions of Somerset and the executor-councilors could potentially have served to undermine an already tenuous regime.

Somerset and the executor-councilors could not see into the future and be assured of Mary's compliance. They could, however, enjoy a measure of security on this issue if Mary accepted the bribe of a landed estate. Moreover, this bribe could be cloaked by claiming a false relationship to Henry VIII's will. The will's bequest of a respectable (although not excessively generous) allowance to Mary enabled Somerset and the executor-councilors to bribe the princess on a massive scale under the cover of performing Henry's will.

Henry's will indicates that he assumed the princesses would live as most spinster English princess lived—in one combined household under crown oversight. His will allocated that each princess should have £3,000 to pay for incidental expenses such as tips, rewards, and gifts. Their household servants would remain as crown servants sworn to the service of the king who would pay their wages. Henry's plan, however, was cast to winds (along with other provisions in the will) when Somerset asked and secured for himself the regency during Edward VI's minority. Because Mary was an all-too-credible alternative to assume the regency, Somerset deemed it necessary to bribe her into passivity by converting the allowance Henry had bequeathed her into a landed patrimony. Somerset sweetened the deal still further by ensuring that her landed revenues considerably exceeded the allowance Henry had left her.

Endowing the princesses with substantial estates that would be reflected in their households was the last thing that Henry VIII would have wished. The king's overriding concern throughout the will is Edward's safety as an underage monarch. This grant to Mary of landed patrimony in lieu of the traditional allowance resulted in her becoming an "overmighty subject" with the resources to challenge Edward's authority in matters of religion and of the succession. Her estate turned Mary into a regional magnate with many livings and offices in her gift. After receiving her patent letters in 1548, Mary formally obtained "lordship" rights the offices and livings associated with her estates. This made her a political patron of considerable local influence in East Anglia. Eventually, Mary would exploit this local influence to raise an army to successfully challenge Jane Grey and enforce her own succession to the throne in 1553. Throughout Edward's reign, the princess maintained that her household and estates were not subject to the crown's policies on religion. Thanks to Somerset's decision to award Mary a landed patrimony, she took possession of the throne in 1553 as an overmighty subject as much as a prince of the blood.

Henry was relentlessly conventional in his provision for his daughters. His bequest to them in his will revolved around their future marital status. Henry's concern over the marriages of his daughters was reflected in the wills of other elite men. More particularly, the strictures Henry placed on Mary's and Elizabeth's freedom of choice was another instance of Henry following testamentary convention amongst elite fathers. Like other contemporary elite fathers, Henry specified that his daughters marry with the consent of the will's executors so as to prevent the princesses from marrying beneath them or "dishonorably."[15]

The Privy Council's decision to convert these bequests into lands undid Henry's attempts to contain and marry off his daughters. Their considerable estates robbed the princesses of any motivation toward marriage. They now wielded authority as two of the country's wealthiest magnates. As events were to play out, the Privy Council would have done better, in terms of their long-term political careers, to adhere to the original stipulations of Henry VIII's will. The conversion of princesses' bequests from "stuff" to property elevated them from the status of barely acknowledged heirs to overmighty subjects. Using crown lands to create overmighty subjects had been a concern of political commentators since the mid-fifteenth century.[16] This was very probably the outcome that Henry had tried to avert.

The patent letters for both Mary and Elizabeth contain a deliberate fraud. Because there were no supporting documents, like a specific bequest in Henry's will or conveyancing documents in process, the patent letters employ unusually vague language when claiming a relationship to Henry's will. The more concrete phrase "by the advice of the Protector [Somerset] and the executors" reveals the true authority awarding estates to Mary and Elizabeth.[17]

In the first uncertain weeks of Somerset's regency, Mary's international connections, blood claims, and domestic political status meant that she, potentially, posed a serious threat to the stability of Somerset's regime. Mary was therefore included in Somerset's wholesale landed bribe of the politically elite. Somerset intended this bribe to quiet any objections to the questionable legitimacy of Somerset's regency. Without supporting documentation, Somerset could not fund his bribe to Mary from the royal demesne since there was no indication that Henry had ever intended to bestow lands on either of his daughters. Somerset twisted the allowance bequest to the princesses to serve as nebulous basis for awarding a very generous patrimony to Mary.

Because the Henrician allowance bequest included Elizabeth, then she, too, must be provided with an estate to further enhance the plausibility that Henry's will had bequeathed land to both his daughters. Yet the political realities of the situation after Henry's death with Mary now being the heir to the throne meant that Elizabeth need not be placated with such generosity as Mary. So Elizabeth received an estate that generated annual revenues that only just met the allowance Henry had bequeathed her.

Mary and Elizabeth began living off their landed revenues in 1547 not because their father had bequeathed patrimonies to them. Rather, their patent letters contain evidence of a legal fraud instigated "by the advice of the Protector [Somerset] and the executors" designed to mask a raiding of the royal demesne to endow Mary with a massive estate.[18] Mary's patrimony was a bribe by Somerset similar in purpose (if not in scale) to the other landed bribes Somerset offered to other members of the political elite. The fraudulent claim that Mary's patrimony originated from Henry's will necessitate that Elizabeth's allowance also be converted to landed revenues in order to lend extra verisimilitude to the patents' claimed relationship to Henry's will.

The princesses owed their estates to the *sui generis* nature of the Somerset regime rather than to their father's generosity. The connection between elite estates and high-stakes politics was pervasive in Tudor England. The unusual nature of Mary's and Elizabeth's roles as heads of elite households and property owners tracked the unusual situation of a government headed by an underaged monarch and a sovereign Privy Council. The 1544 Act of Succession had created the opportunity for the female succession, but it was the Privy Council's decision to confer princely estates on Mary and Elizabeth that gave them the financial and military resources to accomplish it.

NOTES

1. The records of these land grants are transcribed in the *CPR 1547–1548*, (London 1924), pp. 6–7, 17, 23, 25, 42, 45, 124, 190, 193, 240, 243–245, 252

2. Harris, *English Aristocratic Women*, p. viii; according to Mary's patent letters, her annual landed revenues were £3,819, see *CPR*, II, p. 22

3. *CPR*, II, p. 20

4. Miller, "Henry VIII's Unwritten Will," p.87; D. Starkey, *The Reign of Henry VIII: Personalities and Politics* (London, 1985), p. 163. G. R. Elton, *Reform and Reformation* (London, 1977), p. 333; Houlbrook, "Henry's Will," p. 898; P. Williams, *The Later Tudors: England 1547–1603*, (Oxford UP, 1998) pp. 34–35; J. Loach, *Edward VI*, (Yale UP, 1999), pp. 26–27

5. Miller, "Henry's VIII's Unwritten Will", p.97; The records of these land grants are transcribed in the *CPR 1547–1548*, (London 1924), pp. 6–7, 17, 23, 25, 42, 45, 124, 190, 193, 240, 243–245, 252

6. *APC*, II, p. 85

7. *CPR, 1547–1548*, pp. 25, 45, 190, 252

8. *CPR*, II, p. 22

9. The total for all the estates of the privy councilors in landed revenues is given in Miller, "Henry's unwritten will," p. 87; Starkey, *The Reign of Henry VIII*, p. 64 suggests that this may be a conservative estimate

10. Houlbrooke, "Wills," p. 896. Somerset would substantially increase his lands and revenues of the course of the next two years

11. Prescott, *Mary Tudor*, p. 102; R. K. Marshall, *Mary I*, pp. 49–50

12. Loades, *Mary Tudor: The Tragical History*, p. 70

13. Hoak, *The King's Council*, pp. 254–262

14. She later told the Imperial ambassador, Van der Delft, that she had no idea of the will's contents, *CSP*, Spanish, IX, 123. Queen Mary's later efforts to suppress the will because of the marriage clause suggest that she had a pretty good idea of the will's

stipulations (the clause stipulated that she must obtain the executors' consent before marrying or forfeit the throne); *CSP* Mary, p. 207, fn. 6. Queen Elizabeth too sought to suppress the will; Levine, *Tudor Dynastic Problems*, p. 113

15. Harris, *English Aristocratic Women*, 57 for instances of other elite fathers placing similar strictures on their daughters

16. Wolffe, *Crown Lands . . .* , pp. 36, 91

17. *CPR*, II, p. 20

18. *CPR*, II, p. 20

Mary's Aborted Flight, 1550

In July 1550, a Flemish warship drew near the Essex coastal town of Maldon. The ship, sent by Mary of Hungary, Regent of the Netherlands for her brother, the Habsburg emperor, Charles V, was on a mission to rescue an highly-placed religious dissident: Mary Tudor. On this covert rescue ship was the Regent's envoy, Jean Dubois, charged with the mission to bring Mary safely out of England. Although Mary had appealed to the Imperial ambassador for years to bring this about, she changed her mind at the last minute. Mary mobilized her household and exploited prevailing gender conceptions to deliberately sabotage Dubois' mission.

Dubois' mission was to land on the English coast where Mary's household would make contact with him immediately. Then the household officers and Dubois would arrange for the princess to be brought aboard his ship. Once the princess was aboard his ship Dubois would then take Mary first to the Flemish court of the Regent and then to the Imperial establishment of the Emperor Charles. The information for this incident comes from a report filed by Dubois to the Regent and is detailed in an unusually long and detailed abstract in the *Calendar of State Papers, Spanish*.[1]

Mary's staff failed to contact Dubois after he landed. This jeopardized the entire mission. The longer the ship was in port, the more suspicious the Maldon townspeople would become of Dubois and his Flemish warship. It took

Dubois a whole day before he managed to track down and meet with Mary's most senior household officer, her comptroller or treasurer, Sir Robert Rochester. Rochester ominously began the meeting by stating he was not sure it was a good idea for Mary to leave England at all. Thoroughly alarmed, Dubois recalled to Rochester how throughout the previous year, 1549, Mary had relentlessly petitioned for asylum at the Habsburg courts. Thus Dubois' mission was the result of a year's worth of planning, mainly by the princess herself. Dubois could not resist reminding the embarrassed Rochester that the thirty-four-year-old Mary had claimed she was "like a little ignorant girl" who placed herself in the keeping of her Imperial relatives.

Dubois insisted that Mary come to his ship that night if there was any chance for her escape to be successful. Instead, much to Dubois' annoyance, Rochester relayed a command from the princess herself ordering Dubois to come to her lodgings for an interview. This would cause further delay since Mary insisted that she could not see Dubois until the evening. This meant effectively that the schedule would be thrown off for another day.

If Dubois was frustrated by this delay, there was worse yet to come. When Dubois presented himself at Mary's lodgings, Mary kept him waiting in the antechamber. To add insult to injury, Rochester appeared to keep Dubois company and regaled him with yet more objections to the proposed escape plan. When the princess finally received him, Mary announced that the earliest she could leave with Dubois was not for two more days yet. No doubt suppressing his annoyance as best he could, Dubois began then and there to work out the details of a new escape plan with Mary.

Before Dubois could finalize the details with the princess and, perhaps, salvage the mission, Rochester interrupted the interview with the news that Maldon officials were about to impound Dubois' ship. According to Dubois, the princess immediately panicked and began wailing "What shall we do? What is to become of me?" Dubois argued that the best thing was for the princess to accompany him back to the ship immediately as originally planned. At this critical juncture, Rochester suddenly remembered that he had heard that the watch in Maldon would be doubled that night.

The bad situation now thoroughly disintegrated. Dubois and Rochester hotly debated whether the princess should leave that night while Mary continued to wail in the background "but what is to become of me?" The tension was broken when Dubois wearily suggested that maybe he should just return to the ship by himself. Suddenly there was silence. In this silence, no one actually acknowledged that this would effectively mean the end of the mission, but the calm that now prevailed spoke volumes. Even more revealing was Mary's parting remark to Dubois. She said, "You see that it is not our fault now."

Some days later, in his report to the regent Mary of Hungary, Dubois noted bitterly that the watch had not been doubled that night as Rochester had claimed.

Furthermore, Dubois learned that his ship had never been in any danger of being impounded. Dubois laid the blame for the failed rescue attempt squarely upon Rochester: "I suspected that the Controller had made out the situation in Maldon to be more dangerous than it was in reality." Dubois left the English coast for good a few days later without Mary.

The reason that I have chosen to break with current scholarly convention and quote so extensively from an abstract in *Calendar of State Papers* is that Dubois' letter to the Regent is abstracted in the calendar in unusual length and detail. Perhaps for this reason, this incident enjoys popularity amongst Mary's modern biographers for its obvious farcical elements.[2] Reading Dubois' letter transparently, as the editors of the *Calendar* surely did, later scholars have suggested that Rochester decided independently that it would be political suicide if Mary left the country. The idea is that Rochester, not Mary, realized that she would have a difficult time enforcing her claim to the throne if King Edward died while she was abroad. Historians assume from Dubois' report that Mary was too politically inept to grasp the complexities of the situation presented by Dubois' ships and, therefore, relied upon the decisive advice of Rochester.

I suggest here that a critical reading of Dubois' letter reveals clues pointing to a very different scenario. Dubois described the details of the failed escape so exhaustively because he was returning to Brussels without the Princess Mary and would have to account to the Regent (and through her to the Emperor) for the deployment of ships and money to no avail. Naturally, his first concern is to exonerate himself of any blame.

Of course, someone must be to blame. It may initially appear that Dubois casts blame overtly on Rochester but covertly upon Mary also. It is this covert blame that has resonated with Mary's twentieth-century biographers. Although Dubois' depiction of Mary may strike modern readers as cloying or relentlessly conventional, it was very much in agreement with the conventions of female behavior found in contemporary conduct literature. Dubois' depiction of Mary is entirely appropriate to the desired behavior of a female—she was passive, needy, and dependent. In other words, Dubois may have tailored his depiction of Mary in order to exonerate rather than blame her. Dubois absolves her of blame because she was merely a helpless female as contemporaries understood the term.

Indeed, it would have been counterproductive for Dubois to disparage Mary too roundly. Dubois was, after all, writing to Mary's maternal relatives. Moreover, rank was important here. Dubois was merely an untitled envoy writing to royalty about royalty. So Dubois exonerates the princess by portraying Mary as an "ignorate little girl" being ruthlessly manipulated by the real villain of Dubois' account, the comptroller, Sir Robert Rochester.

Dubois' self-interested, though understandable, concern with blaming others for the failed rescue attempt does open the door for reading his letter critically.

We cannot take everything he wrote at face value. He surely had an agenda. If one would rather not claim so much then one must at least search for outside confirmation of his depictions. Were there, for instance, other accounts that indicate that Mary completely relied upon her servants, upon Rochester in particular, to make important political decisions for her? Had Mary ever allowed an household officer, like Rochester, to act on his own initiative and determine her future?

What evidence survives for Mary's relationship with her servants presents a stark contrast to the depiction of Dubois in his letter to the regent. I have argued in chapter 2 that there is enough evidence to indicate that a "culture of reverence" persisted in her preaccession household. All surviving evidence suggests that Mary's servants were acutely conscious of her rank, exalted ancestry from two royal houses, and potential future as a sovereign ruler.

In fact, other evidence indicates that Rochester in particular was overawed by Mary. As detailed in chapter 2, Rochester chose imprisonment in the Tower rather than attempt to pressure Mary into conforming to the king's orders regarding religion. Rochester's misgivings appear to have been confirmed by Mary's reaction to the very idea that her servants could exert any kind of influence upon her on politically sensitive issues. A few months after Dubois left England, Mary informed a delegation from the privy council that she would never blur the distinction between mistress and servant by asking their advice on political or religious matters. The privy council registers record her as declaring that the princess would "wurst endure" her servants "to move her in any suche mattiers."[3]

Either Mary and Rochester's relationship had undergone a sea change in the weeks following Dubois' departure or Dubois' depiction is a less-than-accurate representation of their relationship. It is hard to credit that Rochester, who would literally rather face death than attempt to overrule the princess, would, a few weeks earlier, have deliberately sabotaged an escape plan she herself had planned for a year if she was still committed to it. It is even harder to credit that Mary would have played along or allowed him to take such initiative.

I am not suggesting that Dubois deliberately misrepresented the dynamic between Mary and Rochester. Rather, Dubois quite accurately represented a staged scene orchestrated by Mary and Rochester. In fact, there are clues in Dubois' report that indicate that it was Mary who sabotaged the rescue and that she allowed, even encouraged, her servant Rochester to take the blame for it upon himself.

There is a telling remark contained in the abstracted version of Dubois' letter that Dubois attributes to Rochester, though the source of the information could only have been the princess herself. Dubois claimed that Rochester was convinced from a recent casting of the king's horoscope that Edward VI would not live out the year. If Rochester knew of this horoscope, it was certainly be-

cause Mary had commissioned it and therefore knew of it also. It was a treasonous offense to cast the monarch's horoscope. It was too great a risk for Rochester
to do this on his own initiative. Just as Elizabeth would commission the casting
of Queen Mary's horoscope, it appears that Princess Mary did the same for her
brother, Edward VI. What this apparent non sequitur in Dubois' letter tells us is
that Mary was convinced from a recent casting of the king's horoscope that she
would soon be inheriting the throne. It was not a good time for her to leave the
country.

The situation in which Princess Mary found herself in the summer of 1550
when Dubois arrived with his "rescue" ship was complicated. She was the leader
of the Catholic opposition to her brother's Protestant regime. It was a regime,
moreover, that was putting ever-mounting pressure on her and her household to
attend the new Protestant service as a show of political loyalty to the crown. As
the heir to childless Edward VI, Mary's conformity was of national importance.
What had helped her to resist this pressure thus far was her blood ties to the
Habsburg imperial family, in particular to the emperor Charles V and to Mary
of Hungary, Regent of the Netherlands. The leaders of Edward VI's government
were unwilling to risk open conflict with Charles V or disrupt the important
wool trade with the Netherlands over Mary's persistent Catholicism. As the
Edwardian government slowly but persistently increased pressure upon Mary
to conform to Protestantism, it must have seemed like good sense, in 1549, for
Mary to canvass plans with the Imperial ambassador to flee the English realm
and seek refuge at the courts of Mary of Hungary and Charles V.

Yet by midsummer 1550, the king's horoscope indicated to Mary that she
would shortly inherit the throne. Then Mary heard that Dubois' ships had left
port, and soon thereafter they were sighted off the Essex coast. What was she to
do? If she went through with the rescue plan then she might forfeit the English
throne through her absence. If she refused the help offered by Dubois on behalf
of the Emperor and the Regent, then she risked alienating her vital imperial
allies. According to Dubois' letter, Mary tellingly referred to the dilemma I have
just outlined: "I do not know how the Emperor would take it if it turned out to
be impossible to go now, after I have so often importuned his Majesty on the
subject." The best strategy that allowed her to remain in England and yet not
frustrate the attempts to render imperial aid was for her to stall for time and
make it appear as if the rescue failed due to circumstances beyond her control.
The best result would be for Mary to be able to claim, "You see now it is not our
fault" that the rescue failed.

It is surely more than a coincidence that this is exactly the scenario that
Dubois depicted. Given what other evidence reveals about the relationship between Mary and Rochester, it is clear that Mary would not have allowed Rochester to sabotage her escape plans if she was still fully committed to them.

Moreover, it should be remembered that Mary was thirty-four years old at the time she was claiming to be an "ignorant little girl" and wailing in the background "But what is to become of me?" It is hard to credit that she was being anything but disingenuous with Dubois. After all, this was the same woman who, a few weeks later, would yell at privy councilors from a second-story window that it was stupid of them to assume that her servants could influence her in any way.

Dubois' portrayal, when interpreted in the light of Mary's history as an householder and Dubois' own agenda in constructing the account, indicates that Mary and her household put on a performance for Dubois that he was only too happy to detail in his letter to the Regent. By allowing Rochester to assume responsibility for the failure of the escape plan, by acting the part of an "ignorant little girl," Mary could hopefully escape blame for the unraveling of the scheme to which the Emperor and the Regent had committed ships and money. Mary's gender and the loyalty of her household servant endowed her with plausible deniability in a tricky and tense political situation. For his part, Dubois could exonerate himself of any blame without insulting the princess to her relatives.

NOTES

1. *CSP, Spanish*, X, pp.124–35
2. See D. M. Loades, *Mary Tudor: A Life* [Oxford, 1989], p.156, and F.M.H. Prescott, *Mary Tudor* [London, 1952], p.139
3. APC, III, p.350

APPENDIX D

Creating and Investing a Prince of Wales

This confusion was, perhaps, exacerbated by the idiosyncratic nature of how the title was bestowed and invested. The royal tradition for designating the monarch's firstborn son as "Prince of Wales" has remained remarkably stable for centuries. The associated procedures and legal status of the title are the same today as they were in late medieval England. The title "Prince of Wales" is (and always has been) in the sovereign's gift. The title is reserved only for the monarch's firstborn son. The sovereign, however, can withhold the title. The monarch can elect not to bestow the title on his or her firstborn son. However, the sovereign does not have complete discretion over the granting of the title. Most important, the monarch cannot bestow the title "Prince of Wales" on anyone but the firstborn son, and that son must be the issue of a legally valid marriage. So Henry VIII could not bestow the title on his illegitimate son, Henry Fitzroy. The other relevant caveat for this study is that at that time the sovereign could not (and never could) bestow the title on a female.[1]

Complicating the issue further is the difference between the "creation" of a Prince of Wales and the formal investing of a royal offspring with the title. Some of Mary's contemporaries erroneously assumed that Henry had bestowed the title upon Mary informally, but they would have simultaneously understood that she had never been officially invested with title. A Prince of Wales is "created" or granted the title by the monarch informally. The sovereign can "create" (designate) his or her firstborn son as "Prince of Wales" shortly after birth, as Edward IV did for his son, the future Edward V, and as Henry VIII would later do for his son, the future Edward VI. This designation can be nothing more than a witnessed verbal declaration that finds confirmation in subsequent written documents. Edward VI's right to the title of Prince of Wales was confirmed by the crown when Henry VIII issued instructions for Edward's first household in which the infant was referred to as "prince of Wales and duke of Cornwall."[2]

"Investing" a prince with the title "Prince of Wales" is another, much more public, matter. When sovereigns designated their infant firstborn sons as Prince of Wales, the investiture often did not take place until years later when the prince was judged of sufficient age to withstand the ceremony. The "investiture" of a prince with the title involves not only elaborate ceremony but also a confirming act of Parliament. The confusion over "creating" and "investing" a royal offspring with the title was aggravated in the sixteenth century by the imprecise terminology employed on this issue even by those most vitally concerned. For instance, the first entry in the chronicle kept by Edward VI refers to his "creation" as Prince of Wales and how this ceremony was to take place but was cancelled when his father, Henry VIII, died and Edward acceded to the throne.[3] Edward, however, was referring to his "investiture." He had held the title "Prince of Wales" since infancy and even signed himself "princeps" in his personal correspondence, but had not yet been invested with the title ceremonially. It was the ceremony that had been cancelled, not Edward's assumption of the title of Prince of Wales.[4]

This disjunction between the designation and the ceremonial investment of a Prince of Wales is something not widely appreciated in the sixteenth century. Edward VI, before his accession, was styled "Prince of Wales" in royal documents even though he never underwent a formal investiture ceremony.[5] In this, he followed in his father's footsteps. After the death of Arthur, Prince of Wales, his father Henry VII declared verbally that his younger son, Prince Henry, was now Prince of Wales. But Prince Henry (the future Henry VIII) did not undergo a formal investiture ceremony, nor was he granted the revenues of the principality as enjoyed by his brother before him. Despite this lack of ceremonial and public confirmation of the title, contemporaries understood in both cases that these princes held the title "Prince of Wales."

It is not surprising, therefore, that some of Mary's contemporaries drew the erroneous impression from her household on the Welsh Marches (which so resembled in scale and function those of preceding Princes of Wales) that she, too, had been granted the title. Given all this ambiguity, it appears that the scale of Mary's household in the Welsh Marches, evoking as it did the establishments of previous male Princes of Wales, was taken as a sign by many that Mary held the title officially.

To ensure that modern readers do not share in this confusion, it is necessary to be clear about this here: Mary was neither created nor invested as Princess of Wales. In the sixteenth century (and at the time of this writing), a woman was not eligible to hold the title in her own right. The designation "Princess of Wales" was reserved only for the wife of the Prince of Wales. There are no official documents generated by the crown that refer to Mary holding the title of Princess of Wales or Prince of Wales.

The designation referring to "princes council" signifies only that spelling has changed over the intervening centuries. The modern word "princess" was often spelled with only one "s" in the sixteenth century. Moreover, the possessive was often not employed and rarely with the type of punctuation common to modern usage. The "princes council" is properly translated into modern idiom as "the princess' council" with the term princess indicating Mary's rank as "my lady princess" rather than as a female Prince (or Princess) of Wales.

Despite this, Mary's princely household in the Welsh Marches associated her very strongly with the Principality. As indicated earlier, this association was compelling enough to persuade foreign and domestic observers into assuming that Mary held the title. Mary was the unofficial Princess of Wales because her household was on such a scale that many observers assumed that she held the title.

NOTES

1. For an extended treatment of the procedures and history of the title, see F. Jones, *The Princes and Principality of Wales* [Wales UP, 1969]

2. BL Cotton Vitellieus C., i., f. 45v

3. J. North, *England's Boy King: The Diary of Edward VI, 1547–1553* [Welwyn Garden City, UK, 2005], p. 16; best modern edition is in W. K. Jordan, ed., *The Chronicle and Political Papers of Edward VI* [London, 1966]

4. Henry's plans for sending the prince to the Welsh marches after his investiture are in *LP*, XIII, pt.1, 1057. BL Cotton Vitellius C., i., ff. 39r–44v (formerly 59r–64v); printed in P. R. Roberts, "A Breviat of the Effectes Devised for Wales," *Camden Miscellany*, 1975

5. BL Cotton Vitellieus C., i., ff. 45v, 46v

SELECT BIBLIOGRAPHY

PRIMARY SOURCES

London: British Library MSS
Arundel, 97, 151
Cotton Caligula D. VII
Cleopatra, E. VI
Cotton Faustina C. ii
Cotton Nero, B. vi
Cotton Nero C. X.
Cotton Otho, X
Cotton Titus B.i
CottonVespasian, C. XIV; F.XIII
Galba B XII
Harleian 589, 1419B, 6807
Lansdowne 840, A.
Royal 14 B. XIX; 17 B XXVIII

Kew: The National Archives MSS
E   23/4/1
      36/219

36/222
101/625/1
101/419/15
101/419/17
101/419/19
101/420/2
101/420/6
101/421/4
101/421/10
101/421/12
101/421/14
101/424/7
101/424/20
101/425/1
305/21/H19

PC   2/2–2/3

PRINTED EDITIONS

[unless otherwise noted, all editions printed in London]

Words in **bold** are reference terms

Acts of the Privy Council of England. New Series., ed. J. R. Dasent [1890]

Ascham, R., *The Schoolmaster* (1570), ed. E. Arber [Birmingham 1870]

Disertissimi Viri Roger Aschami, Angli Regiæ Olim Maiestati à Latinis Epistolis, Familiarium Epistolarum Libri Tres, Magna Orationis Elegantia Conscripti, Nunc Prostremò Emendati & Aucti . . . ed. E[dward] G[rant] [1581]

"The Examination of Robert **Aske**," M. Bateson (ed.), *English Historical Review*, V [1890], pp. 550–573

Calendar of Letters, Despatches and State Papers Relating to the Negotiations between England and Spain. Preserved in the Archives at Vienna, Simancas, and Elsewhere [1912]

Calendar of the Patent Rolls. Preserved in the Public Record Office [1924]

Calendar of State Papers and Manuscripts, Relating to English Affairs, Existing in the Archives and Collections of Venic, and in other libraries of Northern Italy, R. Brown (ed.) [1867]

Calendar of State Papers, Domestic Series, of the Reign of Mary I, 1553–1558, preserved in the Public Record Office, Revised Edition, C. S. Knighton (ed.) [1998]

Calendar of State Papers, Foreign Series, of the Reign of Edward VI, 1547–1553, Preserved in the State Paper Department of Her Majesty's Public Record Office, W. B. Turnbull (ed.) [1861]

Camden, W., *The Historie of the Most Renowned and Victorious Princesse Elizabeth, Late Queene of England . . .* [1630], W. T. MacCaffrey (ed.) [1970]

Castiglione, B., *The Book of the Courtier (Venice, 1528)*, ed. C. Singleton [New York, 1959]

Cavendish, G., *Thomas Wolsey, late Cardinal his Life and Death*, R. Lockyer (ed.) [1962]

The Chronicle of Queen Jane and of Two Years of Queen Mary . . . , J. G. Nichols (ed.), Camden Society, no. XLVIII [1850]

Chronicle of the Grey Friars of London, J. G. Nichols (ed.) [1852]

Clifford, H., *The Life of Jane Dormer, Duchesss of Feria*, J. Stevenson (ed.) [1887]

Duwes, G. *An Introductory for to Learn to Read, to Pronounce, and to Speak French [1532?]* R.C. Alston (ed.), Facsimilie [Menston, UK, 1972]

The Literary Remains of King Edward VI, J. G. Nicholas (ed.) [1857]

Chronicle and Papers of Edward VI, W. K. Jordan (ed.) [1966]

"State Papers relating to the custody of the Princess Elizabeth at Woodstock, in 1554 . . . ," Manning, C. R. (ed.), *Norfolk Archaeology . . .* , 4 (1855): pp. 133–226

Elizabeth I: Collected Works, L. S. Marcus, J. Mueller, and M. B. Rose (eds.) [2000]

Elizabeth I: Autograph Compositions and Foreign Language Originals, J. Mueller and L. S. Marcus (eds.) [2003]

Queen Elizabeth I: Selected Works, S. May (ed.) [2004]

The Word of a Prince: A Life of Elizabeth I, M. Perry, (ed.) [Suffolk UK, 1990]

Elyot, Thomas, *The Book Named the Governor, 1531* [facsimilie: Menston, UK, 1970], ed. R. C. Alston

The Defense of Good Women (1540) facsimile ed. E. J. Howard [Ohio, 1940]

"The Count of Feria's Dispatch to Philip II of 14 November 1558," *Camden Miscellany*, ed. M. J. Rodríguez-Salgado and S. Adams, 4th ser., vol. 28 [1984]

Fœdera, Coventiones, Literæ, et cujuscunque generis Acta Publica, inter reges angliæ, et alios quosvis Imperatores, Reges, Pontifices, Principes, Vel Communitates . . . ed. Thomas Rymer, 3rd edition [1751] [fascmilie] [Hants., UK, 1967]

Forrest, W., *The History of Grisild the Second: A Narrative, In verse, of the Divorce of Queen Katharine of Aragon (1558)*, ed. W. D. Macray [1875]

Foxe, J., *Acts and Monuments of These Latter and Perillous Dayes . . .* [John Day, March 20, 1563]

Foxe, John *Acts and Monuments [. . .]. The Variorum Edition.* [online]. (hriOnline, Sheffield 2004). Available from: http://www.hrionline.shef.ac.uk/foxe/. [Accessed: 2000–August 2007]

Correspondencia de Guitierez Gomez de Fuensalida, ed. A. P. y Mélia [Madrid, 1907]

Guistinian, S., *Four Years at the Court of Henry VIII.; Selection of Despatches . . .* , tr. Rawdon Brown, 2 vols. [1854]

Harrison, W., *The Description of England: The Classic Contemporary Account of Tudor Social Life* G. Edelen (ed.). [1968]

The Privy Purse Expenses of Henry VIII, N. H. Nicholas, (ed.) [1827]

Of Household Stuff: The 1601 Inventories of Bess of Hardwick [2001]

"The **Household** Account of the Princess Elizabeth, 1551–2," ed. Viscount Strangford [Percy Clinton Sydney Smythe], *The Camden Miscellany*, 2 [Camden Society, 1853]

A Collection of Ordinances and Regulations for the Government of the Royal House-hold made in divers reigns from King Edward III to King William and Queen Mary. Also Receipts in Ancient Cookery [1790]

The **Inventory** *of King Henry VIII*, vol. 1, D. Starkey (ed). [1998]

"**Inventory** of the Wardrobe, Plate, &c. of Henry Fitzroy, duke of Richmond and Somerset; and an Inventory of the Wardrobe, &c. of Katherine of Arragon [sic], at Baynard's Castle," J. G. Nichols, (ed)., *Camden Miscellany*, 1st seris, vol.3, part 3 [1855], pp. 1–41

Letters *& Papers, Foreign and Domestic of the Reign of Henry VIII*, J. S. Brewer (ed). [1870]

The **Lisle** *Letters*, M. St. Clare Byrne (ed). [Chicago, 1981]

The Diary of Henry **Machyn**, *Citizen and Merchant-Taylor of London, From A.D. 1550 to A.D. 1563*, J. G. Nichols, (ed). [1847]

The Privy Purse Expenses of the Princess **Mary**, F. Madden Madden (ed.) [1831]

Mayer, J. *A Patterne for Women* [1619]

Pollock, L., ed., *With Faith and Physic: The Life of a Tudor Gentlewoman* [New York, 1993]

The **Proclamations** *of the Tudor Queens*, ed. F. A. Youngs Jr. [Cambridge UP, 1976]

Religion, *Politics and Society in Sixteenth-Century England*, I. Archer (ed), Camden Fifth Series, vol.22 [2003]

Rivals *in Power: Live and Letters of the Great Tudor Dynasties*, ed. D. Starkey [1990]

Haynes, S., *A Collection of* **State** *Papers Relating to the Affairs in the Reigns of King Henry VIII, King Edward VI, Queen Mary and Queen Elizabeth From the Year 1542 to 1570 . . .* [1740]

The **Statutes** *of the Realm* [Records Office, 1810–1828], ed., A. Luder, vol.3

Strype, J., *Ecclesiastical memorials . . .* , 7 vols. [1781–1816]

"The Narrative of Richard **Troughton**," F. Madden (ed.), *Archaeologia*, xxiii, (1831)

Tudor *Royal Proclamations*, Hughes, P. L. and Larkin, J. F. (eds) (1969)

Wingfield, R., "Vita Mariae Reginae," ed., D. MacCulloch *Camden Miscellany*, XXVIII, Fourth Series [London, 1984], pp.181–301

Wriothesley, C., *A Chronicle of England during the Reigns of the Tudors, From A.D. 1485 to 1559* ed. by W. D. Hamilton [Camden Society, 1877?], Vol.2

SECONDARY SOURCES

[unless otherwise noted, all editions printed in London]

Adamson, J., ed., *The Princely Courts of Europe: Ritual, Politics and Culture under the Ancien Regime, 1500–1700* [1999]

Airs, M., *The Tudor & Jacobean Country House: A Building History* [Gloucestershire, UK, 1995]

Alsop, J. D., "A Regime at Sea: the Navy and the 1553 Succession Crisis," *Albion*, XXIV (1992): 577–90.

Amussen, S., *An Ordered Society: Gender and Class in Early Modern England* [Oxford, 1988].

Antrobus, J., *Hatfield: Some Memories of Bishop's Hatfield and its Past*, 4th ed. [Hatfield, UK, 1933]

Asch, R. G., ed., *Princes, Patronage and the Nobility: The Court at the Beginning of the Modern Age* [Oxford UP, 1991]

Barley, S. L. and Tittler, R., "The Local Community and the Crown in 1553: The Accession of Mary Tudor Revisted," *Bulletin of the Institute of Historical Research*, 136 (1984): 131–140

Beard, G., *Upholsterers and Interior Furnishings in England, 1530–1840* [1997]

Bell, S. G. *The Lost Tapestries of the City of Ladies: Christine de Pizan's Renaissance Legacy* [California UP, 2004]

Bennett, J., *Women in the Medieval English Countryside: Gender and Household in Brigstock before the Plague* [Oxford UP, 1987]

Bennett, J., "Medievalism and Feminism," *Speculum*, 68 (1993): 309–331

Bennett, J., *Ale, Beer, and Brewsters in England: Women's Work in a Changing World, 1300–1600* [Oxford UP, 1996]

Bennett, M. J., "Edward III's Entail and the Succession to the Crown, 1376–1471," *English Historical Review*, 113 (1998): 580–609

Bindoff, S. T., "A Kingdom at Stake 1553," *History Today*, vol.3, no.9 (September, 1953): 642–648

Bingham, C., *Darnley: A Life of Henry Stuart Lord Darnely Consort of Mary Queen of Scots* [1995]

Brigden, S., *New Worlds, Lost Worlds: The Rule of the Tudors, 1485–1603* [New York, 2000]

Britnell, R., *The Closing of the Middle Ages? England, 1471–1529* [Oxford, 1997]

Brooks, C., "A Law-Abiding and Litigious Society," from *The Oxford History of Tudor Stuart Britain*, ed. J. Morrill [Oxford UP, 1996], pp. 139–155

Brown, J. C., "A Woman's Place was in the Home: Women's Work in Renaissance Tuscany," pp. 206–222 from M. W. Ferguson, et al., eds., *Rewriting the Renaissance: The Discourses of Sexual Difference in Early Modern Europe* [Chicago UP, 1986]

Bush, M. *The Pilgrimage of Grace: A Study of the Rebel Armies of October 1536* [Manchester UP, 1996]

Cañeque, A., *The King's Living Image: The Culture and Politics of Viceregal Power in Colonial Mexico* [New York, 2004]

Church, S. D., *The Household Knights of King John* [Cambridge UP, 1999]

Clutterbuck, R.., *The History and Antiquities of the County of Hertford . . .* [1815]

Collins, A. J., ed., *Jewels and Plate of Queen Elizabeth I: The Inventory of 1574. Edited from Harley MS.1650 and Stowe MS.555 in the British Museum* [London, 1955]

Comensoli, V., *Household Business: Domestic Plays of Early Modern England* [Toronto UP, 1996]

Cross, C., *The Puritan Earl: The Life of Henry Hastings, Third Earl of Huntingdon* [New York, 1966]

Davis, N. Z., *Women on the Margins: Three Seventeenth-Century Lives* [1995]

Day, R., *The Tudor Age* [1985]

Dickens, A. G. (ed.), *The Courts of Europe: Politics, Patronage and Royalty* [1977]

Doran, S., *Monarchy and Matrimony: The Courtships of Elizabeth I* [1996]

Doran, S., "Elizabeth I Gender, Power & Politics," *History Today*, (May 2003), 53/5

Dowling, M., *Humanism in the Age of Henry VIII* [London, 1986]

Duffy, E, *The Stripping of the Altars: Traditional Religion in England 1400–1580* [1992]

Eaves, R. G., *Henry VIII and James V's Regency 1524–1528: A Study in Anglo-Scottish Diplomacy* [Lanham MD, 1987]

Elias, N., *The Court Society* [Oxford, 1983]

Ellis, S. G., *Tudor Frontiers and Noble Power* [Oxford UP,1995].

Ellis, S. G., "A Crisis of the Aristocracy? Frontiers and Noble Power in the early Tudor State," from *The Tudor Monarchy*, ed. J. Guy [1997], pp. 330–339

Ellis, T. P., *The First Extent of Bromfield and Yale, Lordships A.D. 1315* [1924]

Elton, G. R., *Tudor Revolution in Government* [Cambridge UP, 1953]

Elton, G. R., *Reform and Reformation* [1977]

Elton, G. R., *England under the Tudors*, 3rd ed. [1991]

Erickson, A., *Women and Property in Early Modern England* [1993]

Ferguson, M. W., et al., eds., *Rewriting the Renaissance: The Discourses of Sexual Difference in Early Modern Europe* [Chicago UP, 1986]

Fletcher, A. *Tudor Rebellions* 2nd ed. [1973]

Fletcher, A. (ed.) w/J. Stevenson, *Order and Disorder in Early Modern England* [1985]

Fletcher, A. *Gender, Sex, and Subordination in England, 1500–1800* [1995]

Gage, J., *The History and Antiquities of Hengrave in Suffolk* [1822]

Given-Wilson, C., *The English Nobility in the late Middle Ages . . .* [1987]

Given-Wilson, C., "Late Medieval England, 1215–1485," from *The Oxford History of Medieval England*

N. Saul (ed.) [Oxford UP, 1997], pp. 102–136

Given-Wilson, C., and Curties, A., *The Royal Bastards of Medieval England* (London, 1984)

Graves, M. A. R., *The Tudor Parliaments: Crown, Lords and Commons, 1485–1603* [London, 1985]

Given-Wilson, C. and Thompson, M. W., *The Decline of the Castle* [Cambridge UP, 1987],

Griffiths, R. A. *Sir Rhys ap Thomas and his Family: A Study in the Wars of the Roses and Early Tudor Politics* [Wales UP, 1993].

Gunn, S. J., "The Regime of Charles, Duke of Suffolk, in North Wales and the Reform of the Welsh Government, 1509–1525," *The Welsh History Review*, 12/4 (December 1985): 461–495

Gunn, S. J., *Early Tudor Government, 1485–1558* [Basingstoke, UK, 1995]

Habermas, J., *The Structural Transformation of the Public Sphere . . .* [Germany, 1962; reprint Cambridge, MA, 1989]

Gunn, S. J., *Virgin Mother, Maiden Queen: Elizabeth I and the Cult of the Virgin Mary* [1995]

Gunn, S. J., *Women and Romance Fiction in the English Renaissance* [Cambridge UP, 2000]

Haigh, C. *The Reign of Elizabeth*, (ed) [Georgia UP, 1987]

Haigh, C. *Elizabeth I* [1988]

Haigh, C. *English Reformations* [Oxford, 1993]

Harris, B. J., *Edward Stafford, third duke of Buckingham, 1478–1521* [Stanford UP, 1986]

Harris, B. J., "Property, Power, and Personal Relations: Elite Mothers and Sons in Yorkist and Early Tudor England." *Signs: Journal of Women in Culture and Society* (1990) 15/3, pp. 606–632

Harris, B. J., "Women and Politics in Early Tudor England," *The Historical Journal*, vol. 33, no.2 (1990), pp. 259–281

Harris, B. J., *English Aristocratic Women 1450–1550: Marriage and Family, Property and Careers* [Oxford UP, 2002]

Haugaard, W., "Elizabeth Tudor's Book of Devotions: A Neglected Clue to the Queen's Life and Character," *Sixteenth-Century Journal*, 12, (1981): 79–105

Heal, F. *Hospitality in early modern England* [Oxford, 1990]

Heal, F. w/C. Holmes, *The Gentry in England and Wales* [Stanford UP, 1994]

Heisch, A., "Queen Elizabeth I and the Persistence of Patriarchy," *Feminist Review*, 4, (1980), pp.45–55

Hepburn, F. "Arthur, Prince of Wales and His Training and for Kingship," *The Historian*, 55, (1997)

Herlihy, D. *Medieval Households* [Harvard UP, 1985]

Hill, C., *The World Turned Upside Down: Radical Ideas during the English Revolution* [1975; 1991]

Hoak, D., *The King's Council in the Reign of Edward VI* [Cambridge UP, 1976]

Holmes, W.C., *The Gentry in England and Wales* [Stanford UP, 1994]

Houlbrooke, R., *The English family, 1450–1700* [London, 1984]

Houlbrooke, R., "Henry VIII's Wills: A Comment," *The Historical Journal*, 37/4 (1994): 891–899

Houlbrooke, R., *Death, Religion and the Family in England, 1480–1750* [Oxford UP, 200]

Howard, M., *The Early Tudor Country House: Architecture and Politics 1490–1550* [1987]

Howell, M. C., *Women, Production and Patriarchy in Late Medieval Cities* [Chicago UP, 1986]

Hoyle, R., "War and Public Finance," from *The Reign of Henry VIII: Politics, Policy and Piety*, ed. D. MacCulloch [New York, 1995], pp.75–99.

Ives, E. W., *Anne Boleyn* [Oxford, 1986]

Ives, E. W., "Henry VIII's Will—A Forensic Conundrum," *The Historical Journal*, 35/4 (Dec. 1992): 779–804

Ives, E. W., "Henry VIII's Will: The Proctectorate Provisions of 1546–7," *The Historical Journal*, 37/4 (1994): 901–914

Ives, E. W., *The Life and Death of Anne Boleyn* [Oxford, 2004]

James, M., *Society, Politics and Culture: Studies in Early Modern England* [Cambridge UP, 1986]

James, S. E., *Kateryn Parr: The Making of a Queen* [Aldershot, UK, 1999]

Jardine, L., *Worldly Goods: A New History of the Renaissance* [1996]

Johnson, P., *Elizabeth I: A Study in Power and Intellect* [London, 1988]

Jones, N. L., *Faith by Statute* [London, 1982]

Jones, F., *The Princes and Principality of Wales* [Wales UP, 1969]

Jones, M. K. and Underwood, M. G., *The King's Mother: Lady Margaret Beaufort Countess of Richmond and Derby* [Cambridge UP, 1992]

Jordan, C., "Feminism and the Humanists: The Case of Sir Thomas Elyot's Defence of Good Women," *Renaissance Quarterly*, 36, (1983), pp.181–201

Jordan, W. K., *Edward VI: The Young King* [London, 1968]

Jordan, W. K., *Edward VI: The Threshold of Power:, The Dominance of the Duke of Northumberland* [London, 1970]

Kantorowicz, E., *The King's Two Bodies* [Princeton UP, 1957]

Kettering, S., *Patrons, Brokers, and Clients in Seventeenth-Century France* [Oxford UP, 1986].

Kimball, E. G., *Serjeanty Tenure in Medieval England* [1936]

Klein, J. L. , ed., *Daughters, Wives & Widows: Writings by Men about Women and Marriage in England, 1500–1640* [Chicago UP, 1992]

Korda, N., *Shakespeare's Domestic Economies: Gender and Property in Early Modern England* [Philadelphia, 2002]

Laynesmith, J. L., *The Last Medieval Queens: English Queenship 1445–1503* [Oxford UP, 2004]

Lehmberg, S. E., *The Later Parliaments of Henry VIII, 1536–1547* [Cambridge UP, 1977]

Levin, C., *The Heart and Stomach of a King: Elizabeth I and the Politics of Sex and Power* [Pennsylvania UP, 1994]

Levine, M., "The Place of women in Tudor Government" from *Tudor Rule and Revolution: Essays for G.R. Elton from his American friends*, D. J. Guth and J. W. McKenna (eds.) [Cambridge, 1982]

Levine, M., *Tudor Dynastic Problems, 1460–1571* [1973]

Levy, S. M., *An Elizabethan Inheritance: The Hardwick Hall Textiles* [1998]

Loach, J., *Parliament under the Tudors* [Oxford, 1991]

Loach, J., *Edward VI* [Yale UP, 1999]

Loades, D. M., *Two Tudor Conspiracies* [Cambridge UP, 1965]

Loades, D. M., *Mary Tudor: A Life* [Oxford, 1989]

Loades, D. M., *John Dudley, duke Duke of Northumberland* [Oxford UP, 1996]

Loades, D. M., *Tudor Government: Structures of Authority in the Sixteenth Century* [Oxford, 1997]

Loades, D. M., (ed.) *John Foxe: An Historical Perspective* [Aldershot, UK, 1999]

Loades, D. M., *Mary Tudor: The Tragical History of the First Queen of England* [Kew, Richmond, UK, 2006]

MacCaffrey, W., *Elizabeth I* [1993]

Marshall, R. K. *Mary I* [1993]

Mattingly, G. *Catherine of Aragon* [New York, 1941]

Mattingly, G. *Renaissance Diplomacy* [New York, 1988]

Mayer, T., *Reginald Pole: Prince and Prophet* [Cambridge UP, 2000]

McIntosh, J. L., "Soveriegn Princesses: Mary and Elizabeth Tudor as Heads of Princely Households and the Accomplishment of the Female Succession in Tudor England, 1516–1558" [Ph.D. dissertation, Johns Hopkins, 2002]

McIntosh, J. L., "English Funeral Sermons 1560–1640: The Relationship Between Gender and Death, Dying and the Afterlife" [M.Litt. thesis, Oxford 1990]

MacCulloch, *Thomas Cranmer* [1996]

McIntosh, J. L., and Whitelock, A, "Princess Mary's Household and the Succession Crisis, July 1553," *The Historical Journal*, 50, 2 (2007): 265–287

Mertes, K., *The English Noble Household, 1250–1600: Good Governance and Politic Rule* [Oxford, 1988]

Merton, C., "The Women Who Served Queen Mary and Queen Elizabeth: Ladies, Gentlewomen, and Maids of the Privy Chamber, 1553–1603" [Ph.D. dissertation, Cambridge, 1992]

Miller, H., "Henry VIII's Unwritten Will: Grants of Lands and Honours in 1547," in *Wealth and Power in Tudor England: Essays presented to S. T. Bindoff*, E. W. Ives, R. J. Knecht, and J. J. Scarisbrick (eds.) [London, 1978], pp.87–105

Murphy, B., *Bastard Prince: Henry VIII'S Lost Son* [Sutton, UK, 2001].

Neale, N., *Queen Elizabeth* [1934]

Neale, N., *The Elizabethan House of Commons* [1949]

Neale, N., *Elizabeth I and Her Parliaments* 2 vols. [1953, 1957]

"The Accession of Queen Elizabeth I," first published in *History Today* (Coronation Issue), May 1953 and subsequently reprinted in *The Age of Catherine de Medici and Essays in Elizabethan History* [London, 1958; 1963], pp. 131–144

Orlin, L. C., *Private Matters and Public Culture in Post-Reformation England* [Cornell UP, 1994]

Orlin, L. C., *Elizabethan Households: An Anthology* [Washington, DC, 1995]

The Oxford History of Tudor Stuart Britain, ed. J. Morrill [Oxford UP, 1996]

The Oxford History of Medieval England, ed. N. Saul [Oxford UP, 1997]

Perry, M. E., *Gender and Disorder in Early Modern Seville* [Princeton UP, 1990]

Pierce, H., *Margaret Pole, Countess of Salisbury ,1473–1541: Loyalty, Lineage and Leadership* [2003]

Political Thought and the Tudor Commonwealth: Deep Structure, Discourse, and Disguise, eds. P. A. Fiedler and T. F. Mayer [1992]

Pollard, A. F., *England under Protector Somerset* [London 1900]

Pollard, A. F., *The Reign of Henry VIII: Politics, Policy and Piety*, ed. D. MacCulloch [New York, 1995]

Pollard, A. F., *Religion and the English People 1500–1640: New Voices, New Perspectives*, ed. E. J. Carlson [Missouri, 1998]

Richards, J. M. "Mary Tudor as 'Sole Quene'? Gendering Tudor Monarchy," *Historical Journal*, 40, (1997): 895–899

Robinson, W. R. B., "Princess Mary's Itinerary in the Marches of Wales 1525–1527: A Provisional Record," *Historical Research*, 71 (1998): 233–252

Roper, L. *The Holy Household: Women and Morals in Reformation Augsburg* [Oxford, 1989]

Rosenberg, C. E. (ed), *The Family in History* [Pennsylvania, 1975]

Ryan, L. V., *Roger Ascham* [Stanford UP, 1963]

Scarisbrick, J. J., *Henry VIII* [London, 1968]

Shell, M., *Eizabeth's Glass* [1993]

Shephard, A., *Gender and Authority in Sixteenth-Century England* [Keele UP, 1994]

Skeel, C., *The Council in the Marches of Wales* [London, 1904]

Slavin, A. J., "The Fall of Lord Chancellor Wriothesley: A Study in the Politics of Conspiracy," *Albion*, 7/4 (Winter, 1975)

Spring, E, *Law, Land and Family: Aristocratic Inheritance in England 1300–1800* [1993]

Starkey, D., "The King's Privy Chamber, 1485–1547" [Ph.D. dissertation, Cambridge, 1973]

Starkey, D., "The Age of the Household" in S. Medcalf, ed., *The Later Middle Ages* [London, 1981]

Starkey, D., *The Reign of Henry VIII: Personalities and Politics* [London, 1985]

Starkey, D., "Intimacy and Innovation: The Rise of the Privy Chamber, 1485–1547,"

Starkey, D., ed., *The English Court:from the Wars of the Roses to the Civil War* [London, 1987]

Starkey, D., *Elizabeth: Apprenticeship* [London, 2000]

State, Sovereigns and Society in Early Modern England, ed. C. Carlton w/ R. L. Woods, M. L. Robertson and J. Block [Gloucestershire UK, 1998]

Stone, L., "The Rise of the Nuclear Family in Early Modern England: The Patriarchal Stage," from *The Family in History*, ed. C. E. Rosenberg [Pennsylvania, 1975]

Thompson, M. W., and Given-Wilson, C., *The Decline of the Castle* [Cambridge UP, 1987]

Thurley, S., *The Royal Palaces of Tudor England: Architecture and Court Life 1460–1547* [1993]

Thurley, S., *Whitehall Palace: An Architectural History of the Royal Apartments, 1240–1690* [1999]

Tittler, R., and Barley, S.L., "The Local Community and the Crown in 1553: The Accession of Mary Tudor Revisited," *Bulletin of the Institute of Historical Research*, 136 (1984): 131–140

Tudor Political Culture, ed. D. Hoak [Cambridge UP, 1995]

Tudor Rule and Revolution: Essays for G. R. Elton from his American friends, ed. D. D. J. Guth and J. J. W. McKenna [Cambridge, 1982]

Usher, B., "Backing Protestantism: the London Godly, the Exhequer and the Foxe Circle," from *John Foxe: An Historical Perspective*, ed. D. Loades [Aldershot, UK, 1999], pp. 105–134.

Vale, M., "The Princely Court in Northern Europe, 1270–1380," *History Today*, 52/7 (July 2002): 11–20.

Walker, G., *Persuasive Fictions: Faction, Faith and Political Culture in the Reign of Henry VIII* [London, 1996]

Walker, G., *Wealth and Power in Tudor England: Essays presented to S.T. Bindoff*, eds. E.W. Ives, R. J. Knecht, and J. J. Scrisbrick [1978]

Westfall, S. R., *Patrons and Performance. Early Tudor Household Revels* [Oxford UP, 1990]

Wiesner, M. E., "Spinsters and Seamstresses: Women in Cloth and Clothing Production," pp. 191–205 from M.W. Ferguson, et al., eds., *Rewriting the Renaissance: The Discourses of Sexual Difference in Early Modern Europe* [Chicago UP, 1986]

Whitelock, A., and MacCulloch, D., "Princess Mary's Household and the Succession Crisis, July 1553," *The Historical Journal*, 50, 2 (2007): 265–287

Williams, G., "Wales and the Reign of Queen Mary I," *The Welsh History Review*, 10/3 (June 1981): 334–358

Williams, G., *Recovery, Reorientation, and Reformation Wales, c.1415–1642* [Oxford: 1987], p. 281

Williams, P., *The Council in the Marches of Wales under Elizabeth I* [Wales UP, 1958]

Williams, P., *The Tudor Regime* [Oxford, 1979]

Williams, P., *The Later Tudors* [Oxford, 1995]

Wolffe, B. P., *The Crown Lands 1461–1536: An Aspect of Yorkist and Early Tudor Government* [1970]

Woolgar, C. M., *The Great Household in Late Medieval England* [1999]

Wright, P., "A Change in Direction: The Ramifications of a Female Household, 1558–1603," from D. Starkey, ed., *The English Court . . .* [1987], pp. 147–173

Yates, F., *Astraea: The Imperial Theme in the Sixteenth Century* [1975]

Printed in the United States
150050LV00004B/6/P